The Rumble of a Distant Drum

The Rumble of

a Distant Drum

The Quapaws and Old World Newcomers, 1673–1804

MORRIS S. ARNOLD

The University of Arkansas Press

Fayetteville   2000

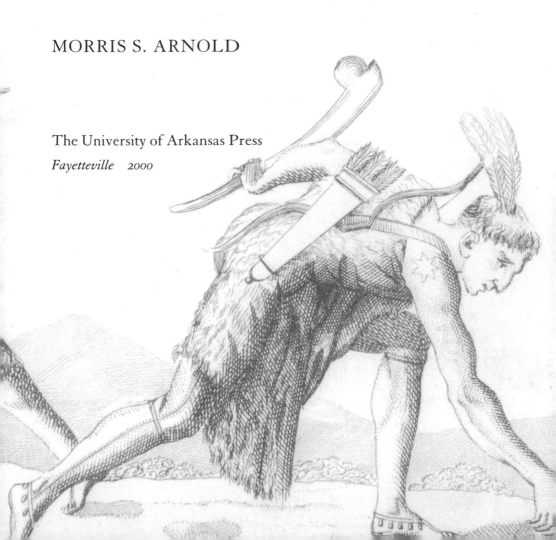

04 03 02 01 00   5 4 3 2 1

Designer: Chiquita Babb

⊗ The paper used in this publication meets the minimum requirements
of the American National Standard for Permanence of Paper for Printed
Library Materials Z39.48-1984.

Library of Congress Cataloging-in-Publication Data
Arnold, Morris S.
    The rumble of a distant drum : the Quapaws and the old world newcomers,
 1673–1804 / Morris S. Arnold.
       p.   cm.
    Includes bibliographical references and index.
    ISBN 1-55728-590-x (alk. paper)
       1. Quapaw Indians—First contact with Europeans. 2. Quapaw Indians—History.
 3. Quapaw Indians—Social life and customs. 4. France—Colonies—America.
 5. Arkansas—History—Sources. I. Title.

E99.Q2 A77 2000
976.7004'9752—dc21
                                                                    99-051769

This project is supported in part by a grant from the
Arkansas Humanities Council and the Arkansas
Historic Preservation Program, an agency of the
Department of Arkansas Heritage.

For my wife Gail

Ah, take the Cash and let the Credit go,
Nor heed the rumble of a distant Drum!
                    —Edward FitzGerald.

I am so biased in its favor, that I am persuaded that the beauty of its
climate influences the character of its inhabitants [i.e., the Quapaws],
who are at the same time very gentle and very brave—for along with
the peaceful qualities that everyone knows them for, they exhibit a
courage without reproach. They have always exhibited an unfailing
fidelity to the French, without being drawn to them by fear or self
interest. They live with the French who are near them more as brothers
than as neighbors, and it is yet to happen that one has seen any misun-
derstanding between the two nations.

                    —Le Page du Pratz,
                        Histoire, 2:291, on the
                        Arkansas country and the
                        Quapaw Indians, 1758.

The Quapaws' attachment to us has led them to follow this settlement
in the various moves that it has made; their private and political inter-
ests won't allow them to move away. Now the floods have caused them
to disperse in such a way that in case of need it would be difficult for
them to gather together and come to our aid. Our common security
depends on the ease with which we can rally to each other's assistance.
Our alliance has always been this way.

                    —Balthazar de Villiers,
                        commandant of Arkansas
                        Post, to Governor
                        Bernardo de Gálvez,
                        22 September 1778.

Contents

Maps and Illustrations

Preface

I owe a large debt to numerous people who contributed materially to the completion of this book, and I am glad to record my thanks to some of them here. The staff at the Eighth Circuit Court of Appeals libraries has responded cheerfully, promptly, and unerringly to my requests for necessary books and articles. Dr. Alfred Lemmon and Mark Cave of the Historic New Orleans Collection, a marvelous facility that is constantly improving its very real usefulness, have provided help in locating and reproducing colonial documents; these gentlemen set an example for others who are engaged in the kind of work that they do. John Crider produced copies of thousands of pages of documents that are housed at the Archivo General de Indias in Seville, and without them this book could not have gotten off the ground. My friends Michael P. Hoffman, George Sabo III, and Jeannie Whayne at the University of Arkansas have read the manuscript, or parts of it, and have provided many useful suggestions for improvement. Malcolm Lewis has helped me understand the cartographic conventions of native Americans.

Chapter 3 of this book is a slightly refurbished version of Morris S. Arnold, "Eighteenth-Century Arkansas Illustrated: A Map within an Indian Painting?" in G. Malcolm Lewis, ed., *Cartographic Encounters: Perspectives on Native American Mapmaking and Map Use* (Chicago: University of Chicago Press, 1998), 187–204, which itself was a reworking of Morris S. Arnold, "Eighteenth-Century Arkansas Illustrated," *Arkansas Historical Quarterly* 53 (Summer 1994): 119–36; and part of chapter 5 previously appeared as Morris S. Arnold, "Cultural Imperialism and the Legal System: The Application of European Law to Indians in Colonial Louisiana," *Loyola Law Review* 42 (1997): 727–44. I am grateful to the University of Chicago Press, the Arkansas Historical Association, and the *Loyola Law Review,* respectively, for their permission to republish these items here.

Carrie V. Wilson, the representative of the Quapaw Tribe for matters relating to the Native American Graves Protection and Repatriation Act, has helped me understand the ways of her tribe. I am especially grateful to members of the tribe, the descendants of the people who lie at the heart of this book, for their encouragement when, though my enthusiasm for the project never waned, my confidence in being able to comprehend what I knew had nevertheless begun to falter. The tribe presented me with a blanket at a traditional Quapaw dinner given in honor of my wife Gail and me in 1998 and offered us the hospitality that the French first remarked on more than three hundred years ago. At that same event, Mrs. Edna Wilson, a Quapaw and member of the Elk Clan, presented me with a silver Quapaw medal that was struck by the Franklin Mint especially for the Quapaws as part of its Indian Tribal Series. Last year, after a dance in my honor which members of the Quapaw tribe requested and participated in at their annual pow-wow, Mr. Ed Rodgers, the chairman of the Quapaw tribal business committee, gave me a tribal flag. The research for this book has made me keenly aware of the cultural traditions behind these kinds of gifts and has thus made them all the more valuable to me. Perhaps this book will, in its turn, prove to be a source of pride for the Quapaws, and serve as a partial recompense for their many kindnesses.

Introduction

Depending on what one counts, this is either my third or fourth book on the subject of colonial Arkansas,[1] and so a reader might reasonably object that it represents a kind of overkill; but the truth is that there is virtually nothing in this book that is in the others. I am convinced, moreover, that what emerges here is the real story of Arkansas Post, or, at the very least, that my other books contained too little about the Quapaws and some other Indian tribes in the area to provide the reader with the full picture of what life at the colonial post was like. One of life's real pleasures is repairing ignorances, and writing this book has mended some major ones of my own.

Some years ago, Daniel J. Boorstin provided us with a useful reminder that when writing about Indians the "opportunities for new insight are legion, as are the temptations to passionate overstatement, pride, romanticism, self-flagellation, and polemics."[2] As scholars more frequently than ever turn their attentions to interracial dealings in general, and to relations between whites and Indians in particular, this is a caveat that very much needs to be kept in plain view. Because the scope and content of race relations are presently matters of deep political concern, debate sometimes generates more heat than light, and not all historians have been able to avoid transforming their research into what is little more than a search of the past for friends.

While all of us may necessarily do that sort of thing from time to time, or to one degree or another, it has seemed to me that theorizing would be greatly advanced by the examination of the huge, unpublished archival resources in France and Spain that bear on the question of how Europeans and Indians interacted during Louisiana's colonial period. I initially chose to write about Arkansas Post, I must admit, because it was close by; but this fortuity proved to be fortunate in the extreme, for the documentary evidence left behind by this tiny and remote community was unexpectedly voluminous, and the parts of it that touched on Indian and white relations were unexpectedly rich. During the twenty years or so that I have been trying to piece together and comprehend the colonial history of Arkansas, I have acquired copies of more than eight thousand pages of unpublished letters, reports, inventories, legal instruments, legal proceedings, and other documents written at, to, from, or about Arkansas Post in the seventeenth and eighteenth centuries; and since, as it happens, Indian affairs occupied much of the local commandant's attention there, these papers have proved especially revealing.

This book relies heavily on this original source material, and not so much on the burgeoning secondary sources (huge amounts of which I have read), to tell its story. That is partly because I did not want my own vision blurred or deflected by what other writers might make of the events that I discovered and described, partly because I did not want the narrative repeatedly interrupted, and partly because I wanted to allow those who participated in the relevant events to tell their own story. One must be alert, of course, not to give participants too much license, because they will tell a self-interested version of what happened. But over the years reliable ways of discounting for this general human tendency have revealed themselves, and the simple truth is that the critical evaluation of evidence goes on constantly every day in every town in this country, not just in its courts of law but elsewhere. One hardly needs to be expert in some arcane branch of hermeneutics to engage in this kind of interpretation; in fact, one cannot get through life without doing so. What is sometimes more difficult to avoid is improperly discounting what is said, that is, inserting oneself into the evidence. For some people, and for all of us some of the time, a document can unfortunately serve more as a mirror than as a window, revealing the reader and not the world on which it opens.

The major aim of this book has been to reconstruct the strategies that the Quapaw tribe and their French and Spanish visitors developed to deal with each other more or less harmoniously for upwards of five or six generations in circumstances that were almost always exigent. This does not make this study by any means unique, but it certainly sets it apart significantly from that great mass of historiography that emphasizes constant interracial conflict on a virtually genocidal scale. In fact, if I am even close to being right about the main contours of eighteenth-century Arkansas society, what manifested itself on the Arkansas River in colonial times was a kinder and gentler kind of imperialism than the sort that is commonly written about.

Understanding this reality about eighteenth-century Arkansas carries with it a transcendental lesson or two. Mega-contexts and generalizations about the relations between whites and native Americans have their honored place, and talk of invasions by powerful outsiders bent on hegemony, or even on genocide, may appropriately capture the situation in some places, in some epochs, and in some circumstances, in the so-called New World. Continental and English jurists, safe in their universities, could spin their theories concerning the rights of conquerors and supposed discoverers to impose their ways on those whom they considered heathen peoples. But time and circumstance frequently worked to make eighteenth-century white Louisianians as much like immigrants as invaders, and reduced the fine talk of metropolitan lawyers to so much academic prattle. The Quapaws, it is true, were caught in a net created by competing European expansionist ambitions, but at the dawn of the nineteenth century the French, the English, and the Spanish were all gone: The Quapaws, on the other hand, still lived not far from where they were when Marquette and Joliet had encountered them one hundred and thirty years before.

I have tried to produce an ethnohistorical account of a wide variety of relations, from the most intimate to trade and military alliances, and I also deal, among other things, with the accommodations and compromises that the two relevant nations made with respect to religious practices and the application of legal principles. The disciplines of law and of economics figure heavily in the narrative and the analysis, and my debt to anthropology is also manifest. My intent has been to provide a descriptive, interpretive, and analytical story that will help the reader understand the main features of the complex cultural mix that characterized an Arkansas that disappeared almost two hundred years ago. Whether what happened there happened elsewhere in colonial Louisiana I cannot say, but it would be very surprising if it did not. Even if it did not, however, the story has to count as one that will help the reader understand how the wider world works.

The society that was created on the Arkansas River in the colonial era was highly complex and rife with a subtlety some features of which will inevitably have eluded recapture. That society's gross outlines, however, seem clearly discernible, and it is evident that they resulted from a strong desire on the part of the Indians and Europeans to find ways to cooperate and survive. It is useless to pretend that a single general theme is retrievable from a record so complicated as the one that these Indians and Europeans left behind, partly because individual exigencies will generate transient cultural artifacts tailored to specific times and events: Any transcendental pattern may thus be only the product of hindsight. There were times, in other words, when the Quapaws' strong cultural will was matched by their ability to work it and times when Europeans had the muscle and resolve to exert a more powerful influence than their Indian neighbors. There were also times when the two nations constructed a new cultural artifact, a third thing. The main truth uncovered here, I believe, is that the society that they created was characterized by a dynamic kind of symbiosis, and this book provides numerous examples of the individual manifestations of that symbiosis.

Because a reader needs room to reflect, ruminate, and even to muse, I have tried conscientiously to avoid simple reductionism in interpreting the events discussed and described, while attempting simultaneously to guide thoughts into useful channels along the way. Paul Greenberg once remarked on the "tendentious quality of the texts" that accompanied an exhibit in a museum that he had visited, and he decried the fact that those texts were "closer to a set of reins and blinders than an introduction to thought."[3] Perhaps the respect that I have tried to pay the reader is what will in the end allow the book to be a window, and my attempt to guide is simply the way that the book reveals itself as a mirror.

While, as I have been at pains to say, the book is not contrived so as to present a single argument, a concluding chapter offers some thoughts on how a proper understanding of what occurred in eighteenth-century Arkansas can be organized around the proposition that the Quapaws were rational economic actors and their choices therefore inevitably and accurately reflected what they perceived their self-interest required at the time. By self-interest I do not mean selfishness: Many rational people have selves that find satisfaction in charitable and altruistic acts. What I am talking about does not differ markedly from what anthropologists mean when they speak of strategies and adaptive behavior, or from what eighteenth-century political writers meant when they spoke of pursuing happiness. Some, moreover, may find neoclassical microeconomic theory especially congenial because it might be less judgmental even than anthropology: To the economist, a lazy person is simply someone who values leisure time highly, the timorous are merely risk averse, homosexuality is nothing more than a preference. In any event, the observation that the Quapaws acted from self-interestedness is not meant to be, nor is it as an objective matter, a disrespectful or cynical observation. It is a recognition of the human and humane character of Quapaw society and of its need and will to survive.

Some readers might like at this point to have some help with a few basic elements of Arkansas colonial history. Arkansas Post was settled in 1686 by Henri de Tonty, partner and protégé of René-Robert Cavalier de La Salle, thirteen years before the establishment of Louisiana on the Gulf Coast: It was thus the first European settlement in what would become Jefferson's Louisiana. (The Post predated New Orleans by some thirty years, and St. Louis by eighty.) Tonty's aim was to establish a trade and military alliance with the Quapaw Indians. Near the confluence of the Arkansas and Mississippi Rivers (see Figure 1), the tiny outpost failed late in the seventeenth century, and its rebirth had to wait until John Law sent some workers to the old site in 1721. The settlement thereafter moved several times, due to floods, the fortunes of war, and changes in its strategic mission, until it finally came to rest in 1779, a little more than a decade after Louisiana's change from French to Spanish sovereignty, on the Arkansas River at the edge of Grand Prairie. This is where the Arkansas Post National Memorial is situated today. It was here, after Spain returned Louisiana to France, that the Arkansas country was finally delivered to the Americans in 1804.

The scene of at least three bona fide battles, and the seat of the Arkansas territorial government from 1819 to 1821, the Post apparently had ceased existing as a real town when its post office closed for the final time in 1941. Even as late as 1972, however, the Geological Survey maps continued faithfully to give to a cluster of houses, presumably the ghost and echo of the old village, the ancient and venerable name of Arkansas Post.

The Indian tribe near which the French settled themselves, and with whom they very soon began to establish the complex relations that are at the focus of this book, called themselves the Kappas (the Americans rendered the name Quapaws), which roughly translates as "the downstream people." They were a Dhegihan Sioux nation, and thus cousins of the Osages, Kansas, Omahas, and Poncas. The French commonly called them the Arkansas because that's what the Illinois Indians called them. The

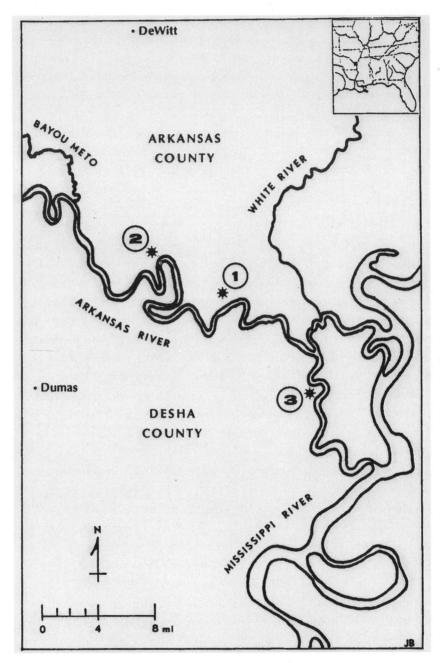

Figure 1. The locations of Arkansas Post, 1686–2000: 1. 1686–1699;
1721–1749. 2. 1749–1756; 1779–2000. 3. 1756–1779.
Courtesy of Arkansas Historical Association

word Arkansas itself evidently means nothing; it is just a proper name. The Quapaws were living on both sides of the Mississippi near the Arkansas River when Marquette and Jolliet first visited them in 1673; whether they were newcomers themselves at that time, or had been there when Soto cut his destructive swath through the area in the sixteenth century, is a matter of some considerable dispute.

The Rumble of a Distant Drum

I

Family Ties:

Dalliances and Alliances

Early French travelers reported that Quapaw rituals of welcome were elaborate and sometimes lasted for days. Henri de Tonty, for instance, has left an account of a four-day ceremony at Kappa in 1689 during which "there was nothing but drumming, feasting, and masquerading after their manner."[1] Visitors to the Quapaws were commonly carried to the villages on the shoulders or backs of their hosts.[2] There they were seated on the chief's roofed scaffold situated in the town square, the floor of which was often covered with willows, fine rush mats, bear skins, or panther skins.[3] Crowds of people gathered round to witness and participate in the ceremonies and feasts.[4]

Not all of the French were able to endure the complete marathon. Father St. Cosme grumbled that the Quapaws' rattles and drums made "a music which is not the most agreeable, while an Indian who was behind us rocked us." He eventually begged off: He and his companions "put some of our people in our place after staying there a little while," and, he recollected with satisfaction, "they had the pleasure of being rocked all night."[5] Father Du Poisson, on the other hand (though he found that the Quapaw dances "as you may well imagine, are somewhat odd"), nevertheless greatly

Figure 2.   The Quapaws dance the calumet to welcome Bossu in 1770.
Frontispiece from Jean-Bernard Bossu, *Nouveaux voyages dans
l'Amérique septentrionale* (Amsterdam: 1777).

admired "the precision with which [the Quapaws] mark time" and found it "as surprising as the contortions and efforts that they make."[6]

Henri Joutel recorded some of his ruminations upon being introduced into Quapaw society in 1687, and while his reactions no doubt were somewhat idiosyncratic, we cannot think that they were altogether atypical of the first impressions of other seventeenth-century French visitors to the Arkansas upon encountering what was for them a strange if hospitable people. "What gave me the most pleasure," he said, "was to see the posture in which they were, being altogether naked, some being painted, each having attached to his belt three or four gourds or calabashes, in which there were some little pebbles or a little corn, in order to make noise, and each with a horse or buffalo tail hanging out back. When they moved, they made a very funny clinking sound, and we had a lot of trouble to keep from laughing when we saw these kinds of figures, though we had to pretend."[7] He also could barely contain himself when he noticed a "waiter at the meals" who "takes care to paint himself with various colors, and seats himself on his backside like a monkey while he keeps his dignity."[8]

We can be sure that the Quapaws had an equally hard time restraining their laughter over the looks and deportment of their visitors, but, alas, we have only one relevant snippet on the subject, and this from Jean-Bernard Bossu, hardly a reliable source: He reported that the Quapaws, who "usually . . . have no hair on their bodies, except on their heads . . . say we resemble animals in that respect," and he claimed that they expressed similar views "when they see us eat herbs and salads."[9]

I.

From the first time that they laid eyes on the Quapaws, most Frenchmen very much liked what they saw: Tonty said that "[i]t may be affirmed that these are the best-formed Savages we have seen";[10] and even Joutel allowed that they "were very well made and lively—the women are better made than those of the last village that we passed."[11] Father Membré, comparing them to the Indians "at the north," who, he said, were "all sad and severe in their temper," pronounced the Quapaws "far better made, honest, liberal [i.e., generous], and gay."[12] Another version of Father Membré's evaluation of the Arkansas Indians has him saying that they were "all so well formed and proportioned that we admired their beauty."[13] Another priest described the Quapaws as the "best made, frankest and best disposed men that we have seen."[14]

It was probably Father Charlevoix, though, who praised the Quapaws' physical appearance most fulsomely. "The Arkansas," he said, "are reckoned the largest and handsomest of men of all the Indians of this continent, and are called by way of distinction *les beaux hommes,* or the handsome men."[15] In 1700, Pénicaut found the Quapaw women "very pretty and white," while, he said, "the men, for the most part, are large and stocky."[16] The only discordant voice in this otherwise extravagant chorus of praise was Le Sueur's: While he admitted that "the men are very tall, large, and well made," he unfortunately found "the women very ugly."[17]

For the most part, too, the early French found the Quapaws easy and tractable. Father Montigny thought that the Quapaws were "very mild," and reported that "they give a warm welcome and have esteem for the French."[18] To Father Membré, they were "cheerful, polite, and generous."[19] And Le Page du Pratz outdid even himself when it came time to describe the Arkansas region and its native people. "I am so biased in . . . favor" of the Arkansas country, he said, "that I am persuaded that the beauty of its climate influences the character of its inhabitants, who are at the same time very gentle and very brave—for along with the peaceful qualities that everyone knows them for, they exhibit a courage without reproach."[20]

There was only an occasional dissent from the highly favorable evaluations of the Quapaws' temperament that one generally encounters in the French sources. The Quapaws were not a race of Tontos ("tonto" is the Spanish word for "stupid"); they had their own personal and national agendas which, as we shall see, they shrewdly pursued, and, quite naturally, they were not inclined to tolerate rude or disrespectful treatment from their visitors. For instance, in 1722 Bénard de La Harpe complained bitterly that the tribe was "very large and of ill will,"[21] but that was only because the Quapaws had refused to help him in his effort to penetrate the upper reaches of the Arkansas River, a reluctance almost certainly caused by their fear that that penetration would result in the French trading guns to their enemies the Osages. La Harpe, moreover, had commandeered one of the Quapaws' boats for his expedition, and then rather oddly condemned them for resenting it.

The French also seemed to exhibit a reasonably detached kind of

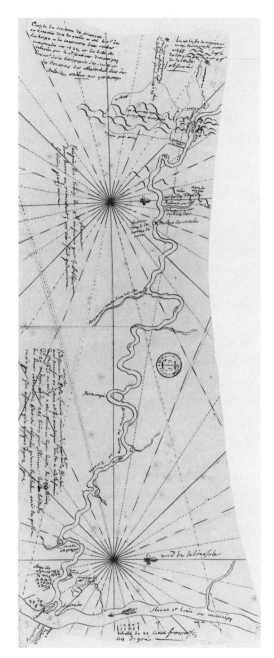

Figure 3. Dumont de Montigny's map of the Arkansas River, 1722, showing Law's concession and the Quapaw villages. *Courtesy of Archives Nationales, Paris*

tolerance when it came to describing the Quapaws' religious practices. Diron d'Artaguiette provides the only real exception: "These are surely the coarsest and most superstitious savages that I know in Louisiana," he wrote, speaking of the Quapaws, and he then went on to describe "a method of healing their sick which is very peculiar." Quapaw "jugglers" would yell loudly to drive out the evil spirits, pour five or six pails of water over the sick person, chase the spirit away, "and, acting as if they had it, they put it out of the tent."[22]

But perhaps partly because the Quapaws usually respected the "black chiefs," as they called the Roman Catholic priests who visited and settled among them, missionaries did not indulge in invective when discussing Quapaw religious practices; instead, they described them, if frequently incorrectly, more or less matter-of-factly. The Quapaws extended a polite and politic invitation to early priests to stay in their country, and even offered one group to build them a house.[23] One priest, speaking of the Tunicas, remarked that "[r]eligion may be greatly advanced among them, as well as among the Arkansas, both those nations being half-civilized," something of an encomium coming from the mouth of a seventeenth-century Christian missionary. But Father Du Poisson's hopes were not that high, and he was on the spot: "Pray to God," he enjoined his correspondent, "that he may give me grace to devote all the strength that I have to the conversion of the Savages; to judge humanly, no great good can be done among them, at least in the beginning."[24]

Bossu, who, in his own self-promoting and crude way, was a writer of the "noble savage" school, had, as we would expect, some very good things to say about Quapaw religion. "Here," speaking of Arkansas, he exuded, "everything is submissive to the will of the Great Spirit or to the Supreme Being. It is here that He is served in a most agreeable manner in a simple, undecorated temple . . . without cunning artfulness on the part of the medicine men or priests. . . . The soul unaided worships Him and offers words of truth to Him. It is sufficient to be conscious of this dear benefactor, this Master of Life."[25] It does not require much imaginative sophistication to make out the anticlericalism in Bossu's observations, which his eighteenth-century readers would have picked up on and appreciated in an immediate way.[26] He is using the Quapaws to bash the Roman Catholic clergy and along with them what he perceived to be an extravagant and materialistic church.

II.

From the foregoing it should be reasonably clear that the Frenchmen of the Arkansas were quite high on the Quapaw nation and would hardly have been averse to establishing various kinds of liaisons with them, including sexual and connubial ones. We first hear of Quapaw women when Robert Cavalier de La Salle approached the village of Kappa in 1682: The Quapaws, he said, "thinking their enemies were upon them, sent away their women and children."[27] Once matters calmed down, however, and it became clear that the French party had no hostile intentions, the women returned and brought their visitors corn, beans, corn flour, and fruits, "in return for the little gifts which we gave them and with which they were delighted because of their novelty."[28] (This incident provides some evidence of Quapaw women's ownership and control of the food supply, a property right presumably bottomed on the fact that the women planted and tended the gardens.) Several French visitors remarked that Quapaw women worked harder than the men,[29] and Bossu allowed that there was "no country where the women are more industrious." According to him, they did the cooking and housekeeping and cared for the children, fetched the game from the woods, dressed hides to make clothes and leggings, and cultivated the gardens.[30]

Quapaw women did not lack for a wide range of foods to serve their families. The Quapaws were accomplished horticulturalists and led a sedentary life most of the year, but they hunted various animals extensively in the winter to supplement their diet and for other purposes. Corn, of course, was an important agricultural product: Early visitors reported that the Quapaws made three different corn crops a year,[31] indicating probably a considerable amount of experimentation on their part (or on the part of tribes with whom they had come in contact) and the development of strains selected for their differing characteristics. Joutel admired a field of four or five square miles from which the Quapaws harvested "corn, pumpkins, melons, sunflowers, beans, and other like stuff, as well as lots of peaches and plums."[32] The French were impressed with the variety of the fruits available at the Arkansas, which included peaches, plums, persimmons (the French always compared these very favorably with their medlars), watermelons, mulberries, and even grapes from which the Quapaws made a wine.[33]

The French found that the food that the Quapaw women prepared was very much to their liking. A great deal of creativity went into dressing up the ubiquitous corn dishes: Sometimes ground corn was "seasoned plentifully with dried peaches, sometimes with turkey";[34] and Joutel tells us that the Quapaws made "several kinds of corn bread"[35] which they served to visitors along with smoked meat and fruit. Jean-Bernard Bossu quite evidently relished the "broiled venison cutlets and sun-dried bear tongues" with which the Quapaws regaled him in 1770.[36] The Quapaws were also excellent at spearing fish,[37] and even, according to Tonty, had domesticated some cocks and hens.[38] The Quapaw women cooked all these in ways that visitors frequently found most agreeable.

Diron claimed, in fact, that Quapaw women did "all the work except the hunting, which is the ordinary occupation of the men, as is also the dressing of the buffalo skins, upon which they paint designs with vermilion and other colors."[39] But the men must also have cleared fields whenever that was necessary,[40] and, of course, they were responsible as well for making war and deciding the course of village and tribal affairs in the council meetings, gatherings from which Quapaw women were excluded. Although women were also excluded, it seems, from some of the dances (as, for instance and for obvious reasons, the dances preparatory to war), they were included in many others, and they participated in important religious rituals like the mourning rites that Father Charlevoix observed in 1721. A smallpox epidemic had devastated a Quapaw village in that year, and Father Charlevoix saw the women in a large graveyard, among "a forest of poles and stakes, weeping over the dead, singing *nihahani* over and over again." One woman, he said, was crying over her son's grave and pouring sagamite (a corn dish) over it; another had lit "a fire beside a neighbouring tomb, probably in order to warm the deceased person."[41]

The nurturing and spiritual qualities, and, not least of all, the practical skills that the Quapaw women possessed, would have made them ideal mates and partners for the French hunters of the Arkansas, who, as we shall see, made their livelihood in much the same way that many Indians sometimes made theirs, namely, by hunting and by trading the product of their hunt for European goods. It was a natural match that could not have failed to occur, especially given the advantages that the Indians themselves saw in establishing family ties, social and cultural advantages that were

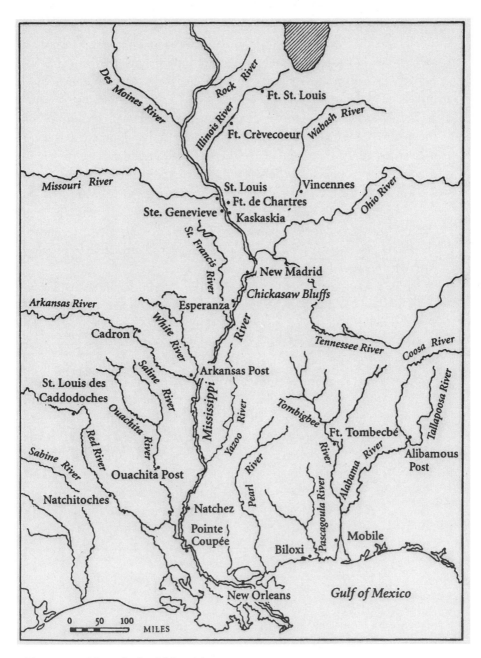

Figure 4. Map of colonial Louisiana.

similar to those that a conjugal connection brought in European society, but advantages that were a good deal broader as well. That was, as we shall see, because in Indian societies families (or rather clans) performed functions that in European societies were performed by governments, including, importantly, the punishment of certain offenses and the making of war.

The French *coureurs de bois* (forest rangers) have long been famous for the manner in which they freely took up with Indian women, and from the earliest times there must have been a considerable amount of intermarriage and concubinage between the Frenchmen of the Arkansas and the women of the Quapaw nation. Quapaw marriage customs allowed for easy divorce[42] and there is even evidence, at least in the very early period, that the Quapaws practiced polygyny:[43] Both of these aspects of the indigenous law of domestic relations would have proved attractive to Frenchmen who ventured into the Arkansas country.

Diron d'Artaguiette demonstrated a keen interest in the sexual habits of Indian girls and women in Louisiana, an interest that seems to have transcended the merely reportorial. "Young girls" of the Illinois tribe, he wrote, despite the best efforts of the Jesuits, "are the mistresses of their own bodies (to use their own expression)."[44] Natchez women, too, were "all precocious in matters of love." Among them, he asserts, there were "very few girls, twelve years old, who have not several lovers, all of whom they make happy." These girls, he said, "generally like all the Frenchmen, to whom they refuse none of their favors, in return for a few glass beads or other trifles."[45] But when it came time to describe the Quapaws, Diron, though he reckoned that their women were "passable for Americans," said that they were "all very well-behaved, for I do not believe that there is a man in the colony who can boast of having had any gallant relations with any Arkansas girl or woman." The interpreters told him (he did not seem to believe it) that Quapaw men "make [the women] believe that they could die if they had the least intercourse with us."[46]

This testimony of Diron's seems at best a bit odd, given the amount of sexual activity that took place between Frenchmen and native Americans in the rest of Louisiana, and it is, in any case, entirely contrary to Du Pratz's version of what occurred in seventeenth- and early eighteenth-century Arkansas. Speaking of Tonty's 1686 Arkansas establishment, he said that "this little settlement [*habitation*] maintained itself and grew stronger, not only because from time to time it has been augmented by some Canadians who descended the Mississippi, but above all because those who formed it had the wisdom to live in peace with the natives and treated as legitimate the children that they had with the girls of the Arkansas, whom they married out of necessity."[47] Bossu, too, in speaking of Arkansas Post, maintained that "some of our compatriots took Indian women for wives in the absence of white women at the start of the settlement,"[48] but it seems quite possible that Bossu was simply following Du Pratz here, whose book had appeared ten years before his, and a copy of which Bossu surely had.

A similar observation about French and Indian relations in the Arkansas country comes from the very early nineteenth century, that is, at the close of the colonial epoch. In describing the newly reacquired Louisiana province to a French audience, Louis Dubroca, speaking of Arkansas Post, reported that "the Canadians who established themselves there in coming downriver found there a delightful climate, a fertile soil, prosperity, and peace." Much of this, to say the least and as we shall see, is an extravagant exaggeration. But the author continued that the "habit that [the French] had acquired in Canada of living with the savages led them to marry the Arkansas girls without any difficulty and these alliances had the happiest consequences." He offered the further comment that "one never sees the least chill between even very different nations whom marriage has united." For the French of Arkansas, the author concluded, this meant that "this trade and reciprocity produced good effects that overcame obstacles thrown up in the course of time."[49] These claims, too, contain not a little puffing, but Dubroca's assertions about intermarriage, like those of Du Pratz and Bossu, are, as will shortly appear, objectively verifiable.

It is certainly true in any case that most French women would have balked at coming to the Arkansas to share the lives of *voyageurs* (boatmen) and *coureurs de bois,* although there were a number, like the ones with whom Father Du Poisson shared a boat on the way up the great river to Arkansas in 1727, who were sufficiently adventurous. These were, in his sardonic words, "girls taken from the hospitals of Paris, or from the *salpêtrière,* or other places of equally good repute, who found that the laws of marriage are too severe, and the management of a house too irksome." He offered, in addition, this interesting evaluation of these young women: "A voyage of four hundred leagues does not terrify these heroines; I already know two of them whose adventures would furnish material for a romance."[50] A few of these adventuresses must surely have ended up at

Louisiana's Arkansas Post. In fact, Father Du Poisson relates that he had come upriver to the Post with "one of those heroines of whom I told you, who was going to join her hero; she did nothing but chatter, laugh, and sing."[51] One writer has claimed that "[a]s New Orleans expanded, the Arkansas Post attracted from that source new members [including] the romantic 'Casette girls' . . . who in 1726 augmented the charm and class of the outpost on the Arkansas River."[52] But there is not the slightest support for this pretty tale, and there can be no doubt that it is wholly fanciful.

While the number of French women who made their way to the Arkansas was certainly not negligible, French men greatly outnumbered them there from the very start, and the more objective record completely bears out the claims of contemporary French writers about European and Indian intermarriage, claims that might, for various reasons, otherwise have to be approached with a certain degree of caution and skepticism.[53] There has been, it is true, a significant amount of genealogical work done on French colonial Arkansas families, but their unions with the Indians have heretofore gone all but unremarked on.[54] That is partly, though not entirely, because that earlier work has concentrated on the gentry and on the merchant and *habitant* (planter) class of the Post and its environs,[55] and thus necessarily to the exclusion of the great bulk of the colonial Arkansas population, especially the *voyageurs* and *coureurs de bois* whose peripatetic ways and virtual invisibility in some records tended to leave only ephemeral traces of their existence. These people frequently escaped the censuses as, for the most part, did the Indians of the region. But there were other classes of people (some of them pursuing hunting, farming, and trading in equal measure) whose lives are more than faintly detectable in the ecclesiastical record. And there they reveal some very interesting details about themselves and their marital and sexual habits.

Father Pierre Janin, the only priest whose services the canonical parish of St. Stephen at Arkansas Post ever enjoyed, left behind a register that he styled "Baptisms of Whites of the Faithful of the Arkansas River," in which he recorded the names of more than seventy infants whom he baptized during his short tenure as pastor there from 1796 to 1799.[56] Despite the register's title, the individual records that it contains positively state that twenty-one of the "white" infants baptized, about 30 percent, were partially of Indian descent. But this is not the whole story: If one eliminates from the record the babies who had no Frenchmen in their recorded

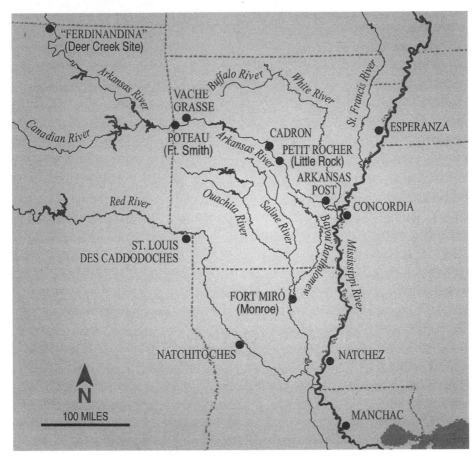

Figure 5.   Map of the Arkansas region in the eighteenth century.

line, mostly those of German or American parentage, the percentage of new Christians with express Indian family ancestry rises to almost 40 percent.

There are, in addition, eleven other entries that reveal that the baptized children had an Imbeau or Francoeur in their direct line, and both of these families are known to have intermarried extensively with the Quapaw Indians.[57] (In 1889, for instance, there were six members of the Quapaw tribe named Imbeau.)[58] These babies, therefore, would have had at the very least Indian collateral kin, and many of them, no doubt, were descended from Indians. Taking these last children into account, even in a conservative way, makes it plain that well over half of the "French" babies whom Father Janin baptized must have had direct and relatively close Indian ancestors.

Finally, when one adds to all this the fact that four of the baptized children not already counted were of unknown parentage, and many others had unknown grandparents on one or both sides, characteristics that tend to indicate some Indian blood, it is about as clear as it could be that the vast majority of the "French" in and around the colonial Post of Arkansas were also Indians to one degree or another, or at the very least had close Indian collateral relatives. This conclusion can only be reinforced by the fact that the people who presented their babies for baptism were probably self-selected Christians, and so the sample of the general Arkansas population that Father Janin's register represents is in all likelihood skewed in favor of people without close Indian kin. That is to say, it seems reasonable that the more European one was in some sense, the more likely one was to have Christian inclinations.

It is also demonstrable that even some of Arkansas's few gentry produced mixed-blood progeny. In 1889, for instance, six members of the Quapaw tribe were named Vallier,[59] no doubt descendants (either of his own making or of his sons') of Joseph Vallière d'Hauterive, commandant of Arkansas Post from 1787 to 1790. François Menard, moreover, the richest man at the Post in the Arkansas colonial period, though he was married to a French woman, fathered a daughter named Constance by an Indian girl named Susana Bonne. Constance was educated by the sisters at the Ursuline Convent in New Orleans, and Menard provided rather generously for her in his will.[60]

All of this documentary evidence amply supports the eyewitness account of a man who was evidently an officer in the American garrison at the Post and who signed himself "A. Stewart." In 1809, in describing the denizens of the Post, he wrote that "the Inhabitants being mostly a Heterogeneous Mass of French and the Arkansas Indians who live 16 miles higher up the river, there are but few families who are not more or less connected with the Natives."[61] Describing the population of Arkansas Post to his readers in 1812, Amos Stoddard reported similarly that "the French to preserve peace with [the Quapaws], and to secure their trade, intermarried with them." The result, he said, was that "[m]ost of the inhabitants of that village are of mixed blood, and the same mixture is observable among the Indians, who are now reduced to a very few in number, and live in two small villages above that of the whites."[62]

III.

Tonty's motive in settling the first Arkansas Post in 1686 was to establish trade with the Quapaws; indeed, Arkansas Post takes its name from the fact that it was a trading post.[63] For a time, however, and partly because France was slow in following up on La Salle's plans for a real settlement among the Quapaws, it looked as though Carolina traders were going to gain an important foothold in the Arkansas country. With the help of Jean Couture, a French ship's carpenter who in 1686 had built Tonty's first Arkansas Post, English traders had traveled all the way from Carolina to treat with the Quapaws; and by the end of the eighteenth century one of those traders had even married into the tribe.

Pierre-Charles Le Sueur, on his way up the Mississippi River in 1700, had encountered an Englishman at the Post, and the French arrested an English trader there the year before, but it is doubtful that French activities in the region alone would have ended British influence in the Arkansas country entirely. It is even possible that the English had a hand in the martyrdom of Father Foucault, missionary to the Quapaws, who was killed by some Koroa Indians in 1702. However that may be, and for whatever reason, there is no mention of English traders among the Quapaws in the early eighteenth century after Le Sueur's visit to the tribe.[64] The general English effort to drive the French entirely from Louisiana during Queen Anne's War, moreover, seems to have been felt only in the most tangential way in the Arkansas country. In 1708, Thomas Welch, a Carolina trader, held a council at the Yazoo River with the representatives of a number of Mississippi River tribes, including the Quapaws, at which he concluded a "peace" aimed at cementing them to the English interest. But Governor Bienville claimed, and he was probably right, that the tribes attending the parley refused to take a part in or even approve the projected English assault on Mobile.[65]

After the failure of the first French post among the Quapaws, which must have finally occurred at the latest by around 1700, there is little evidence of French activity in the region until 1721, when John Law's ambitious colonizing schemes caused the establishment of fewer than a hundred Europeans and a small garrison at the site of Tonty's former outpost.[66] Father Du Poisson commented in 1727 on the existence at this Arkansas Post of a few Frenchmen who had learned only enough of the

Quapaws' language as was "necessary that they should know for trade."[67] Trading was therefore evidently one of the activities of these Frenchmen, but whether they were trading for subsistence or for export Du Poisson does not say. There certainly was some trade with the Quapaws for food-stuff, especially in the early days before the French became reasonably well established.[68] Du Poisson also claimed that "only the excellence of the climate and of the soil here kept them" at their settlement, so the denizens of Arkansas were apparently engaging in some form of agriculture as well.[69] About a decade later, in 1738, Father Vitry, writing of Arkansas Post, noted that a "few Frenchmen attracted by the hope of trade with the Indians, are settled nearby."[70]

The proposition that Indians conceived of trade as mutual gift-giving is frequently advanced,[71] and is sometimes true, but they certainly did not usually do so, and in their very early dealings with the French of the Arkansas the Quapaws clearly revealed their appreciation of the difference between reciprocated gifts and bargained-for market exchanges of the ordinary sort. One of Father Du Poisson's letters from the Arkansas country in 1727 is quite instructive on the sharp distinction that the Quapaws were capable of drawing, and did draw, between the two kinds of transactions. An unidentified Quapaw, probably a chief, wanted to sing the calumet to the good father to incorporate him into the Quapaws' tribal arrangement. The Quapaws carefully explained to the Jesuit priest that they meant to present him with something "without design," that is, that they did not want to trade but were intending to establish a relationship of an ongoing character that would involve reciprocal duties of support and maintenance between the donor and the donee. As they said, in the context of a calumet adoption ritual, the idea was that Quapaw and Frenchman should make gifts to each other, an exchange not bargained for but aimed at creating a fictive kin relationship between an Indian and a Frenchman, in which, in this instance, the Frenchman became an adopted "father" and the Indian an adopted "son."

So, Father Du Poisson was told, after such a relationship was created, "I should make him [the Quapaw] sit down, and should give him food as to my own son; and when he returned a second time to see me, I should say: 'sit down, my son; look, here are vermillion and powder.'" The exchange therefore was not an arms-length, one-time transaction; it involved mutual gifts that created a superintending familial and fiduciary environment,

Figure 6.   Engraving of Quapaw warrior painting an arrow on a tree as a declaration of war. A. Antoine de Saint-Gervais, *Nouvel album des peuples ou collection de tableaux* (Paris: 1835), 98.

where the duties of kinship, and the wants, needs, and deserts of the parties, measured the obligations that each party owed.

The Quapaws further explained that, on the other hand, a regular market trading arrangement involved an offer to exchange "with design," that is, for a bargained-for price. In such a relationship, they said, for example, if a Quapaw cast some game at the foot of a Frenchman, the Frenchman would simply ask him, "For what dost thou hunger?" In other words, he would ask what the Quapaw wanted in exchange, that is, the price of the game. When a Quapaw then gave Father Du Poisson a painted (*mataché*) buckskin, and the good father asked him what he wanted in return, the exasperated Indian responded, "I have given without design," and then asked rhetorically, "[A]m I trading with my father?" Only a few minutes later, however, the Quapaw said that "his wife had no salt, and his son no powder." In other words, the Indian wanted to give Du Poisson things because the Indian was the son, and he wanted Father Du Poisson to give him things because Du Poisson was the father. Goods in this fictive kin relationship changed hands because of the reciprocal obligations inherent in family ties.[72]

It is clear from Father Du Poisson's letter that he comprehended the main outlines of what was being said to him, but he wrongly suspected that the whole thing was a ruse to extort goods from him, and he did not, moreover, want his relationship with the Quapaws to be "materialistic." In this, he certainly misunderstood both the Quapaws' motives and their sincerity. On the other hand, one needs clearly to understand that the Quapaws were not acting in a disinterested way in choosing whom they wanted as a "father": As the Spanish would soon discover when they succeeded the French in Louisiana, the Quapaws had no interest in having paupers for fathers. This was because the Quapaws understood full well what their obligations of defense and support were as sons, as they understood what those duties were when the shoe was on the other foot and they were cast in the paternal role.[73]

The Quapaws, in any case, were more than a little interested in acquiring European goods, and had been for a considerable time. Though Marquette and Jolliet may have been the first white men whom the Quapaws had ever actually seen, by the time of their arrival at the Arkansas in 1673 the Quapaws had already acquired some European trade goods, including knives, hatchets, and beads.[74] The Spanish, either of New Mexico or of Florida, were almost certainly the indirect suppliers of some of these goods: Possible middlemen for the Florida trade included the Taogrias who lived on the Tennessee River, some of whom were reported coming from the Arkansas in 1700,[75] and Wichitas or Caddos could have passed on European goods from New Mexico.[76] Some of the goods that Marquette saw may well have been French, since he reported that the Quapaws had acquired some of their trade items from "an Illinois town to the west."[77] Joutel says that the Quapaws traded plates that they made in exchange for bows and arrows, probably with the Caddos.[78]

The Quapaws, of course, were especially keen to have guns for offensive and defensive use against their enemies. Their longtime foe the Chickasaws had probably had guns for some time. Marquette reports meeting armed Indians on the Mississippi, who the Quapaws said "were their enemies who cut off their passage to the sea, and prevented their making the acquaintance of the Europeans, or having any commerce with them."[79] It seems very likely that these Indians were Chickasaws. In 1687, Joutel told the Quapaws that he and his party "intended to go to our country and bring [guns and munitions] back to them, and that we would even bring back people to go to war with them. Then we would destroy all their enemies and make peace everywhere." This news, Joutel reports, "made them cry out with joy and they told us not to be long in coming."[80]

La Salle evidently had left no guns with the Quapaws in 1682, but they had certainly acquired them by 1687, because Joutel reports that at three of the Quapaw villages the Quapaws saluted his arrival with volleys from their muskets;[81] Joutel remarked that he did not know if they had gotten these guns from Tonty or from upriver (*pays d'en haut*).[82] Nor does he say whether the Quapaws as yet had horses, but since he does not report that his mounts had caused any particular stir on his arrival, it seems a reasonable guess that there were already at least a few in the Quapaw villages. Joutel's party, at any rate, left all their horses at the Post to go on to the Illinois by boat[83] (a decision that they later regretted), so horses would have become familiar to the Quapaws at least by 1687. Joutel also left the two Frenchmen living at the Post some powder, balls, gunflints, knives, hatchets, beads, rings, needles, and "other trifles and utensils," so that they could trade with the Indians.[84]

The list of trade goods that Commandant Gamon de Larochette had on hand in 1758 helps complete the view of the kinds of items popular among the Quapaws. For hunting and war, he could offer them Tulle guns, trade guns, powder, lead, flints, balls, wormscrews, and salt; for clothing, he stocked blankets, trade shirts, shoes, Limbourg (a lightweight woolen cloth, often of red or blue), twilled woolen serge, another cloth called *sempiterne* that resembled this last, beads, wool ribbon, and even shoes (probably for the soldiers or inhabitants). Larochette also had white and blue paint on hand that the Indians used for decorating their faces and bodies. One of Larochette's competitors, the Post's storekeeper Étienne Layssard, had vermilion paint for sale, among other things,[85] and the king's store had in stock, in addition to the goods already mentioned, two-point blankets, three-point blankets, breechcloths, awls, strike-a-lights, folding knives, and butcher knives. One could even buy four kinds of nails, candles, flour, and biscuit at the government store, along with rum and brandy, these last two not intended for the Indian market, a prohibition, we must believe, more often violated than observed.[86]

Trade with the Quapaws themselves may never have been particularly lucrative. It infrequently receives mention in the records, and when it does, it is rarely to extol its importance. In the 1740s, for instance, Bienville complained that the Quapaws were lazy because they would not produce even one thousand deerskins a year; about thirty years later Villiers wrote that the trade with the Quapaws was not worth sending an agent to their village and that the Quapaws took the few skins that they had to the English to exchange for liquor.[87] On the other hand, in 1758 Commandant Larochette wrote to New Orleans to request goods for the Quapaw trade (which the government may have been advancing to him on credit);[88] and he and Layssard were engaged in an ongoing contretemps over whether the commandant was entitled to a monopoly over the Quapaw trade,[89] so it must at least have been worth something. In the same year, the French built a house near the fort at Arkansas Post "to give lodging to the Indians allied with us when the business of the service calls them there,"[90] and, no doubt, for the Quapaws' use when they came to the Post to trade as well. Furthermore, a decade later, Alexandre Chevalier DeClouet asked for a monopoly over the Quapaw trade.[91]

Whatever may have been the Quapaws' attitude about trading with the residents of Arkansas Post, they were certainly anxious to restrict the Post merchants' trade with other tribes. They were especially troubled by the prospect of guns reaching the Osages, and so when La Harpe appeared at the Post in 1722 and made inquiries about the upper reaches of the river, he could get no information whatever from the Quapaws, who, La Harpe noticed, seemed unhappy with his expedition.[92] When he asked for a boat, though the Quapaws had more than thirty of them, they refused; and when he commandeered one, he was forced to return it in response to a show of force by the Quapaws. Fabry de la Bruyère met with a similar reception in 1741. Although he did finally manage to obtain five boats from the Indians for his expedition upriver, it was only "with much difficulty,"[93] and when he returned to the Post to get some horses, the Quapaws refused to sell him any. Then, for good measure, the Quapaws frustrated his attempt to acquire horses from the Caddos by providing him with guides who led him around in the wilderness for forty-five days without finding the Caddo villages, the route to which they had to know perfectly well.[94]

IV.

In their efforts to establish a political and military alliance with the Quapaws, the French very early on discovered that the chief of the Kappa village was the great chief of the entire Quapaw nation;[95] but they learned at the same time that a Quapaw chief, even a great chief, could not command. He was entitled only to cajole his people into joining enterprises that he believed worthy of them or necessary to the nation's welfare. Joutel maintained, for instance, speaking of the Quapaws, that "they obey their chiefs only in part and as far as they wish," and that "the chiefs aren't received as such until they perform some good deeds [belles actions], and on condition that they be generous with what they have, and make themselves commendable in some way in order to draw the young people to them." Joutel explained that that was "why, when one makes them a present, they [i.e., the chiefs] get the least of it, because they distribute it to the young people and to the warriors."[96]

The motive for the chief's gift-giving had, as Joutel recognized, a prudential aspect, but socio-legal obligations to share were almost certainly imposed in many situations among the Quapaws. It could hardly have been otherwise in such a small society the members of which were bound by elaborate kinship connections, biological and otherwise, and whose fund of assumptions about how a moral world was ordered had become embedded in their behavorial patterns. Bossu described this aspect of Quapaw culture in an embarrassingly unsophisticated way, but, despite his evident desire to exploit the Quapaws as a way of criticizing what he saw as so regrettably missing from his own culture, his description probably captures the essence of the Quapaw attitude toward the duty to share. "Americans," meaning Indians, he says, in general "derive indescribable joy and pleasure from helping the widow, the orphan, the old, and the poor."[97] He also "found admirable among the men whom we have the barbarity to call barbarians" the fact "that there are no paupers at all among them who go about begging for a living." He thought it a shame that Europeans did "not imitate the Americans, among whom the widow and orphan are fed at public expense," and praised Indians for employing "those who cannot do strenuous work" at making spears for fishing or bows and arrows for hunting.[98]

The diffusion of power in Quapaw society was in sharp contrast to the situation that obtained in hierarchical societies like that of the Natchez, where "the chief has great authority over the people of his tribe, and he makes them obey him." The French realized that this was "not so with most of the other tribes," including the Quapaws; "they have chiefs who are chiefs only in name; everyone is master, and, notwithstanding, no seditions are ever found among them."[99] This aspect of the Quapaws' government was adverted to again and again by the French who dealt with them.

In 1739, for instance, when Lieutenant Coustilhas came to Arkansas Post to enlist the Quapaws' aid in the second French attempt to bring the Chickasaws to heel, the Quapaws responded respectfully that "the Frenchman is our father; we were worthy of pity, and he has supplied our needs, and we listen to the words of our father." But, the Quapaw chiefs cautioned, "you know that we are not the masters of our warriors. We speak to them, but we cannot compel them to listen to us." The chiefs assured the lieutenant that they would "hold councils in our village, and will invite our people to follow you," but the French, they said, should "not blame us chiefs, if we do not give you the men whom you ask for."[100] It took the Quapaws three weeks to raise the requested number of warriors, and then only from two of their three villages, but even so, Father Vitry warned, "[t]he agreement may be arbitrarily broken at any time." "The Indian is independent," he cautioned, "and likes his freedom; if you press him for one thing, he will choose the other."[101]

The French and the Quapaws, however, frequently found common ground in their animosity to the Chickasaws. Quapaws and Chickasaws had evidently been at odds for some time, perhaps not engaged in war in the European sense (we do not know), but rather in a potentially endless chain of reciprocated homicides, each of which was regarded as a just and required retaliation for ones that had preceded it. These kinds of killings were no doubt sometimes precipitated by disputes over hunting territory, but they were probably not part of territorial wars in the European sense: The aim of killing was not to gain territory, but to avenge deaths. It is also true that peace might well involve gaining and losing territory, but that would not have been its aim. In other words, the Quapaws, as an original matter, may not have fought over territory, but they did have altercations that territorial claims gave rise to.

While the Chickasaws made overtures of peace to the Quapaws in April of 1727,[102] nothing seems to have come of the effort, and the Natchez massacre of 1729, in which the Chickasaws connived, an attack that rocked the very foundations of colonial Louisiana, hardened the parties' position in such a way as to make peace between them impossible for many, many years. Although the French of Louisiana seem to have recognized that the massacre had at bottom been the fault of an arrogant French commandant's attempt to force the Natchez off their ancestral lands, Governor Périer resolved to exterminate them, an aim in which he all but succeeded.

Périer was sure (or said that he was sure) that the Natchez uprising signaled the beginning of a general Indian revolt in the colony. Early in 1730, wild and false rumors that "war was breaking out high and low" circulated throughout the province, even including reports that the Caddos and the Wichitas had attacked and destroyed part of the Quapaw nation, that the Quapaws had retired to join their "allies" the Osages, and (most disturbing of all) that the Quapaws had killed "five or six Frenchmen who were among them [*chez eux*]."[103] The French were relieved two months later to learn from pirogues coming from the Illinois country that "the Arkansas have remained faithful to us," and that the Quapaws "were delighted to have news from us because they were beginning to believe that we had been entirely destroyed as our enemies were maintaining in order to convert to their side the nations who were wavering."[104] Father Le Petit reported that the Quapaws had "made a solemn oath that, while one *Akensa* should be remaining in the world, the *Natchez* and the *Yazous* should never be without an enemy."[105] Périer subsequently learned that the Chickasaws had sent embassies to the Quapaws to try to recruit them into their war effort against the Choctaws and the French, but without success.[106]

According to Bossu, the Quapaws, "following the Chief's advice, wanted no part of the Natchez' plot to massacre the French," and in 1751 were "still at war with the Chickasaws among whom the Natchez found refuge,"[107] indicating, perhaps, that the Quapaws had even had advance notice of the Natchez plan to destroy the French in their neighborhood. However that may be, Bossu is certainly right that the Quapaws harried the Chickasaws, and joined in the government's organized war efforts against them, throughout the entire French colonial period.

It was the Natchez revolt of 1729, and the deep panic that it understandably inspired in the Louisiana French, that led directly to the reestablishment of a garrison at the Arkansas Post, which had been without one since 1726. The Quapaws, Governor Périer wrote, "are so necessary for us that one cannot do too much in their favor." It was, he said, "their situation and their attachment to the French [that] kept the English from passing over the Mississippi" after the revolt at Natchez. Because "the Chickasaws have done everything to seduce this nation from us," he resolved to send Pierre Petit de Coulange to command at the Arkansas Post; "without this precaution," he predicted, "the Chickasaws would have succeeded" in undermining the Quapaw alliance.[108]

In the spring of 1731, Périer dispatched a convoy of four boats containing a large contingent of seventy men to the Arkansas with orders to reestablish the military post, but the attempt was thwarted, and the convoy was turned back, when the Natchez attacked it on the Mississippi, killing two Frenchmen and wounding two others.[109] Although the French finally achieved their goal late in 1731 or early in 1732, the "fort" that they built at the Arkansas did not even have a stockade, a matter for complaint from the Quapaws, who wanted one in which to shelter their families in case the Chickasaws attacked their villages. This was a well-founded fear, for by the summer of 1732 the Quapaws had already attacked a party of Chickasaws, one or two of whom they had taken prisoner and burned to death in their village. The Quapaws also complained that they had not received any presents and had not even been paid for the scalps that they had taken.[110] In 1733, Périer wrote that Ensign Coulange had "made himself loved to the point that" the Quapaws "have made war continually [on the Chickasaws] even though I have had nothing to give them except promises";[111] and the next year a very large force of one hundred and fifty Quapaw warriors sallied forth to scour the Mississippi for the Natchez.[112]

The Quapaws also participated in the First Chickasaw War in 1736[113]

Figure 7.   Engraving of Quapaw warriors marching to attack an enemy
village. A. Antoine de Saint-Gervais, *Nouvel album des peuples ou
collection de tableaux* (Paris: 1835), 100.

and performed important scouting services in preparation for the equally
abortive Second Chickasaw War of 1738.[114] Seventy Quapaw warriors,
moreover, in response to a personal visit from Governor Bienville,[115] arrived
at Chickasaw Bluffs early in 1740 to contribute to the effort there,[116] whereupon, greatly impressed by the firing of the French howitzers, they opined
that the French "were not men but great spirits" and "offered to carry the
bombs and six-inch mortars to the Chickasaws on their shoulders!"[117] But
only ten days later, put off by Bienville's endless temporizing, the Quapaws
abandoned the field and returned home.[118]

After the disastrous denouement of this campaign, the Chickasaws soon
resumed their raids on Mississippi shipping and continued to terrorize and
harry the Arkansas French when they ventured out on the great river,[119] and
in 1743 the governor got word that the Chickasaws had united with some
Abekas and Cherokees with a mind to attack Arkansas Post.[120] Governor
Vaudreuil immediately persuaded the Quapaws to engage Chickasaw war
parties, and one such foray in 1744 resulted in two Chickasaw scalps.[121] It

is little wonder that the next year Vaudreuil learned that the English were trying to convince the Quapaws to settle on their side of the Mississippi with promises of cheap goods. The Quapaws, the governor cautioned, were "a very numerous nation . . . , friends of the French," whom the French needed as allies against the Chickasaws and the English party among the Choctaw nation; and the Quapaws had warned the French that they could not continue to do business on the basis of prices that were then current.[122] In 1746, however, the Quapaws brought the governor five more Chickasaw scalps. The governor's private evaluation was that although he had "had some trouble drawing them from the lethargy in which I found them, they appear at present to be in our interest." Two more scalps followed early the next year, which led the governor to instruct the Arkansas commandant, Lieutenant Montcharvaux, "to pay them generously for scalps and to tell them of my satisfaction."[123]

In 1748, the Chickasaws and some disaffected Choctaws raided some of the French settlements along the Mississippi, and, as usual, the colonial government looked to the Quapaws to retaliate. Ten bands of Quapaws, two hundred warriors in all, went out to search the Margot and Yazoo Rivers and to prowl the "roads of the Chickasaws and Choctaws and the places that our enemies are accustomed to frequent." One Quapaw party stayed at Natchez for a few days, time enough to "let the garrison get its wood, gather corn and tobacco outside the fort, and perform some other work that they could not have got done without this help."[124] Two years later, the governor wrote that the "Arkansas are always in our interest and make frequent sorties against the Chickasaws, from whom they have got some eighteen scalps." They had also killed six Choctaws and captured four; these last the governor had released to the Choctaw nation, "which produced," he said, "a very good effect."[125]

The long-rumored attack on the Post at last materialized in May of 1749 when a force of Chickasaws, Abekas, and perhaps a few Choctaws in the English interest struck and overwhelmed the small *habitant* population gathered around the tiny fort at Louisiana's *Poste aux Arkansas.* The success of the foray, which resulted in the deaths of a number of male settlers, and the capture of several women and children, could only have emphasized the strategic importance of the Quapaw alliance, for that success had resulted largely from the fact that the Quapaws had just the year before removed their villages five or six miles from the Post. After the attacks, therefore, the French relocated their fort and settlement to the Indians' neighborhood for greater security.[126] The French and Spanish of the Arkansas were thereafter keen on maintaining a proximity to the Quapaw villages in order to prevent future such debacles.[127]

The English, for their part, never seemed to abandon hope of one day dislodging the Quapaws from their alliance with the French. In 1751, they attempted to form a pan-Indian league to "attack the various posts of this continent," and were sending necklaces to "all the nations of the Wabash [i.e., Ohio]" and the Mississippi, and to the Osages as well, to enlist them in the intrigue. Some Illinois, it seems, were inveigled into signing up, and so "even the Arkansas were not exempt" from English importunings: The English party among the Illinois sent an embassy to the Post, but when Captain Delinó, the Post commandant, "discovered the real reason for the proceedings of these deputies," the emissaries, "seeing their plan discovered, retired with the presents and necklaces of the English." Governor Vaudreuil ordered the Post commandant to "make sure that the Arkansas do not have any dealings with English traders." "We do not need," Vaudreuil said, "to have trouble stirred up in this nation, which up to the present time has never given the French any reason to be unhappy."[128]

The French and Quapaw alliance remained so firm and unshaken, even in the face of sustained English attempts to undermine it, that the Chickasaws resorted to dissembling to cause the French to suspect the Quapaws of treachery. In 1754, a man named La Morlière and several other Frenchmen were killed in the environs of Natchez, and Quapaw tomahawks were ominously left in plain view on the cadavers. The Natchez commandant thus assured the governor that the Quapaws had committed this atrocity, and, besides, he said, some of his soldiers had recognized the perpetrators as Quapaws who had recently danced the calumet at Natchez when they had passed by.

Governor Kerlérec confessed that this evidence of Quapaw perfidiousness "was hard for [him] to believe, because of the protestations of fidelity that the Quapaws had made [him] and the good treatment that they had always afforded" his predecessor Governor Vaudreuil. But since the Natchez commandant was very concerned for the safety of the Arkansas Post, the governor assembled a council of war, which decided to send sixty men, including some crack Swiss troops, to the aid of Captain Charles Marie de Reggio, who was commanding at the Arkansas.

Pierre Henri d'Erneville, who was put in charge of this expeditionary force, learned on arriving at the Post that the "Chickasaws had played a trick with the tomahawks that had been left on bodies of Chickasaws by war parties that [the Quapaws] had sent last year to the environs of [the Chickasaws'] villages." The Chickasaws had simply saved the Quapaw tomahawks and left them later on the bodies of the slain Frenchmen in an attempt to deflect blame onto the Quapaws. While the charade failed in its ultimate purpose, which was to cause a serious and even permanent rupture in the French-Quapaw relationship, it had nonetheless cost the French a lot of money, time, energy, and other resources, not to mention considerable anxiety. It had also thrown them off the track of the true miscreants for a time.[129]

Showing up at Arkansas Post in 1754 with a force of sixty soldiers and with the aim of accusing the Quapaws of murdering Frenchmen was a matter of not a little delicacy. But d'Erneville, evidently, was up to the task. Kerlérec congratulated him roundly on the success of his mission and on his diplomacy in executing it. "You have done an excellent turn with respect to your mission to the Arkansas," the governor exuded. "Far from having humiliated and mortified [the Quapaws], you have flattered them greatly by persuading them that you had been sent to bring them help. You drew every advantage possible by making something good out of an enterprise the only real object of which was vengeance."[130]

II

An Animal and Human Refuge

We have seen that after the French came to the Arkansas country in the seventeenth century they had enjoyed a considerable success in making conjugal, trade, and military connections with the Quapaws, connections that overlapped and interlocked, thus providing some significant stability for Indian and European alike during the three generations or so that the French claimed sovereignty over the Louisiana region. The main economic activity that sustained these alliances, and both parties to them, was the exploitation of the abundant animal resources of which the Arkansas could boast for most of the eighteenth century. The richness of these resources was never substantially threatened, because during "the entire colonial period, Arkansas remained relatively empty of human beings."[1] It was the animals of the Arkansas country, and the nature of the small European population that they drew there, that would give the region its distinctive character and would provide a reputation for it that endured throughout its colonial epoch and well into the American epoch as well.[2]

I.

The general reader will, of course, have been conditioned long ago to associate the buffalo with the Great Plains of the Midwest and of Texas, but the truth is that there was scarcely a place in the continental United States that it did not inhabit, even in historic times, and the Arkansas region was no exception. Buffaloes seem to have been impressively plentiful in Arkansas during the seventeenth and eighteenth centuries.[3] In the southeast part of the state, the Le Boeuf (buffalo) Swamp and Bayou and, in the northwest, the Buffalo River and the Vache Grasse (fat cow) Prairie, serve to remind us of the extent of the animals' former range. And numerous travelers' accounts, some upwards of three hundred years old, reveal to us the buffaloes' now abandoned haunts rather fully.

In 1673, Father Marquette, while descending the Mississippi in the environs of the St. Francis River, remarked on "the number of wild cattle that [he] heard bellowing," which made him "believe the Prairies [were] near."[4] There were certainly some small prairies close to the great river in the region that the good father was describing, but buffaloes also found cane a congenial forage, and the banks of many of Arkansas's rivers in the eighteenth century sported huge canebrakes that would have attracted buffaloes in large numbers, especially in the winter.[5] (In fact, there are more than one hundred places in fifty-six counties, and over sixty streams, named after cane in the state of Arkansas.)[6] Some of these brakes probably sprang up in the abandoned Indian fields created by the devastating epidemics that struck the native peoples in the sixteenth and seventeenth centuries. There is evidence, too, though not in Arkansas, that Indians managed the buffalo population by burning cane at appropriate intervals to ensure that it was not crowded out by competing woody vegetation.[7]

Early travelers on the Mississippi commonly depended on the buffaloes that they killed en route to sustain themselves during their voyages. In the late seventeenth century, Father La Source reported that from Chicago to the Arkansas country "the bison and cows are so numerous that you cannot lack provisions if you have powder and balls."[8] Father St. Cosme, descending the Mississippi from the Illinois region, saw buffaloes "almost every day during [his] voyage to the Akanseas."[9] In fact, he reported that his party "had so great a quantity of meat along this river, as far as the Acanseas," that they "passed several herds of buffalo without caring to fire

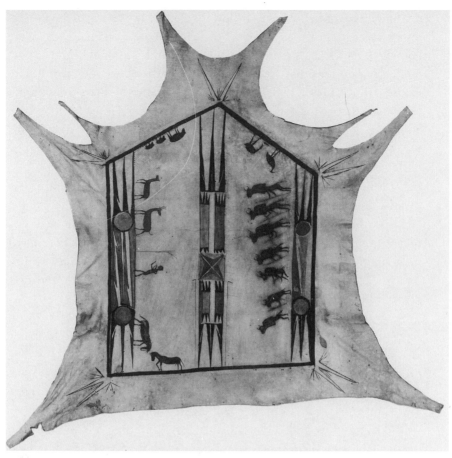

Figure 8.   Robe of the buffalo dancers, painted by Quapaw artist or artists in middle of the eighteenth century. *Courtesy of Musée de l'Homme, Paris*

at them."[10] Matters had not changed at all thirty years later. Writing from Arkansas Post, Father Du Poisson explained that while "[n]ot the smallest settlement is found between here and the Illinois," travelers to the upper country "seldom fail to kill some wild cattle, which are much relished by people who have only *gru* [corn mush] for food."[11]

Although in the seventeenth century buffaloes were also numerous from the Arkansas River all the way down to the Gulf of Mexico,[12] by the middle of the eighteenth century they seem to have been scarce below Natchez or the Yazoo River.[13] In 1721, La Harpe had already fretted about the buffalo becoming rare in the lower colony: He commented on meeting two pirogues that year on the Mississippi "with Canadians who were going to New Orleans with five thousand pounds of salted beef [i.e., buffalo]." He said that they "had killed eighty cattle above the great Pointe Coupée, which proves that it is important to prohibit hunters from killing these animals beyond their needs, for fear that this type of hunting may become rare in these regions."[14] And two years later, Diron, making his way up the Mississippi to inspect the Arkansas settlement, reported that the buffaloes, normally numerous after the Yazoo River, had gone missing. He lamented that his party was "reduced to Indian corn, without either meat or flour, and with no hope of killing any buffaloes from here to the Arkansas." The reason for this unusual scarcity of buffaloes, he said, was that the Quapaws were hunting them along the river and had "caused these animals to withdraw into the back country."[15] In the Arkansas country itself, however, Diron opined, game was so plentiful that even "the most worthless Frenchman can kill a buffalo in this region."[16]

After leaving the Arkansas country to proceed to the Illinois, Diron reported killing buffaloes at will.[17] Early one morning, in fact, his party saw a buffalo swimming across the Mississippi, whereupon, he said, they proceeded to hitch their "boat to it for more than a quarter of a league, after which we killed it." About noon the same day, he landed "to go after a herd of more than a hundred buffaloes, both bulls and cows." They "killed five and wounded more than twenty," but they "cut out only the tongues," leaving the rest behind.[18] Bossu, a few decades later, also noted that there was not a single village or house between Arkansas Post and Fort de Chartres in the Illinois, but that along the way there were herds of buffaloes that yielded abundant provisions to voyagers. French travelers, he said, often hired Quapaws to keep them supplied with game on the way to the Illinois country: The Quapaw hunters ventured out in the morning ahead of the main group, killed buffaloes along the riverbank, and left the meat along the shore for the convoy to pick up as it passed.[19]

The environs of the Arkansas River were also a favorite haunt of the buffalo. The Quapaws and their European visitors hunted them on the Grand Prairie just to the north of Arkansas Post[20] and found buffaloes plentiful up the river as well.[21] During his failed expedition up the Arkansas River in 1722, Bénard de La Harpe killed numerous buffaloes for the maintenance of his troop;[22] but, oddly, about thirty years later, Fabry de la

Figure 9.   Detail from the robe of the buffalo dancers. *Courtesy of Musée de l'Homme, Paris*

Bruyère (who launched an abortive attempt to reach Santa Fe from Arkansas Post), had two buffaloes killed at the Post and salted one of them "to take along to the Forks [i.e., the juncture with the Canadian River], not counting on any more game" after setting off.[23] Bossu, who claims to have visited Arkansas Post in 1770, asserted that the banks of the Arkansas "shelter a multitude of buffalo" among other animals.[24] The buffalo was plentiful along the Ouachita River as well, though by the late eighteenth century they were no longer common in its lower reaches.[25]

But it was the St. Francis River country that was an especially productive spot for buffalo hunters.[26] It was probably the neighborhood of the St. Francis and White rivers that Father Du Poisson had in mind when he spoke of New Orleans hunters who came regularly to the Arkansas region "to the country where there are cattle": They would dry the buffaloes' *plats côtés* (flanks) in the sun, he said, and salt the rest.[27] In the spring, these hunters descended the Mississippi "to supply the colony with meat." According to the good father, one Canadian hunter had only recently returned downriver to the capital with "four hundred and eighty tongues of cattle that he and his partner alone had killed during the winter."[28] Commandant La Houssaye was so high on the advantages of this region that in 1752 he even proposed removing the Post to "the St. Francis River where cattle [i.e., buffalo] are abundant, and where there is more subsistence."[29]

Du Pratz seconded Du Poisson's enthusiastic appraisal of the excellent hunting opportunities in the vicinity of the St. Francis River. Those precincts, he said, were "always covered with herds of buffaloes, despite the hunting expeditions made to the region every winter." It was there, he revealed, that "the French and the Canadians go to lay in stores of salted meats for the inhabitants of the capital and the neighboring plantations; they are helped by the Arkansas natives whom they hire for this purpose." He revealed an interesting technique used by the hunters: "They choose a tree from which to make a pirogue," he claimed, "the middle of which they use for a salting tub which is closed on both ends, leaving enough room for only one man at each end."[30]

Francisco Bouligny was moved to remark in the late eighteenth century on the continued bountifulness of the hunt in the Arkansas region. "[A]ll the countryside from Pointe Coupée up to Illinois," he reported, "is heavily populated with animals, particularly with buffalo or wild oxen, deer, and bears." He noted enthusiastically that "without exaggeration, it can be said that the world does not have a country where more excellent and abundant meats can be taken out or with greater ease." He gave an illustration of the bounty to be found in Arkansas. "Four hunters go out with a pirogue from New Orleans up the Mississippi River to Arkansas," he said, "where they spend forty or fifty days. Entering by either the White River or the Saint Francis River, they go to some meadows where cattle are so abundant that in two or three days they kill enough to fill the pirogue with the fat of cattle [buffalo tallow] and the tongues or oil of bears alone and they return to New Orleans. Behind them they leave an infinity of meat scattered in the fields which is not used at all."[31] "These lands are so plentiful," he concluded, "that the accounts made daily by the hunters who cross them do not seem believable to us."[32]

The buffalo was put to many uses in the Arkansas country. It was, as we have seen, a favorite food of Indian and Frenchmen alike. Dumont de Montigny, indeed, was high in his praise of it: "The flesh of these wild cattle," he opined, "is excellent, as is that of the cow and the calf; it has an exquisite taste and natural gravy [*jus*]."[33] Du Pratz reported that "buffalo is the principal meat of the natives, and for a long time has also been that of the French." He maintained that "the best part is the hump, which is extremely delicate." The Indians, he claimed, "hardly kill anything but the cows" because "the flesh of the males smells musky," a difficulty that could, he says, easily be obviated if only the natives "as soon as the animal died would cut off the testicles as one does with stags and bears."[34] Buffalo meat was salted, smoked, or, in the case of the flanks, sun dried, in order to preserve it for later use. (The town of Sallisaw, near the Arkansas River in modern-day Oklahoma, must surely owe its name to the French word *salaison,* which means the method of curing meat by salting it.)

The Arkansas region provided huge quantities of salted buffalo meat to various users. For instance, in 1740, a French officer at Fort St. Francis reported that a "boat from Arkansas arrived and brought . . . eight thousand pounds of *salaison*" for the French troops that were assembled there in preparation for an attack on the Chickasaws.[35] New Orleans, and the lower colony in general, also consumed a lot of Arkansas meat. The buffalo's tongue and the hump ribs were the choicest parts, and officials at the Post frequently sent salted buffalo tongues to officials in New Orleans as gifts and tokens of esteem.[36] At times, the governor promulgated tariffs to fix the prices of meat and other animal products in the New Orleans market, including buffalo meat in general and buffalo tongues in particular, though, as we would expect, these tariffs were not very faithfully adhered to.[37]

Another important product that was exported from the Arkansas was buffalo tallow, produced by rendering the animal's fat, and used for candles, soap, and even for caulking boats.[38] An inventory of an Arkansas Post estate executed in 1743 contains buffalo tallow, and, indeed, according to the Post storekeeper in 1759, it was tallow that "makes up the small commerce of this river."[39] Bossu reported that Quapaw women "melt the [buffalo] suet in copper kettles to make tallow cakes which they sell or trade to the French or English for European merchandise."[40] Le Page du Pratz, always at the ready with advice, recommended that it was best to hunt the old bulls "who could barely walk," because they were easier to kill and so fat that "one could draw at least one hundred pounds of tallow from each" of them.[41]

Large amounts of this commodity were drawn from the Arkansas region. In 1775, François Menard, who would become, if he was not already, the principal merchant and richest man at the Post, landed a contract for ten thousand pounds of it for use in the shipyards in Havana;[42] and five years later a boat from the Arkansas sank in the Mississippi with a cargo of nine thousand pounds of buffalo tallow.[43] Though the usual hunt began at the beginning of the winter, because at that time the coat was thicker, the meat was fatter and juicier (buffalo meat is very lean), and the animal would produce more tallow, the Indians occasionally hunted buffaloes in the summer because the hides produced then would not require as much preparation if they were destined to provide spring or summer clothing.

In the early days of the fur trade in Louisiana, buffalo hides were an object of great interest. Indeed, La Salle sought and received a monopoly over the trade in buffalo hides in the Illinois country,[44] a monopoly to which Tonty succeeded, and Tonty was at pains to say that he was impressed by the availability of buffalo hides in the Arkansas country when he visited there.[45] Both he and La Salle "repeatedly evinced an interest in buffalo hides."[46] But in the early eighteenth century the trade in those hides was all but abandoned because of a lack of a market for them,[47] and they seem to have figured hardly at all in the trade in and around Arkansas Post during the colonial period.[48] A memorandum of about 1760 offered the suggestion that at Arkansas Post one "could even make quite a considerable commerce in big peltries [grosses peltries]," possibly including buffalo hides, but indicating that there was virtually no trading for skins at the Arkansas at the time.[49] In 1776, Lieutenant Governor DeMézières reported that thirty-six thousand deerskins had been exported from Natchitoches during the year, but only one hundred twenty dressed buffalo hides.[50] The relative price per pound of these two items no doubt figured in the decision of which to exploit and export, especially with transportation costs as high as they undoubtedly were.[51]

We shall probably never know exactly how the Quapaws hunted buffaloes,[52] not because contemporary French writers did not purport to tell us, but because their reports are altogether untrustworthy. The Baron de Lahontan claims to have encountered three or four hundred Quapaws in March of 1689 hunting buffalo on the Mississippi in the environs of the Missouri River. This account, except for the very large number of Quapaws that the baron reports, is not in itself difficult to believe. But the alleged

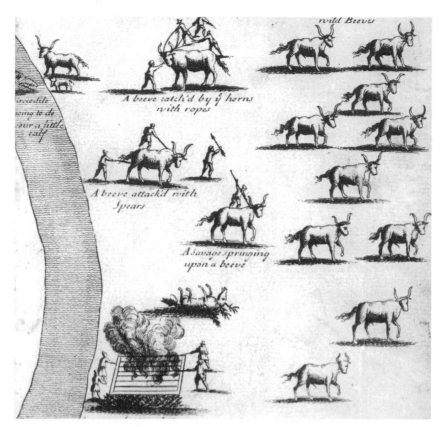

Within the engraving, the following labels appear:

wild Beeves

A beeve catch'd by y̆ horns with ropes

A beeve attack'd with Spears

A Savage springing upon a beeve

crocodile going to de vour a little calf

Figure 10. Engraving purporting to show the Quapaws' methods of hunting buffaloes in 1689. Baron de Lahontan, *New Voyages to North America* (London: 1735), 1:106.

encounter follows hard on the baron's story of his trip up the mythical "Long River," an account that historians have long known to be nothing but a tall tale. The proximity of this tale to the description of the meeting with the Quapaws decreases the value of that description more than a little, even if its very content did not all but entirely discredit it.

In any case, Lahontan asserts that the Quapaws entertained his party with a display of their buffalo-hunting prowess, and he included in his book a plate that, he says, depicts the various methods that the Quapaws employed to take the animal—including lassoing them, attacking them with spears, even jumping on them to run them through! His illustration also includes a scene showing the Quapaws smoking their kill.[53]

Not to be outdone, when Jean-Bernard Bossu came to record an alleged visit to the Quapaws almost a century after Lahontan's purported meeting with them, he included in his book an even more magnificent plate than Lahontan's, and in an ornate neoclassical style, complete with a reviewing stand in which Indians (with feathers) and colonial Europeans (with tri-cornered hats) are shown standing shoulder-to-shoulder surveying the scene—this last perhaps suggested by Lahontan's claim that the Quapaws had put on a hunting exhibition to regale his party. Like Lahontan, Bossu depicts the Quapaws smoking the slain buffalo. It is a splendid scene indeed: The Quapaws are shown riding horses and brandishing crescent-shaped blades on long poles, with which they are slashing the tendons of a fleeing buffalo's back legs so as to bring it down. Bossu had topped Lahontan yet again. But not only is this scene far too elaborate to be accurate, we can, as it happens, give proper credit to the story's true fabricator, for it appears that Bossu did not even bother to invent his own tale.

The credit belongs instead to Le Page du Pratz, who had announced portentously to his readers in 1758, more than a decade before Bossu's book was published, that he had hit on a way to hunt buffalo that "some say the Spanish of New Mexico employ." His method would be cheap, he claimed, because horses were cheap in Louisiana and "one feeds them practically for nothing." He explained: "Each hunter mounts a horse and is armed with a crescent . . . , the inside of which ought to be quite sharp. The top of the crescent ought to have a socket for inserting a pole or shaft." The riders, he continued, could simply pursue the buffaloes and cut their hamstrings, thus felling them easily. "One can judge by what I just said," he concluded, "what profit some hunters would realize on the hides and tallow of these buffaloes."[54]

It follows from all this that Frenchmen's accounts of Quapaw buffalo-hunting techniques are interesting historiographically but not very useful for the purposes of sober history. If one had to guess, it would seem more probable than not that eighteenth-century Quapaws and Frenchmen alike simply approached the buffaloes from their downwind side ("nose to the wind," as the eighteenth-century phrase went) and shot them. This is just what Du Pratz recommended in another place in his book, and he advised that it was best to aim at a buffalo "just below the shoulder in order to kill it on the first shot; for if it is only wounded, it will charge a man."[55]

La Harpe reveals that the Indians had by 1722 already passed on to the

Figure 11. Engraving purporting to show the Quapaws' methods of hunting buffaloes in 1771. Jean-Bernard Bossu, *Nouveaux voyages dans l'Amerique septentrionale* (Amsterdam: 1777), 102.

Louisiana French a trick that nineteenth-century buffalo hunters relied on to increase their kill and to reduce the risk of injury to themselves. When hunters encountered a herd, they first killed "the old bull and the old mother," because then "none of the herd takes flight," they being "accustomed to following their elders as being the most experienced." As a result, La Harpe says, the entire herd could be destroyed with little difficulty.[56]

Bears, too, were much hunted in and exported from the Arkansas, occasionally for food[57] but usually for the oil that could be rendered from their fat.[58] Bears seem to have been extraordinarily numerous in the region, and bears' oil is mentioned in an early French memorandum on Louisiana as an important Arkansas export; indeed, Arkansas was famous for its bears well into the nineteenth century.[59] Dumont de Montigny has left a memorable account of the utility of these animals. Louisiana Indians, he asserts, would eat bears only if they were very lean: "In any other condition, it is only the four feet that one can eat; the rest is only fat." But, he continues, "it is precisely this fat itself that is very advantageous to the country for the

Figure 12. Quapaws selling bear meat at Chickasaw Bluffs in 1820, by Fleury Generelly. *Courtesy Special Collections, Tulane University*

great quantity of oil that it furnishes, of which one makes a general use in this province."

The Indians, Dumont explained, after they killed a bear would cut it into pieces "which they throw into a kettle under which they light a fire. The flesh, which is only fat, melts little by little and renders itself finally altogether into oil." From one bear, Dumont maintains, "one sometimes draws more than one hundred and twenty pots [240 liters] of this oil. The savages trade a lot of this with the French. It is very beautiful, very healthy, and without any bad taste." It was used in cooking "stews and fried foods" and it was "even very good on salads" as a dressing. When frozen, he said, it was "of a dazzling whiteness" and the French spread "it on bread as a substitute for butter."[60] C. C. Robin agreed with Dumont about bear's oil, pronouncing it "quite attractive," and calling it "fine and delicate"; but he reckoned that the fattest and largest bear would provide about eighty pots [160 liters] of oil, an estimate that was no doubt a good deal more realistic than Dumont's.[61]

Du Pratz has left us a detailed description of how bear's oil was produced and processed. After the Indians killed a bear, he explains, they would then kill a deer. They cut the deer's head off and peeled the skin down from the neck "as one would do a stocking," removing all the meat and bone as they went, in order to make a seamless sack of the deer's skin. They cut the skin off at the hams, scraped and cleaned it inside, and sealed all the holes but the neck with a glue that they made from a mixture of the deer's tallow and a little ash. The Indians then cooked the bear meat and fat together in earthen pots to separate them from each other. When the oil cooled, they poured it in the skin cask, which, Du Pratz says, the French then called a "fawn of oil."[62]

After the oil was traded to the French, it was sometimes subjected to further processing. According to Du Pratz, the French melted the fat in a kettle and added a handful of laurel leaves to it. When they sprinkled in salted water, he claims, the decoction would emit a great roar and a thick smoke would rise that drew out with it what little bad odor remained in the fat. The fat was then transferred to a pot in which it was allowed to set for eight to ten days, after which a very clear oil had risen to the top. The French then carefully skimmed the oil off with a spoon. This oil, Du Pratz assures his reader, was "as good as the best olive oil and serves the same purposes." Below the oil was a lard as white as pork lard but softer. It served, he said, "for all cooking needs, even for white sauces, without any discernable after-taste or any bad odor." More than that, the lard was "at the same time a sovereign remedy for all pains," presumably as a balm, and he claimed that it had cured him "of rheumatism in the shoulder."[63]

Deerskins, it seems, did not figure prominently in the economic activities of Arkansas denizens. Bienville complained in an undated mémoire, perhaps from the 1730s, that the Quapaws were "very lackadaisical and lazy" and depended "entirely on the work of their women for the necessities of life, and hardly could they furnish from their hunt a thousand deerskins a year."[64] The deerskin trade was very important to the economy of eighteenth-century Louisiana generally,[65] but, to judge from the records at least, this was a trade in which Arkansas denizens, white and Indian, did not incline themselves to engage for most of the eighteenth century. It was otherwise for the Englishmen who lived on the opposite bank of the Mississippi: Commandant Orieta reported that the British had purloined twelve thousand deerskins and six thousand pounds of beaver from the White and St. Francis rivers during February and March of 1776 alone.[66] The next year, Captain Villiers complained about trespassing Englishmen "who hunt only for deer and beaver," scaring off all the game, and he indicated that the Arkansas hunters were interested in other game, presumably buffalo and bear.[67] Very late in the colonial epoch, however, and early in the American period as well, the Osages, Choctaws, and Chickasaws provided huge numbers of deerskins to Arkansas Post traders.[68]

Deer was surely a common item in the French and Quapaw diet, yet even here, oddly, there is mostly silence. Dumont was moved only to remark rather laconically that "[d]eer meat is also very useful" and that Louisiana deer were larger than the European ones and had "horns like a stag." Deer, he said, were the sheep of colonial Louisiana—that is, the colonists boiled or roasted them. He also reported that "in the woods and the prairies on the bank of the Arkansas there were stags and does in great number."[69]

There were but few furs produced in the Arkansas region during the colonial period. Marquette remarked in 1673 that the Quapaws "do not know what a beaver is, their riches consisting in the hides of wild cattle,"[70] by which he meant that buffalo hides were the only peltry that the Quapaws had to trade. Fifteen years later, however, Father Douay reported seeing beaver and otter skins being burnt in heaps, probably because the way to the Canadian market was not open.[71] Because of the relatively warm climate of the Arkansas region, it turned out that its furs were not much sought after, but the records nevertheless occasionally refer to beavers being shipped from the Post. In 1770, for instance, Pierre Favrot complained to Desmazellières about an abortive business deal that had involved peltries, including twenty-four pounds of beaver.[72]

In the late eighteenth and early nineteenth centuries the fur trade at the Post evidently acquired some momentum, but it seems that the bulk of the furs were produced by Arkansas's European residents and by tribes other than the Quapaws. John Treat, the government Indian factor (trader) at Arkansas Post in the early American period, mentioned the junction of the Black and White rivers as "the general crossing Place both for the Chickasaws, many of the Cherokees, and almost all the Delawares, who cross and recross, with considerable Quantities of Beaver, as well as other Peltry."[73] He revealed, moreover, that in the last years of the Spanish colonial period, the Osage trade had produced twenty-five to thirty-five hundred beavers annually at the Arkansas Post, and that by late February of 1806 eighteen thousand pounds of beaver furs had already passed through

Figure 13.   Illustration of Illinois Indians in New Orleans in 1732 with *plat côté* (buffalo ribs), *suif* (tallow), and *huille dourse* (bear's oil) for sale. These same products were the most important exports of the Arkansas region during much of the eighteenth century.
Photograph by Hillel Burger, courtesy of Peabody Museum, Harvard University

the Post—only half of what he "expected to be shipped throughout the season terminating the first of May."[74] Bearskins and a few packs of "small furs" (raccoons, foxes, otters, and wildcats) were also shipped from the Post with some frequency, at least in the early American period.[75]

Given the abundance of the animal resources in the Arkansas country, it is little wonder that a mémoire on Louisiana written about 1750 had already described the "principal occupation" of the Frenchmen at Arkansas Post as "hunting, salting meats, and trade in tallow and bears' oil."[76] Indeed, the numerous letters, reports, memoirs, travel accounts, and contemporary publications completely confirm Captain Philip Pittman's 1765 description of Arkansas Post as a place where the "people subsist mostly by hunting, and every season send to New Orleans great quantities of bear's oil, tallow, salted buffaloe meat, and a few skins."[77] That the skin and fur trade became lucrative in the very late colonial period is seemingly confirmed by Captain Pierre Rousseau's observations in 1793. While ascending the Mississippi in his Spanish war galliot, he reported that just below Natchez he met "two pirogues which had come from Arkansas, loaded with peltry and salted meat belonging to Mr. Menard"; and two weeks later he encountered another boat from Arkansas Post on its way to New Orleans "loaded with furs and dried salted meat."[78]

II.

Neither Father Du Poisson nor Father Vitry mentioned the existence of professional white hunters at the Arkansas in the 1720s and 1730s, but that does not necessarily mean that they were not there. Father Vitry had not arrived at the Post until late October, and the hunters may by then have already set off on their annual campaign. Because of the hunters' itinerate habits, and the impermanence of their hunting camps, moreover, the priests may simply not have regarded them as worth mentioning. French hunters may well have been attracted to the Arkansas region in significant numbers in the 1740s because of the declining population of the Quapaws, which in 1748 was said to have been "greatly reduced due to illness among all on that river."[79] By 1752, the Natchez commandant could report, moreover, that the Quapaws were "rapidly decreasing in number and weakening due to disease and the loss of warriors."[80]

For whatever reason, white hunters had indeed become quite numerous at the Arkansas by the 1740s: A census of 1749 reveals that eleven hunting parties comprising a total of forty men were on the Arkansas River, a total of nine hunters were on the White and St. Francis rivers, and sixteen *voyageurs* were "at the Post to return to the hunt." These last would have been at the Post to re-equip themselves for the winter campaign, indicating in turn the presence of merchants there who were in the business of outfitting them. The *voyageurs* on the rivers, Commandant Delinó pointedly noted, "had stayed on the rivers despite the orders that one had given them."[81]

From what we know of the Spanish period, it seems altogether likely that the hunters who had refused to return to the Post were hiding out from their creditors. The census of 1749 thus very probably bears the imprint of a sociological pattern that had developed early in the history of the settlement. In 1766, in fact, a letter from the Post complains of "vagabonds and bankrupts" who had already been numerous on the Arkansas River for more than twenty years, that is, since the 1740s.[82] As we shall see, the relationships laid bare by this census virtually defined the kind of community that Arkansas Post would be during the entire time that it was part of the colony of Louisiana.

The opportunity for trade with the Quapaws, foreign Indian nations, and local European hunters was one of the main attractions of the Arkansas region, and virtually all of the commandants of the Post were dedicated merchants from the earliest times, sometimes even in ways that conflicted with their official duties. In 1735, for instance, Pierre Louis de Coulange, Louis Boucher de Grandpré, and two other Frenchmen formed a business partnership, and they had substituted their goods for government munitions loaded on a boat that had called at the Post, thus compromising the safety of the colony. Coulange was ordered to jail in Fort de Chartres for six months for his part in the affair, and, Governor Bienville said, he would have been cashiered from the service altogether but for his exemplary conduct in the war effort against the Chickasaws.[83]

Some fifteen years later, Captain Delinó, having learned that new troops had arrived in New Orleans, and fearing that he might lose his command at the Arkansas, "one of the best in the colony, left his post without permission"; and in his absence the corporal whom he had left in charge and his entire garrison had deserted, taking "all that they could carry, not only from the king but from [Delinó] as well."[84] We may presume that the Arkansas was called "one of the best in the colony" in this instance because it was more lucrative than many others, and again we have an example of the commandant's private interests adversely affecting the performance of his public duties. This must have happened at the Arkansas with some regularity, since it was unusual in the extreme for a commandant not to engage in trade. Commandants who did not do so were so rare that Governor Vaudreuil felt moved to remark about Jean-François de Montcharvaux, Delinó's predecessor at the Arkansas, that he "never was susceptible to any trade, even in the posts where he commanded, which nothing proves so much as the poverty to which this officer is reduced."[85]

Early in the Spanish period, Commandant DeClouet at various times asked the governor for monopolies on the Quapaw and Osage trade,[86] and just three years later Captain Leyba revealed that he was deeply involved in trade on the Arkansas. He complained loudly to the governor about the number of competitors with whom he had to contend at the Post. "This

Figure 14.   Captain Alexandre Chevalier DeClouet, commandant of Arkansas
Post from 1768 to 1769. *Courtesy of Dupré Library, University of
Southwestern Louisiana*

post is fully supplied with all goods and drinks," he reported. "Many of the
farmers [*habitants*] here are traders," he continued, "and in addition there
are other people settled here who have no other business but trade." His
immediate difficulty was that on his arrival at the Post he had found that
the other Post merchants had "already made the advances to the hunters
and Indians for this year," and thus when the hunters returned to the Post
they would have to pay their creditors and would not have anything left

over to trade to him. He therefore asked the governor not to license any more traders for his post, which, he believed, would be the only way that he could survive.[87] After Leyba left the Arkansas, Francis Vigo, a soldier of the garrison, was allowed to go upriver to collect some debts that Leyba had been unable to collect before his departure.[88]

Perhaps Captain DuBreuil put the matter most plainly in 1784 after he had used up his personal supply of munitions defending the Post against a British attack the previous year. He had repeatedly asked the Spanish government to replace those supplies, but to no avail. He therefore wrote Governor Miró with more than a little urgency, explaining again that "the powder and balls were mine," and begging that they be replaced with munitions of an equal quantity and quality. "I have to make a living for myself," he pleaded, "in a land where almost everyone is a hunter, and they value munitions more highly than silver."[89]

Given this state of affairs, it can hardly be surprising that Captain Balthazar de Villiers would set his fertile and inventive mind to the promotion of economic growth at the Post by devising means to protect the rights of the small and fragile merchant-capitalist class that he was trying to nurture there[90]—a class, not incidentally, to which, as we shall see, he himself belonged in an active way. Not long after he took possession of his command at the Arkansas, Villiers attempted to persuade Governor Unzaga not to allow any merchant to trade any higher up the Arkansas River than the Post itself. The merchants ought to be concentrated at the Post, he argued, because of the way their principal business, equipping hunters for their yearly campaigns, was financed. The hunters were almost all desperately poor: Captain Desmazellières had revealed in 1770 that "these poor hunters are so feckless that they don't know how to do anything but shoot a *fusil* [gun]," and that most of them owned "nothing but their guns."[91] Since equipment was therefore necessarily sold to them on credit, to be paid for from what the hunt produced, if traders introduced themselves upriver during the hunting season, they would buy up all the peltries, tallow, bear's oil, and salted meats that the hunters had, leaving nothing to satisfy the Post merchants for their original outfits.

According to Captain Villiers, some of the hunters of the Arkansas would go to the most extraordinary lengths to avoid their creditors. Upwards of forty of them, he said, had repaired upriver "on the branches of this river near the Panis [i.e., the Wichitas]," and had had the product of their hunt smuggled past the Post (presumably to New Orleans) without settling up with the Post merchants who had outfitted them. In the Wichita village they lived a "libertine, insubordinate, and vagabond life— at the risk even of being killed by the Osages."[92] Villiers claimed that "there were many refugees among [the Wichitas] who are more dangerous even than the natives."[93] Some of these Frenchmen, he asserted, had achieved a prominence in the councils of the Wichitas and had participated in (and even instigated) raids against the French and Anglo-American hunters on the Arkansas. Sometimes these mounted Wichita war parties numbered as many as two hundred horsemen, and, while the losses that they inflicted contributed materially to Villiers's financial ruin, he did note that some good might nevertheless come from the hunters' perfidiousness. The raids, he remarked, not without a little ironic satisfaction, "inspired a terror in [the Anglo-Americans] that is going to keep them away from the neighborhood for a long time."[94]

Lieutenant Governor DeMézières of Natchitoches, it would seem, knew what he was talking about when he charged that the Arkansas River above the Post was inhabited largely by miscreants. "Most of those who live there," he claimed, "have either deserted from the troops and ships of the Most Christian King or have committed robberies, rape, or homicide." Indeed, for him the Arkansas River was "the asylum of the most wicked persons, without doubt, in all the Indies."[95] There is every reason to conclude that many of the European residents of Arkansas were outlaws not just in the popular but in the technical sense as well, because they forswore any attachment to the European nations that claimed sovereignty over the region. Some of the hunters, commandants occasionally grudgingly admitted, would indeed respond to orders to return to the Post, as one of the Francoeurs did in about 1766;[96] and Desmazellières described the hunters Darbonne and Antoine Lepine as "honest men" in 1770.[97] But these kinds of evaluations of the hunters' character were few and far between.

It would appear that the virtually unremitting complaints about the moral character of many of the denizens of the Arkansas River were not simply the product of class prejudice on the part of the Louisiana gentry who, as we have seen, constantly registered them.[98] From the days of Law's ambitious colonization schemes, Louisiana had attracted numbers of French criminals, deserters, and other undesirables, and many of these people were necessarily without the means or the skills to make respectable livings. They would have found in the wilds of the Arkansas region a congenial retreat, and in the life of a hunter a vocation that required very little capital and no technical training to pursue.

When various eighteenth-century commandants and officials, including Villiers, complained about the vagabonds, libertines, and deserters who made their home on the Arkansas River, moreover, they were not merely engaged in generic, deprecatory name-calling: They were using terms of art with a fixed socio-legal meaning that contemporaries would have understood in an immediate and specific way. Vagabonds, for instance, were vagrants, many of whom were deported to Louisiana in large numbers in the early eighteenth century, and libertines were people who lived insubordinate lives.[99]

One means to which commandants at the Arkansas had very early made resort to ensure the hunters' return was requiring them to leave their families at the Post while they were on their campaigns. Villiers explained that he had made some exceptions to this rule, as, for instance, for a hunter named Barthelemy, who was trustworthy and whose family was so numerous that they would find it difficult to support themselves at the Post. This was a privilege, Villiers said, that would "ordinarily serve only to perpetuate a class of vagabonds who were delighted to find a means to escape from all jurisdiction." But the simplest way to ensure the hunters' return, Villiers posited, was to make all merchants and traders settle at the Post where they could pursue "their business . . . with every freedom." He knew, he said, that this was the rule and custom already established at Natchitoches and at Pointe Coupée.[100]

Governor Unzaga probably understood and shared Villiers's concern for the nascent merchant class at the Post; at least there are no recorded complaints that he failed to heed Villiers's animadversions after he received them. But when Bernardo de Gálvez became governor in 1777, New Orleans mercantile interests prevailed on him to give passports to individuals to trade upriver from the Post. The most prominent of these traders was Andrés Lopez, who had a partner in New Orleans named François Bearnoud,[101] and to whom Gálvez granted a license "because as a vassal of the king he ought to have a right to this benefit, and my intention is that all trading men (except those of bad conduct and of unruly life) should enjoy it and that there be no exclusion." His general plan, he revealed, was to grant a similar license to any qualified person who asked for one.[102]

This news greatly agitated Villiers, not least because he was himself a merchant and deeply in debt, and he wrote a long response to Gálvez, laying the local situation open to him and attempting to get him to retreat from his free-trade position. Villiers expostulated that the New Orleans interests who had prevailed on the governor to allow Lopez to come to Arkansas simply did not understand local conditions and particularly the way business was done at his post. He patiently explained that there were thirty-five to forty parties of hunters on the Arkansas River at that time, most of whom had outfitted themselves at Arkansas Post (although some of them had been equipped at Pointe Coupée or New Orleans). The hunters had passports for only a year, at the end of which time they were obligated to return to the Post, pay their outfitters, and then pay their other debts. Once all their debts were paid, they were free to sell what they had left over, either at the Post or at New Orleans. But, as Villiers had already explained to Unzaga, if traders were to go upriver with goods and liquor during the hunters' sojourn there, they would draw off all the product of the hunt, leaving nothing for the outfitters, and the liquor would cause serious disruptions to the hunters' operations. The hunters were, Villiers reiterated, "almost all faithless and dishonest vagabonds," who, if resupplied, would simply continue their campaigns, never to return to the Post, thus ruining those who had made them advances.

Villiers had nevertheless allowed Lopez to enter on the river, though subject to some very narrowly tailored restrictions, because the governor had ordered it and because by sheer happenstance he had promised the Osages to send them a trader to Cadron in an effort to bind a rather fragile peace that he had just arranged with them. He sent along his corporal, Louis Boulard, to keep an eye on things, and he forbad Lopez to furnish any equipment to the hunters, to sell any hunting party more than three pots of liquor, or to buy any products of the hunt unless a hunter had met with an accident and could not otherwise finish his campaign. But Villiers entreated Gálvez not to repeat the mistake that Gálvez had made with Lopez: "Nothing is more vexatious," he allowed, speaking with the force of considerable past experience, "than to have sown well and to see the profits reaped by others at the capital."[103]

Only about a week after Villiers had written with such urgency to the governor (and probably even before his letter had reached New Orleans), Governor Gálvez granted two more licenses to trade on the Arkansas River, one to William Brun and the other to Remis Fotin. In granting these licenses, the governor waxed panegyric yet again on the virtues of economic liberalism, repeating his intention "that all men of good conduct should participate in the common benefit as vassals of the king," and asserting that for "one person alone to enjoy it to the prejudice of others would be offensive to his royal will and to the law of nations."[104]

But Villiers soon wrote Gálvez yet another letter, telling him that Lopez had inveigled them both by smuggling large quantities of liquor up to the Post, much more than Gálvez had allowed him in his passport, and had been selling it upriver. "This will cause a rebirth of the disorder and confusion on this river," Villiers gloomily predicted, and "the people who have made advances to the hunters are going to be ruined." The hunters, he reemphasized, were "a bunch of professional drunks [*ivrognes de profession*]" who were "going to forget their engagements and sacrifice everything to satisfy their penchant." He feared that he himself would be a victim of Lopez's machinations, that as a result he would not be able to export anything from the Post to New Orleans that year, and that he would therefore never be able to pay the large expenses that visits from Indian nations constantly caused him.[105]

Whether or not it was this last argument that moved Gálvez off his lofty attachment to the principles of free trade, he soon wrote to Villiers that he was not going to grant any more licenses to trade outside the Post. He had become convinced that Villiers's suggested way of managing things would "make all the *habitants,* merchants, and hunters happy," and would still allow everyone to "participate in the benefits that trade offers, since all are equal subjects of the same king and thus there ought not to be any monopoly [*privilegio*]."[106] After hearing of the way that Lopez had behaved, moreover, Gálvez vowed that he would fix it so that Lopez would never again return to the river.[107]

Having wrung these important concessions from the governor, Villiers turned his hand to drafting some local legislation to regulate the activities of hunters and to protect the rights of the merchants at Arkansas Post. On 26 January 1778, Villiers published an ordinance at the Post that, among other things, provided that anyone who got paid on the river by hunters without his authorization would have to deposit at the Post what he had received until the payer returned, and a failure to do so would give rise to an obligation on the part of the payee to pay the payer's debts. The ordinance also rendered null and void any notes, conveyances of goods, obligations, or bills of sale executed on the river between hunters, and any goods acquired by virtue of the transactions to which these instruments related had again to be deposited at the Post, under a like penalty. Finally, in order to discourage clandestine shipments in fraud of creditors, all returning hunters had to declare any product that they were carrying in their pirogues that did not belong to them, "under penalty of answering for the entire debt of the debtors of bad faith with whom they had conspired."[108]

Despite Gálvez's promise not to allow trade anywhere but the Post, he and later governors nevertheless occasionally granted licenses to persons who wanted to trade on the rivers that were under the jurisdiction of the Arkansas Post commandant. In fact, incredibly, in 1778, barely three weeks after Villiers had promulgated his ordinance, Gálvez revealed that a boat was coming up to the Post loaded with goods intended for none other than Andrés Lopez himself, and the governor directed Villiers to give Lopez a license to go upriver to sell them, "unless it is contrary to the order and disposition taken on the division of the posts of commerce *[el repartimiento de los puestos de comercio]*."[109]

Similarly, Governor Miró, Gálvez's successor, because he wanted to do Juan Baptista Duchassin a favor for unrevealed reasons, granted him a license in 1789 to trade on the White River,[110] which drew the predictable howl from Commandant Vallière, who protested that "this will be a great prejudice to the creditors." (Vallière, moreover, expressed his respectful opinion to the governor that it did not make sense to him that someone who did not have anything invested in an enterprise ought to reap its fruits.)[111] Miró also gave Juan Baptista Imbeau a license to trade on the Arkansas River as the agent of Madame Villiers, the former commandant's relict, as a way of helping her pay her husband's debts.[112] Captain DuBreuil put no obstacle in Imbeau's way because Imbeau was a trustworthy man of good character. But when François Menard presented him with a passport from Miró to go upriver to trade with the Osages, DuBreuil balked because, he said, Menard had openly admitted in conversations with Post merchants that he would use the "opportunity to get hold of all the credits that they have with their hunters by selling them goods." DuBreuil explained that since he knew Menard, "who is capable of doing worse things," he had forbidden him to go upriver but had given him the option to commission someone else to go in his place.[113]

In 1789, Captain Vallière, having evidently received an ambiguous passport from Governor Miró, wrote that it had "not been convenient for [the licensee] to pass to the rivers," because he wanted "to go not only to collect his debts but also to trade," and this last would be "a great prejudice to the other creditors."[114] Travel up the rivers for debt collection, so long as the priority rules were adhered to, seems on the other hand to have been unobjectionable; so when Miró ordered Vallière to allow the merchant Pedro Nitard, who wanted to abandon the Post altogether, to go upriver to collect his debts,[115] Vallière gave the governor no difficulty about it.

While it is not easy to believe that there were not other abuses like the ones that had engaged so much of Villiers's attention (there were said to be two hundred white hunters "established on the upper part of the" Arkansas River in 1786),[116] the commandants' letters do not contain further signs of systematic anxiety about such abuses until the very end of the colonial period. At that time, Captain Vilemont tried his hand at a kind of quasi-legislative process that reveals as much about prevailing ideas concerning government and legislative jurisdiction as it does about the merchants' notion of a proper economic order. On 16 January 1798, six Arkansas Post merchants (Vilemont said that this was all there were at his settlement) set their hands to a document entitled "Articles of the Agreement of the Merchants of the Post of Arkansas." It contained five numbered articles.

One of the articles provided for a *pro rata* division of a hunter's product among his other creditors after he had satisfied his outfitter. Other articles quite predictably forbad trading on the river, for the same reasons that were so minutely and vividly outlined by Villiers, and prohibited clandestine shipments by the hunters in fraud of creditors. The parties agreed to heavy penalties in case of breaches of the agreement. Most interesting, perhaps, was the article of the agreement that contained the rudiments of a recording system designed to protect creditors: It provided that hunters' obligations evidencing their debts to their equippers had to be executed "by judicial act before *Monsieur le Commandant*, who will keep a record of them," so that merchants would be on notice as to who had the first call on the hunters' product that another article of the agreement created in favor of outfitters. This last article seems to have contained a slip of the pen: It provided that the first outfitter ought to have priority, whereas it seems almost certain that the merchants had meant to prefer the last outfitter. This lapse, in any case, as we shall see, was corrected in due course.[117]

Captain Charles de Vilemont, before whom the merchants' agreement was executed, wrote a private letter to the governor, in French (in addition to an official letter in Spanish transmitting the agreement), indicating his belief that the "agreement is just and equitable for [the merchants'] respective interests and will settle subsequent difficulties, and anyone has the freedom to trade openly on the Post." He nevertheless (as he had to) wisely submitted himself to whatever it pleased the governor to ordain with respect to the matters that the articles of agreement sought to govern.[118]

What it in fact pleased the governor to ordain was eleven rules that featured an assurance that "trade on the post ought to be free for all the people who live there," prohibited trade elsewhere than at the Post, and forbad clandestine shipments in fraud of creditors. All of these principles, as we have seen, had been embodied in the articles of agreement. The governor's rules, however, differed from those contained in the merchants' agreement in two important respects. First of all, his ordinances provided that if a hunter had anything remaining after paying his outfitter, then his other creditors should be satisfied according to the age of their debt (with preference to those who had had their notes witnessed by the commandant), and not *pro rata* as the agreement had provided.[119] Second, the last (i.e., most recent) outfitter, not the first outfitter, was to be preferred to any other creditor, and he was also given a first option to reequip a hunter who had paid him off. (Perhaps this last was an attempt to reward the outfitter by giving him a right of first refusal to a good credit risk.) Gayoso also directed Vilemont to convoke the merchants, along with two hunters elected by a majority vote of the hunters, to fix penalties for offenses against the ordinance and then to send them to him for his approval.[120]

Vilemont dutifully convened the assembly that the governor had ordered and held an election to choose two from the merchant class and two from the hunter class to devise penalties for those who contravened Gayoso's ordinance. This makeshift legislative body then fixed penalties of a month in jail and a fine of twenty-five pesos against any hunter who traded goods upriver and three months in jail and a fine of five hundred pesos against the merchant who had supplied him. Other stiff penalties were imposed for other kinds of violations.[121]

It is not altogether clear whether the governor intended his ordinance to replace the merchants' agreement completely, because, after all, the private undertaking could theoretically survive the ordinance even with respect to those particulars in which it differed from the ordinance. That is because the legislative provisions determining priorities among credi-

Figure 15.
Pierre Lefevre's grave in Mount Holly Cemetery, Little Rock. Lefevre was an important Indian trader at Arkansas Post. *Photograph by Gail K. Arnold*

tors would presumably have been subject to contractual adjustment. But the penalties, at any rate, would be enforced in a different way. In case of a breach of the agreement, only a party to it could enforce it, and then only in a civil action on the contract, and only against another party to it. In case of a breach of the ordinance, on the other hand, the penalties could be enforced against any violator by way of a prosecution on the complaint of any person or even *ex officio* by the commandant.

Although the governor and other officials of the Louisiana colonial government frequently employed the rhetoric of free enterprise, the words had at best a rather specialized meaning in their mouths. First of all, as we have seen, licenses to hunt or trade were not granted to people "of bad behavior," a condition no doubt salutary on its face, but also doubtless subject to abuse. Second, tariffs were occasionally imposed on goods destined for the Arkansas, fixing the prices at which they could be sold, in order to quiet Indian complaints.[122] More fundamentally, however, a great deal of ingenuity had been devoted to creating rules governing creditors' rights that had the effect of physically limiting trade to the Post itself, that is, to the merchants' village that was in the immediate vicinity of the fort. Pierre Lefevre, a *habitant* who lived two miles from the Post on the Arkansas River, informed one of his creditors that the Post merchants had forced him to close his store at his *habitation* (plantation) because "they say that all the trade has to be at the Post" in order to secure the priority that outfitters enjoyed. When he complained to Governor Carondelet about this state of affairs, he received what had long been the stock reply: Lefevre could trade as freely with the Indians as any of the *habitants* of Arkansas Post could "without any other restriction than having his store on the Post [*dans le poste*]" for security purposes and "so that everyone can know what payments the Indians are making that are prejudicial to those who out-fitted them."[123]

With respect to trade with foreign Indian nations, moreover, as opposed to trade with the Europeans, Spanish officials did not even pretend to be votaries of the free market. Monopoly rights to trade with certain Indian tribes were regularly parceled out as payment for services rendered to the state or to serve other special governmental purposes. For instance, in 1787 Captain Vallière asked Governor Miró for an exclusive right to trade with the Abenakis who were hunting on the Arkansas River, because Vallière had no other way to pay his debts. The little trade that the Quapaws engaged in, he said, they carried on with the other merchants at the Post.[124] Miró responded by simply authorizing Vallière to name whomever he wanted to the Abenaki trade.[125] Vallière subsequently farmed the trade out to another individual whom he supplied on credit,[126] and by 1791 there were more than two thousand pesos owing him from his Abenaki trading rights.[127] Exclusive rights to trade with the Abenakis and the Cherokees on the White River were granted later to Captain Vilemont and to Andrés Fagot, and in 1802 Captain Caso y Luengo asked the governor to grant him those privileges because he needed reimbursement for the costs of entertaining and feeding visiting Indians, for which, unlike the situation that prevailed at some other posts, there was no allowance from the royal treasury.[128]

Most remarkably, despite Governor Carondelet's stern admonition to Vilemont in 1796 that "under no circumstances" was he "to grant permission to any trader to go trade with the Osages at the place called *Cadran bleu* [i.e., Cadron] or any other place, since the exclusive trade has been granted to Auguste Chouteau" of St. Louis, five years later Governor Casa-Calvo granted Joseph Bougy "the trade with the Indians on the Arkansas River for three years" as an exclusive privilege.[129] Casa-Calvo could only have been referring to the Osage trade, since the only other Indians on the river were the Quapaws, and if they were meant there is little question that the governor would have said so in terms. (After the American takeover, John B. Treat, the United States Indian factor at the Post, reported that "under the Spanish Government . . . the Osage trade was held out to the highest bidder.")[130] The same month, Casa-Calvo gave François Vaugine a license to send traders and hunters to the St. Francis River for a year.[131]

A final example will make the point that economic liberalism played little part in Spanish trade policy at the Arkansas where foreign Indian tribes were concerned. In 1801, Casa-Calvo wrote Vilemont that he was not under any circumstances to grant any license or passport to anyone who asked his permission to trade or hunt on the Ouachita River: The Baron de Bastrop had obligated himself to build a fort and a strong house at his own expense at Ouachita Post and at Catahoula, the governor reported, and had been granted the exclusive trade of the Ouachita for ten years in recompense.[132]

It seems, however, that the Quapaw trade, partly because it was small, and partly because granting a monopoly on it would have been hard to enforce and would have caused numerous difficulties at the Post, was usually open to anyone during the Spanish period. As we noted earlier, DeClouet had asked for a monopoly on trade with the Quapaws in 1768,[133] but it is doubtful that he acquired it. It is certain, at any rate, that several private parties traded with the Quapaws in the 1770s. The Quapaw chiefs complained of prices in 1770, claiming that the French had sold them a Limbourg blanket for ten deerskins, and now such a blanket cost twenty-five deerskins. They asked the governor to set a tariff and "to make the traders obey it."[134] That same year, the commandant wrote that one Tounoir was charging twenty deerskins for a Limbourg blanket when it used to cost only eight;[135] so when a trader named Diard came up from New Orleans late in that year with goods for the Quapaw tribe, the governor sent along a tariff that he directed Desmazellières to enforce strictly.[136] In 1779, some Post merchants accused Villiers of engrossing the Quapaw trade to himself, but he denied it vehemently. His version was that he had agreed with the Quapaw chiefs that their hunters would supply him with meat for himself and his troop, after which they could sell to whomever they wished. According to him, the Quapaws were free to trade with the Post *habitants* for anything except brandy, and he branded any allegation to the contrary as a "calumny," the perpetrators of which ought to be punished.[137]

The extent to which Indian hunters were incorporated into the credit system operating at the Arkansas is difficult to gauge precisely, because, for various reasons, none of them necessarily having to do with the frequency of their involvement, the Indians' trading arrangements with the whites do not often figure in the surviving records. We do, however, get occasional glimpses of the merchants of Arkansas Post extending credit to Indians, enough to give us some confidence that such dealings were not unusual and indeed were rather commonplace.

A chance remark in 1770 about the return to the Post of "all the free Indians who were on this river with their wives" is probably a reference to Indian hunters who were "free" in the sense that the product of their hunt was not subject to a prior lien in favor of a creditor, thus indicating, by inference, that there were indeed Indians to whom merchants had extended credit.[138] More definite proof of Indian involvement in the credit system came a year later when, as we noted earlier, Captain Desmazellières remarked to the governor that the merchants at the Post "have already made advances this year to the hunters and the Indians";[139] and two years later still Commandant Leyba informed the governor that springtime "was when the hunters come in to pay and something is received from the Indians."[140] Pierre Lefevre seems to have made a specialty of dealing with Indian hunters in the later colonial epoch,[141] and the accounts of his bankruptcy estate from the early American period reveal that Indians from several tribes, including Abenakis, Cherokees, Chickasaws, and Quapaws, were deeply indebted to him.[142]

Other very early American records make it completely clear that members of Indian tribes then frequenting the Post were extended credit on a regular basis. For instance, in 1805 John Treat wrote that there were twelve or thirteen traders at the Post, and that "those traders all have given large credit to the Indians, furnishing them with whatever may be necessary for a hunting excursion";[143] and the next year Treat reported that he had had to extend credit to Indian hunters to ensure a successful trade since the competition did so on a regular basis.[144] It would seem virtually certain that these nineteenth-century Arkansas Post merchants were simply continuing a practice that had already been established by their French and Spanish predecessors in the eighteenth century.

The fact that French traders were extending credit to Indians, however, does not necessarily mean that the Europeans who claimed sovereignty over Louisiana could expect to rely on their legal system to enforce the rights of creditors in case an Indian debtor defaulted. The extent to which the intricate regulatory scheme aimed at protecting creditors' rights was enforceable would, of course, figure in the determination of whether to extend credit in the first place, and this would influence in an important way the degree to which cooperation between the races would occur. The question of how successful the Europeans were at incorporating Indians into their legal system is thus a crucial one, and it turns out that the surviving evidence on this point leads to some very definite and revealing conclusions that we shall examine in detail in due course.

III.

Events relevant to French and Spanish attempts to establish trade with the Wichitas on the upper reaches of the Arkansas River are instructive in a number of ways. For one thing, they expose to view the extent to which the Quapaw trade was insufficient to satisfy the demands of Arkansas Post merchants and others for the products of the hunt. The population of the Quapaw tribe, as we have seen, was greatly diminished during the course of the seventeenth and eighteenth centuries by disease and war, no doubt considerably reducing the commercial value of the alliance to the French. Warfare influenced trade in another way as well, because it meant that Quapaw men could devote less time to the hunt. It seems likely that the Quapaws came during the course of the eighteenth century to depend not on trade but on annual presents from the French and Spanish governments, and on special rewards for raids on tribes antagonistic to the French and Spanish imperial interests, to satisfy their desire for European goods. By 1765, Captain Pittman could write of the Quapaws that "they hunt little more than for their common subsistence,"[145] so it is not surprising that the French would have pressed upriver in search of other trading partners.

The Caddoan speakers whom we have learned to call the Wichitas, and whom the French called the Panis, were a tribe with which Arkansas colonial traders tried very hard and very early to establish a connection.

According to the Quapaws, a man named Pichart and five other French-men of Law's concession had tried immediately after arriving at the Arkansas in 1721 to travel high up the river to acquire horses from the Wichitas, but the Osages had ambushed and killed them.[146] As it turned out, though the Osages had in fact attacked the party, the Frenchmen escaped and reached the Wichita villages, where they were well received.[147] But it would seem that regular and consistent contact between the Wichitas and the denizens of Arkansas Post proved at first elusive.

Governor Bienville had exhibited a keen interest in establishing an alliance with the Wichitas during his governorship. He wrote that they "were a very bellicose nation and irreconcilable enemies of the Paducahs [Apaches], from whom they make many slaves and take numbers of horses." They were fine horsemen, he said, especially in combat, and they covered themselves and their mounts with an armor "of very thin leather impenetrable by arrows." "They still have eight hundred men spread out over several villages on the vast and magnificent plains," he wrote. "Trade there," he remarked wistfully, "would be very good, but few Frenchmen have been up there. They are cannibals."[148]

It appears that an alliance was in fact eventually established by the Arkansas Post commandant with the Wichitas sometime in the 1740s, and that, for a time, the Wichitas figured prominently in the economy of the Post, though tracking their various groups, their movements in the eighteenth century, and the frequency, nature, and extent of their contacts with the traders and hunters of the Arkansas is a matter of not a little complexity. But there is reason to have a great deal of confidence in the main outlines of the story, and it is important to attempt its telling, because of the light that it can shed on French and Indian relations on the Arkansas River in the colonial period.

The Wichita tribe that was probably the largest in the historic period was the Taovayas, who were most likely located on the Verdigris River near present-day Neodesha, Kansas, when Claude-Charles Dutisné visited them in 1719.[149] Another significant Wichita group was the Tawakoni, with whom, among other tribes, La Harpe made contact the same year on the Arkansas River, perhaps near Leonard, Oklahoma, thirteen miles south of Tulsa.[150] The Tawakoni relocated to the Red River around 1737,[151] and the Taovayas and other Wichita groups relocated to two sites on the Arkansas River in Oklahoma just south of the Kansas border and near the river's junction with Deer Creek, some of them perhaps as early as 1716.[152]

While much of the foregoing is admittedly conjectural, it is quite evident that by about 1746, and continuing for a number of years thereafter, the hunters and traders of the Post of Arkansas and the Wichitas at Deer Creek had developed a close relationship. French hunters from the Post and the Wichitas were engaged in a common enterprise, hunting buffalo, bear, and deer, and producing hides, salted meat, tallow, and bear's oil, not only for consumption in the lower Louisiana colony, but, interestingly, also for export to the French Islands and even to Europe.[153] The Wichita men, it appears, furnished horses and helped in the hunt, and the Wichita women prepared the hides, rendered the tallow and oil, and prepared other products for shipment. In return, the Wichitas received the usual trade goods, including guns and munitions.[154] As one eyewitness to relevant events in 1750 described the enterprise, "the French hunters (hunting being their livelihood) go up to these *pueblos* of *Jumanes* [i.e., Wichitas] on the Arkansas River in pirogues, in which they return with peltry, fat and lard of the bison, bears, and deer, their access being facilitated by friendship with the *Jumanes*."[155]

This account, and others, in conjunction with archaeological evidence of a large hide-producing operation in the Deer Creek Wichita village alongside the remnants of considerable quantities of European trade goods, provides unmistakable evidence of Indian and European cooperation of some sort, though its exact contours are not easy to discern. It is unclear whether the French and the Indians were partners in the venture (sharing losses and gains), whether they were engaged in independent hunting operations with the French buying the Wichitas' product, or whether the Wichitas were simply hirelings who were paid for their labor. It is not impossible that all of these business configurations obtained at some point while this alliance lasted. What is clear, however, is that a "thriving business . . . had developed by 1748 through the cooperation of the French hunters and the Wichita living in villages"[156] at and near the Deer Creek archaeological site. It may even be probable that the Wichita alliance accounted for the fact that, as we saw, the command at Arkansas Post was by 1751 considered "one of the best in the colony."[157]

The census taken in 1749 at the Post of Arkansas that has already been alluded to may well have been occasioned by the movement of population into the Arkansas area in response to this alliance. Just ten years before, Governor Bienville had written ruefully of his Arkansas Post that there were "only a missionary and three *habitants* there who do nothing."[158] The new census, however, enumerated not only eight *habitant* families (along with fourteen slaves) in the village itself, but also sixty-five *voyageurs* "who live as much on the rivers as at the Post." Among these last were eleven *bourgeois* (employers) and twenty-nine *engagés* (employees) who were on the Arkansas River "despite the orders given them previously." There were, in addition, five *voyageurs* on the White River, and four on the St. Francis. The Arkansas *voyageurs* no doubt were like those of Canada who were both hunters and petty traders, well practiced at dealing with Indians, and flexible enough to work out a comfortable economic relationship with the Wichitas either as partners, buyers, or employers. It is probable that a number of those reported on the Arkansas were engaged in the Wichita-related enterprise high up the river, where a French flag flew proudly in the Indian villages.[159] It seems that this arrangement was, however, not destined to endure. By 1758, the Wichita villages were apparently relocated to the Red River,[160] and it appears that the heyday of the operation, whatever its exact form, lasted from about 1747 to 1752.[161] Thereafter, Arkansas Post merchants derived their livelihood mainly from dealings with white hunters and sporadic trade with some Osage bands and intruders from east of the Mississippi.

Though the Quapaws' value as trading partners diminished during the course of the eighteenth century, the nature of the European population that was drawn to the Arkansas region did nothing to reduce the Quapaws' value as military allies. Many of the itinerant hunters of the Arkansas frequently forswore any allegiance to European sovereigns,[162] and a militia company was not formed in the region until 1780, as part of the effort to improve military readiness during the American Revolution.[163] These circumstances, coupled with the fact that the Arkansas garrison was regularly tiny and frequently undisciplined, meant that French and Spanish authorities had to rely heavily on Quapaw gunmen for both offensive and defensive purposes. And, as luck would have it, an artifact that dramatically memorializes the French-Quapaw military alliance has survived to provide instruction on one of the ways in which these two very disparate peoples had achieved an important kind of symbiosis by the middle of the eighteenth century.

III

The French and Quapaw
Alliance Illustrated

The fact that the French and the Quapaws forged a military alliance during Arkansas's colonial period has, very surprisingly, been preserved in an engaging work of art that was probably executed around 1740 or 1750. The survival of this artifact, especially such a beautiful and instructive one, is more than we have the right to expect, and it illustrates the extent to which the French had come to depend on the Quapaws by the middle of the eighteenth century. Its preservation also allows us to see an aspect of the Quapaws (their artistic prowess) that surviving documents only hinted at and provides us with a chance at a fuller appreciation of Quapaw national character than we could otherwise have acquired. It is, moreover, a permanent, tangible record of the centrality of French-Quapaw cooperation to a proper appreciation of the colonial history of Arkansas.

I.

In the Musée de l'Homme in Paris, there is a splendid painted buffalo hide (see Figure 16) that may well do much to illuminate the colonial history of Arkansas.[1] Measuring about 7 ½ feet by 5 ½ feet, it features two feathered calumets, four Indian villages, a French village or fort (see Figure 18), and representations of the sun and moon. Above the three villages that are grouped together are written the words Ackansas, Ouzovtovovi, Tovarimon, and Ovqappa. Ackansas (Arkansas), as we already saw, is the generic name that the Illinois Indians (and thus the French) applied to the Quapaw Indians;[2] the other words are the names of the three individual Quapaw villages of the eighteenth century—more usually written these days as Osotouy, Tourima, and Kappa.[3] (The Quapaws were frequently referred to as the Quapaws of the three villages.)[4] Though there are a number of objects on the skin, the main events portrayed are a battle between the Quapaws and another Indian tribe (from which the Quapaws emerged victorious) and a scalp dance performed in the Quapaws' villages in celebration of their victory (see Figure 17). A line, which runs through the French village or fort, connects the Quapaw villages with the battle site.

II.

A recent publication suggests, albeit quite tentatively, that the painting on this skin might well be the work of Illinois Indians.[5] In support of this supposition the author adduces, first of all, the tradition that the skin was part of a larger collection of Indian painted hides assembled by French travelers, notably Father Marquette, in the Illinois country. It is not easy to put much stock in an uncorroborated oral tradition; and in fact, all that we know certainly about the early custody of the skin is that it was in France before 1789.[6] But the surest indications of an Illinois origin, the argument continues, are four of the elements that the painting features, all of which were very much at home in eighteenth-century Illinois: Conical Indian dwellings covered with cane mats, European houses like the ones occupied by French colonial missionaries and merchants, dancers whose faces are painted red and black, and calumets.[7] It is certainly true that these elements are consistent with an Illinois origin. They are, however, equally consistent with a Quapaw origin, and, indeed, it would seem evident from other considerations that will be identified that such a provenience is much more likely.

First of all, some of the Indian houses that are pictured (those of the Quapaws' enemies) may indeed be conical like those of the Illinois. There is nothing, however, that justifies a conclusion that they were covered with

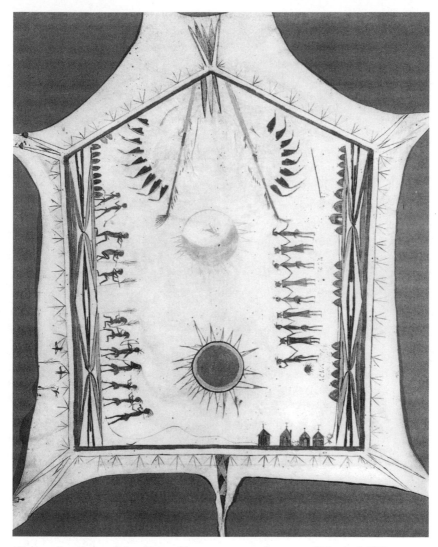

Figure 16. Robe of the three villages, ca. 1750. *Courtesy of Musée de l'Homme, Paris*

mats; from all appearances, they might just as well have been bark-covered, as were those of the Quapaws.[8] The other houses, the ones in the Quapaws' villages, however, conform exactly to the descriptions left by some late seventeenth- and early eighteenth-century travelers who described Quapaw houses as round;[9] and even if, as some scholars have posited, Quapaws lived in long huts with curved roofs,[10] what the skin may be showing is the gable end of a long hut. The profile section of such a building will be virtually indistinguishable, if at all, from the section of a circular dome, and, moreover, the French buildings on the skin seem to be shown with their gable ends forward. (By resorting to this strategy, incidentally, the artist can make room for more buildings.) Additional support for the proposition that the skin is showing long huts in section is that only one of the Indian buildings shows a doorway; and if the huts were dome-shaped it would seem to have been natural to depict the parts of them that contained entrances rather than their featureless elements. The large house with the door, shown with deliberate prominence in the village of Kappa (see Figure 17), could well be "the large council cabin built . . . in the middle of the village" of which Bossu wrote in 1750,[11] the same structure, presumably, that he spoke of twenty years later as "the large cabin of the Council of the Nation."[12] It would seem, therefore, that there is no particular reason to think that the houses in the villages marked with Quapaw names are anything but Quapaw houses.

Houses of vertical logs were common in colonial Louisiana towns from the Gulf Coast to Indiana and from the earliest times. There is therefore no reason to assume that this feature necessarily connects the skin to the Illinois country. Since the French houses are shown hard by the Quapaw villages, they would in any case almost certainly have to be those of Arkansas Post, not some Illinois settlement—whatever the origin of the painting. So much must surely be obvious.[13] But, as luck would have it, we may be able to say a great deal more about these buildings than that they were in Arkansas sometime during its colonial period. As we have seen, in 1732 Pierre Petit de Coulange reestablished the garrison at Arkansas Post in order to counter attempts by the Chickasaws to frustrate and undermine the French colonial effort.[14] He built a military establishment there that, according to a description written in 1734, consisted of four buildings: A barracks, a prison, a dwelling house with a fireplace (no doubt for Coulange and his wife), and a powder magazine, all built in typical French colonial fashion using vertical logs.[15] Our skin shows a French establishment with four buildings, only one of which has a chimney, and clearly illustrates the vertical-log *bousillage* construction of one of the buildings (the one on the far left of Figure 18). This almost eerie correspondence would seem to exceed the bounds of mere coincidence, especially since no other eighteenth-century Arkansas military establishment of which we have a

Figure 17.   Detail from the robe of the three villages depicting a scalp dance and the Quapaws' villages. *Courtesy of Musée de l'Homme, Paris*

detailed account so exactly matches this description. Coulange's site was abandoned and the Post was moved after 1749 when the Chickasaws attacked it, killed some of the *habitants,* and carried off a number of women and children into slavery.[16] So it would seem that what we may have here, incredibly, is a relatively realistic picture of the Post of Arkansas as it existed in the 1730s and 1740s. There is, therefore, no apparent reason to believe that the French buildings shown on the painting have any connection with the Illinois country. Indeed, there is every reason to think that what is depicted is Arkansas Post.

The Illinois Indians, it is true, did paint their faces red and black—not to mention other colors.[17] But so did the Quapaws, in common with most of the other Indians of Louisiana.[18] In 1687, Henri Joutel encountered a Quapaw chief who, "to the End he may appear the finer, . . . never fails to besmear himself with Clay, or some red or black Colouring they make use of"; he also observed some Quapaw dancers "all besmear'd with Clay, of Black or Red, so that they really look'd like a Company of Devils or Monsters."[19] In 1699 the Jesuit Father Gravier gave a chief "a box of vermillion to daub his youth."[20] Virtually a full century after that, John Pope happened on an aging Quapaw who "was in Mourning, having his Face blacken'd over with a Commixture of Bear's Oil, Charcoal and Turpentine: Just under his Jowls were two Streaks of red and white, which ran parallel to each other."[21] Red, the color of blood, is the color that warriors chose to paint their faces, as Bossu is careful to tell us twice. "The war dance is very interesting to see," he reports: "All the young men are painted red."[22] The lead dancer in the painting, moreover, is shown holding a rattle (see Figure 17), a favorite rhythm instrument of the Quapaws that European visitors frequently mentioned. Father St. Cosme, whose baroque ears found the Quapaws' music "not the most agreeable," said that these rattles were "gourds with pebbles in them,"[23] though others asserted that seeds and glass or enamel beads were used to produce the sounds.[24] (There are accounts, too, of Quapaws employing drums, bells, and even reed flutes in their dancing,[25] though none of these instruments is in evidence on the skin.) The women dancers, moreover, are wearing their hair in cylindrical rolls around the ears, a style that the naturalist Thomas Nuttall says was preferred by unmarried Quapaw women.[26] There therefore appears to be no reason to assume that the dancers are anything other than Quapaw.

Finally, the Illinois Indians, it needs saying, were hardly the only tribe to whom the calumet was of importance: It figured centrally in Quapaw rituals of welcome, alliance, adoption, prayer, war, and peace from the very beginning of European contact with them.[27] The black and white feathers attached to the calumets on the skin may well be those of an eagle, which is what the Quapaws used to adorn their calumets. It may not be irrelevant that the calumets depicted have red tips: Father Gravier said in 1700 that red was the color of the war calumet among the Quapaws.[28]

There seems no very good reason, therefore, to posit that our painted skin has a connection with the Illinois Indians or the Illinois country. Its content conforms perfectly with what we know of the Quapaws and of Arkansas Post in the eighteenth century. The painting, moreover, literally has Arkansas written all over it, and it concerns itself with events that feature the Quapaws. These are all facts that tend to indicate a Quapaw origin for the painting. It is noteworthy too that Quapaw folklore included

Figure 18. Detail from the robe of the three villages picturing the French fort on the Arkansas. *Courtesy of Musée de l'Homme, Paris*

a story about the moon being inhabited by a man who held a trophy head in his hand,[29] and our skin features a man on the moon who is clutching something.

Furthermore, the Quapaws were famous throughout Louisiana for their hide paintings. As early as 1687, Henri Joutel had been moved to remark on the "buffalo hides that the [Quapaws] have the industry to dress and paint with a kind of red coloring that is quite pretty,"[30] which the Quapaws hung in their dwellings to divide them into compartments. Thirty-five years later, Diron d'Artaguiette reported that Quapaw men had by then achieved a wide renown for "the dressing of buffalo skins, upon which they paint designs with vermilion and other colors." These skins, he added, "are very highly prized among the other nations."[31] Father Du Poisson, who owned at least one of these Quapaw painted hides, called them *matachés,* which he defined as skins "painted by the Savages in different colors, and on which they represent calumets, birds, and beasts." Quapaw *matachés* made of deerskins "can be used as tablecloths," he noted, while those of buffalo hides served as bedcovers.[32] He also attested to the Quapaws' interest in artistic matters: "They are in ecstasies when they see the picture of Saint Régis that I have in my room . . . *Oukantaqué,* they exclaim, *it is the Great Spirit!* . . . They place themselves in different parts of my room and say, each time smiling: *He is looking at me; he almost speaks, he needs only a voice.*"[33] The Quapaws' artistic ability and interest in artistic matters furnishes further evidence that our painted skin is of Quapaw origin.

But the most probative clue to the painting's Quapaw provenience is its subject matter. One has to ask why the Illinois Indians would go to the trouble of painting a picture that shows the Quapaw Indians defeating an enemy and celebrating a victory, for this, as we have said, is the substance of the principal events that the skin depicts. This has been recognized as putting a difficulty in the way of an Illinois provenience for the painting, but to counter this difficulty the observation is offered that the "Illinois and Quapaws were constantly at war."[34] As it happens, that is not true: The Illinois and Quapaws were fast friends.[35]

As early as 1680, a Frenchman familiar with the Illinois country recorded that the Illinois tribes and the Quapaws had at some previous time formed a kind of confederation the purpose of which was to make war on the Iroquois, and he recalled having visited an Illinois village of four hundred huts and eighteen hundred warriors, some undisclosed number of whom were Quapaws.[36] In the next century, the Illinois and the Quapaws stood resolutely with the French during both of their disastrous wars against another common enemy, the Chickasaws.[37] After France abandoned Louisiana in the wake of the Seven Years' War, moreover, the two old Indian allies participated in the pan-Indian resistance usually, if somewhat misleadingly, called Pontiac's rebellion, and they coordinated their opposition to the imposition of English rule in their respective territories.[38] After the Spanish took possession of the Arkansas country, various groups of the Illinois (including Kaskaskias and Peorias) took refuge there, and a large contingent of them was even incorporated for a time into one of the Quapaw villages.[39] Far from being "constantly at war," therefore, the tribes of the Illinois confederacy and the Quapaws were instead constant and unshakeable allies.

Even if it were true that the Illinois and Quapaws were enemies, that would tend rather to deepen a mystery than to solve one: Why would the Illinois want to record a victory by their enemies? If the painting is of Indian origin, as it seems certainly to be, it would seem far more likely that it was the product of a Quapaw artist, since its evident aim is to record and laud a successful Quapaw military adventure. We know that Indian paintings frequently aimed to celebrate and memorialize the exploits of an individual or a group. They often served as mnemonic devices that "enabled a successful warrior to advertise his achievements to the community at large."[40] It is beyond unlikely that a tribe or some member of it would want to recall a disgrace or defeat, or even record the virtues and accomplishments of another tribe. While it is of course impossible to prove a negative, I know of no recorded instance in which that occurred.

For all of the reasons adumbrated, based on what we can deduce from this painted hide itself as well as what we know generally about Indian painting, a Quapaw provenience for the painting is highly likely. Indeed, it would seem to me to be all but certain.[41]

III.

What else can we say more or less reliably about this remarkable artifact? If we assume for the moment, for reasons already indicated, that it illustrates events involving the fort constructed in 1732 and attacked in 1749, we can make a reasonable guess concerning the identity of the Quapaws' defeated enemies. They would almost surely be the Chickasaws, with whom, as we have said, the Quapaws were already at war when La Salle treated with the Quapaws in 1682,[42] and against whom they struggled for most, if not all, of the French colonial period. The Chickasaws' complicity with the Natchez who destroyed the French settlement at Natchez in 1729 and their steadfast attachment to the English aim of subverting the French effort in Louisiana, as we have seen, prompted the colonial government to strengthen its presence at the Arkansas. After the Natchez turned back an attempt by an expedition of more than seventy men to reach the Arkansas country in 1731, Pierre Petit de Coulange and twelve soldiers at last established themselves early the next year on the Arkansas River. French troops had been absent from the Arkansas for about seven years, so it is a safe bet that the Quapaws would have engaged in their favorite calumet ceremony to resurrect the military alliance. Perhaps it is this event that the calumets on the skin commemorate.[43]

A troublesome embarrassment in the way of a completely confident reading of the skin is that the order in which the Quapaw villages are arranged (or named) on it does not correspond with the configuration that early eighteenth-century travelers ascribed to them. The sources for the 1730s are in unequivocal agreement that the first village encountered on the Arkansas River on the way up to the Arkansas Post was Tourima (with Tonguinga), followed by Osotouy, and then Kappa, this last directly across from the Post.[44] The skin, on the other hand, portrays Kappa first, followed by Tourima and Osotouy. The skin, in fact, depicts the order in which the villages appeared on the river in 1777, when the Post was located close to the Mississippi in Desha County.[45] It is possible, however, since the names of the villages may have been added sometime after the skin was painted,[46] that a mistake was made when they were affixed. (We have no idea who did this, of course, or how much, if anything, he or she knew of the region.) It is also possible that the skin deals with a time after 1748, when, on account of flooding, the Quapaws moved their villages above the fort to *Écores Rouges*.[47] There is no record of exactly where the Quapaws were located at that time, nor do we know the order in which they arranged themselves on the river.

We do know that they remained hostile to the Chickasaws after the 1749 attack on the Post: Later that year, they pursued the attackers down the Mississippi and produced twenty-five Chickasaw scalps,[48] and the next year they sent the governor eighteen more.[49] In 1751 Governor Vaudreuil exulted that the "Arkansas still continue to be attached to us and are making frequent raids on the Chickasaw, from whom they have quite recently brought back some scalps."[50] Since the line on the painting shows the Quapaws moving from their villages, through the Post, and on to the battle, the skin just might have to do with engagements that occurred after the attack of 1749, when the fort in fact lay between the Quapaws and the Chickasaws.

But whatever the exact date of the occurrences recorded, the conclusion that the vanquished foe is the Chickasaws is more or less irresistible because there is simply no other tribe to which the events illustrated can be reasonably connected. There were, it is true, Quapaw raids against the Koroa in 1702 and 1730,[51] but at the earlier of those two dates there was no French settlement at the Arkansas, and most probably there was no settlement there in 1730 as elaborate as the one pictured.[52] Other Quapaw engagements of a minor sort with the Tunicas and the Natchez find mention in the records of the 1730s, but they were of a limited character.[53] There were also difficulties between the Osages and French hunters from Arkansas in about 1720, and a few Osages attacked some Quapaws in 1751;[54] there is, however, no record of Quapaw retaliation in either case. It is doubtful, then, that the skin has any connection to any of these events.

According to Bossu, as late as 1770 the Quapaws still abhorred "the *Chikachas* dogs who have become our implacable enemies since they killed and burned some Frenchmen, along with the *chief of prayer* (a missionary)."[55] (This was an allusion to the disastrous denouement of the First Chickasaw War in 1736, when a large number of Frenchmen were taken captive and burned to death in the Chickasaw villages.) We cannot therefore completely discount the possibility that the skin deals with a time after 1759, when the downriver fort that has come to be called Fort Desha was finally completed.[56] It, too, may have had four buildings, but the punctuation in Captain Philip Pittman's 1765 description of it makes it difficult to know exactly how many buildings it contained; and he does not record the number of fireplaces.[57] But there is no record of Quapaw war parties being sent against the Chickasaws, or anyone else, from this location during the French colonial period, which makes this possibility less likely.[58] Of course, if the skin was painted after the French period, which is not impossible, the enemy could well have been Osages, against whom the Quapaws sent numerous war parties from Fort Desha.[59] But further corroboration that the enemy were Chickasaws is provided by the fact that the Chickasaws' houses were square or rectangular with thatched roofs,[60] and the profiles of the enemies' houses on the skin are consistent with that.

IV.

The representations of the sun and the moon in the painting probably served a dual purpose. First of all, they are likely to be of religious significance. Diron d'Artaguiette reported in 1723 that the Quapaws "worship the moon, to which they are accustomed to pray every evening,"[61] and Bossu later asserted that "they fear the devil, called the Evil Spirit, and worship the sun and the moon."[62] Father Gravier remarked that the Quapaws regarded the calumet as the "pipe of the sun, and in fact they proffer it to him to smoke when they wish to obtain calm, rain or fair weather."[63]

It may also be that the representations of the sun and moon were aligned in a way intended to provide the viewer with an east-west directional axis with which to read and interpret the skin:[64] If so, then the Quapaws are shown venturing up the Arkansas River (more or less east to west), turning north through Arkansas Post (on Lake Dumond in present-day Arkansas County), and then heading east to engage the Chickasaws (see Figure 19). The Quapaws regularly employed a land route to raid the Chickasaws

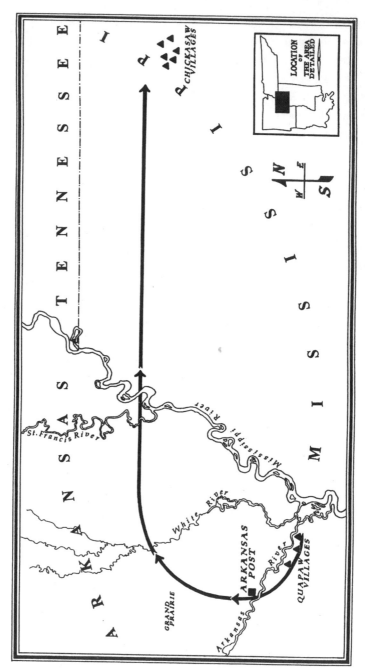

Figure 19. A proposed cartographic interpretation of the robe of the three villages.

that ran north and then east of the Post and crossed the Mississippi River just above the mouth of the St. Francis River. In the 1730s, the French spent a great deal of time scouting this so-called *chemin des Chickachas* for use in their abortive schemes to conquer the Chickasaws.[65] If this interpretation is correct, this skin would be the oldest known original Indian map,[66] and it establishes a possible European influence on the arrangement of the contents of the painting. If, on the other hand, the skin portrays a sortie against the Osages during the time that Arkansas Post was located downriver, the proposed cartesian content of the skin is entirely undone, since the Osages lived northwest of the Quapaws, and Arkansas Post was east of the Quapaw villages. In that case, the skin does not maintain cardinal direction at all, and the line that unites the Quapaw villages, the fort, and the battle site is merely the thread of a story in a diachronic picture,[67] without directional significance, indicating only that the Quapaws first went to Arkansas Post from their villages and then proceeded to engage the enemy.

It would not in any case be at all surprising if the Quapaws were producing maps in the eighteenth century. Indeed, it is well established that "[s]ome if not all of the Indians of North America could draw maps at the time of their first contact with white people";[68] and from "the earliest contacts, Amerindians have transmitted to Euro-Americans spatially-arranged information about the lands, coasts, waters, places, routes and resources of North America."[69] We don't know if the Quapaws were doing this sort of thing when Europeans first met up with them, but, if not, they certainly would have learned quickly to do so thereafter.

Any hypothetical rumination about the Quapaws' ability to make maps by the mid-eighteenth century is rendered unnecessary by events that occurred at Arkansas Post in 1737. On 21 October of that year, Bernard de Vergès, a French engineer, arrived at the Post to secure the Quapaws' help in locating and surveying a road to the Chickasaws to facilitate a French attack on that tribe. This was an effort to which the Quapaws were ideally suited to make a contribution, for, as we have seen, they were making frequent raids on the Chickasaws and were therefore in a position to know the best and most direct routes to their villages.

During their talks with Vergès, various Quapaw chiefs described three different ways to reach the Chickasaw villages from Arkansas Post. A Quapaw village chief named Buagrès then told Vergès that "he knew an excellent road a little above the St. Francis River to which he would guide me if I wished, and that the other two roads were not good for transport [*charrois*]." Buagrès, Vergès reveals, "at the same time traced on the drawing board a map of this country for me, and gave me a description of it, with a great deal of good sense and intelligence." It is not likely that Vergès could have had this much enthusiasm for the chief's map if he did not at least have some confidence that it preserved cardinal direction (a confidence that he would have developed from his discussion with Buagrès), for otherwise the sketch would have been useless to him.[70]

Because of the combination of native American and European elements, some evident and others more conjectural, that we have identified in the content of this marvelous painted skin, we are left to wonder whether it was not, at least in design if not in execution, a collaborative effort between a Quapaw Indian and a Frenchman. Perhaps, even, it represents the work of what may, as a cultural matter, be the same thing, namely, one of those French and Indian *métis* for whom Arkansas Post was famous in the eighteenth century.[71] Such an artifact would come down to us as an appealing epitome of the cultural symbiosis that Indians and Europeans achieved in the six generations that they lived and died together on the Arkansas River during Louisiana's colonial period. Most satisfying of all, it appears that a native American (or *métis*) artist has bequeathed us the only known depiction from the colonial era of the first European settlement in what became Jefferson's Louisiana. De Batz, Dumont de Montigny, and Le Bouteux, all Frenchmen, provided us with views (some sophisticated, some amateurish) of early eighteenth-century French dwellings in lower Louisiana,[72] but none of these stooped to record the sights available in the remoteness of the Arkansas region. Now we can take advantage of the profoundly evocative power of pictures to help reconstruct lives that were passed in eighteenth-century Arkansas and to comprehend the significance of the events that shaped them and gave them content.

IV

French and Spanish Hearts as One?

It is apparent that the French had succeeded in establishing a significant rapprochement with the Quapaws during the six or seven decades that the French had lived among them, the most remarkable surviving artifact of which is the hide painting that we have just been at some pains to describe and interpret. When it fell to the Spanish to take possession of Louisiana, they were keenly aware of the success that the French had enjoyed with the Quapaws, and so they sought to create in the Quapaws the impression that the Spanish were really Frenchmen at heart. Despite some rather extraordinary efforts directed to that end, however, the Spanish, largely because of constant English attempts to undermine them, were not able to achieve their aim entirely. The Quapaws, for their part, quite aware of the advantages of competition, became more than adept at playing on the Spanish and the English to their advantage.

I.

With the end of the Seven Years' War in 1763 came the end as well to French claims to North America. Louisiana found itself divided: Spain got New Orleans and that portion of Louisiana that lay west of the

Mississippi River; England took all the rest and named it West Florida. The French moved promptly to execute their treaty obligations by putting the English in possession of Mobile and Natchez, and they cooperated in the English effort to occupy the Illinois country by way of a convoy from New Orleans. But their Indian allies proved difficult to mollify. Most of them felt betrayed, and it is likely that their own notions of international law were offended by the peace.

The Quapaws, Bossu credibly maintains, were "appalled by this cession." He said that they had "repeated . . . what they had said in my first trip: that the first white men they saw were French whom they welcomed to the exclusion of all other people, but now they were astonished to see that we had deserted them without even giving any reason for it." Bossu further claimed that the Quapaws had said that "they never would have expected this after having sacrificed themselves for our nation in the war we waged into the homeland of the *Chikachas* who had given refuge to the *Natchez* after they massacred our compatriots who had settled among them."[1]

It is well known that a pan-Indian resistance to the English, conventionally referred to as Pontiac's rebellion, frustrated English attempts to establish hegemony in the Illinois region. What is not so well known, though we have already alluded to this briefly, is that the Quapaws at first participated in this resistance even though their territory was not to be occupied by the English, for whom they had for two or three generations been developing a cordial and reciprocated hatred. Partly, it seems, at Pontiac's urging, they had resolved to blockade the British convoy sent from New Orleans to take possession of the upper country, and it required some diplomatic persuasion, accompanied by the usual presents, to deflect them from this ambition.[2]

Shortly after Governor Antonio de Ulloa arrived in Louisiana in 1766, in a first, abortive attempt to assert Spanish control there, Ensign Le Gros de La Grandcour wrote to him from the Arkansas to announce that a Quapaw chief and some warriors had come to the Post to "learn the news." "I gave them the news on your behalf," La Grandcour said, "as having arrived in this colony." The ensign claimed that the Quapaws were "delighted [*charmées*] by this news and by the praise that I gave them from *monsieur le gouvernour.*" The chief and the other Quapaws, he assured the new governor, promised to "carry you in their heart to the same extent that they had carried all the French."[3] The Spanish, for their part, attempted

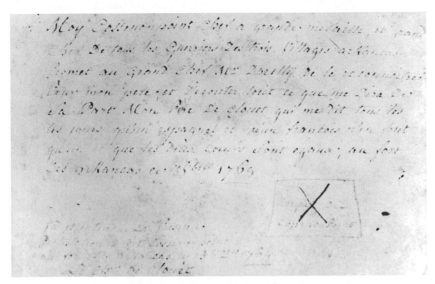

Figure 20. Undertaking by Quapaw chief Cassenonpoint to recognize
Governor O'Reilly as his father and to listen to his words,
15 October 1769. *Courtesy of Louisiana State Museum, New Orleans;
on loan to the Louisiana State Museum from the Louisiana Historical
Society*

to transfer the Quapaws' affection for the French to themselves by repeatedly assuring them, in what must have been the Indian idiom, that "the
two hearts were one," a phrase that even appears in a kind of oath of allegiance to the Spanish king to which Great Chief Cassenonpoint subscribed
his mark in 1769, on the very same day that the *habitants* signed their own
declaration of loyalty to their new Spanish masters.[4]

When the French in New Orleans revolted against the Spanish in 1768
and expelled Governor Ulloa, DeClouet reported that the Quapaws were
much disquieted,[5] and only a few weeks after Alexander O'Reilly arrived
with a great military force in New Orleans to restore Spanish rule, the
Quapaws appeared at DeClouet's house to learn "to what objects they
ought to be attached and what was the name of the great chief." The commandant told them that "the great king of Spain was the one to whom
they ought to be faithful, that today he was their master, and that Mr.
O'Reilly, the great general, represented the person of the king to help them
in their needs."

The Quapaws' inquiry had been generated by the seditious efforts of the English who had no sooner taken possession of the east bank of the Mississippi than they had begun to try to dislodge the Quapaws from their alliance with the Spanish. The English became very aggressive in their efforts to undermine Spanish influence among the Quapaws, and they never missed an opportunity to emphasize the weakness of the Spanish presence in Arkansas. Englishmen urged the Quapaws not to have any faith "in a piece of paper" (presumably the treaties ending the Seven Years' War and ceding the western part of Louisiana to Spain) and maintained that the English were "going to be the only ones staying in the colony." DeClouet had his hands full trying to "erase from the minds of [the Quapaw] young people the bad speeches of our neighbors."[6] He advised Governor O'Reilly that the Quapaws were saying that "your arrival caused the first moment of their unhappiness," a sentiment, he said, "that could only have come from the floating saloons of the English on the river."[7]

The aftermath of the revolution in New Orleans upset the Quapaws considerably. General O'Reilly had executed the leaders of the revolt, and the English of course had lost no time in attempting to turn this event against the Spanish. Desmazellières reported that the Quapaws had asked him "if it were true that the Spanish were bad," and he told O'Reilly that "the English had told them that as soon as you arrived in the colony you had killed five Frenchmen." The commandant had responded to the Quapaws' query with a stupid lie that they could not possibly have believed, namely, that "the Frenchmen who had been killed had lost their minds and that it was the French chief who had asked that the executions be carried out."[8] The English even told the Quapaws that if the Choctaws attacked them it would have been the Spanish and the French who had caused it.[9]

It is altogether likely that the execution of the French leaders of the revolution left the Quapaws with a deep distrust of the Spanish. It is certain, in any case, that the Quapaws openly expressed a preference for a French commandant over a Spanish one, a preference that was encouraged and shared by the French *habitants* at the Post.[10] In 1771, the Quapaw chief Guatanika, on his way to visit the governor in New Orleans, called on Alexandre DeClouet to ask his help in persuading the governor to appoint DeClouet commandant at the Arkansas in place of Leyba, a Spaniard. It seems even that DeClouet had told the chief that he would soon relieve the Arkansas commandant and bring the Quapaws lots of presents.[11] The next year, Governor Unzaga told Leyba that a Quapaw chief had asked him to relieve Leyba of his command.[12]

If the revolution in New Orleans and its aftermath provided a shaky foundation on which to build a Quapaw alliance, the Spanish nevertheless bent every effort to ingratiate themselves with this important Indian ally. In this attempt, they mostly imitated the policy of the French who had been developing close relationships with Indians in Louisiana for three generations. It was imperative for the Spanish to try to fathom and evaluate Quapaw governmental arrangements if they were ever going to make alliances with them on which they could effectively rely.

Like the French, the Spanish were keenly aware that the Quapaws did not have a hierarchical political organization, with leaders who could guarantee the course of public affairs and demand obedience to their orders. Like many other North American Indian societies, the Quapaws probably operated mainly on the basis of consensuses developed in their monthly or extraordinary councils (although majority votes seem to have resolved some issues),[13] and a chief's influence and power varied with his reputation, exploits, persuasive abilities, and the wisdom and general reasonableness of his advice and opinions. So when Arkansas commandants wanted to be certain of tribal support for a particular resolution or plan, they sought the consent of the largest possible number of individual Quapaws. As Captain Leyba put it, with some exaggeration, "it is necessary to make all of them happy, since among these people every voice is equal—the great and the small."[14] So in 1773, when the Quapaws prevailed on Leyba to choose their "interim governor" to serve during the great chief's minority, Leyba, to minimize future complaints from the Quapaws, "asked them one by one if they were happy [with his choice], and they all answered that they were."[15] And a year later, to cement a pledge by the Quapaws to expel Englishmen from their villages, Lieutenant Orieta "had each one of the chiefs and other *considerados* promise me individually" to do so.[16] He was delighted to inform the governor that "they unanimously and of a common accord had resolved to seize" the Englishmen.[17]

One of the ways in which France and Spain tried to cajole the Quapaws into affective allegiances with them, and to knead the Quapaws' political institutions into arrangements with which the Europeans could reliably deal, was by the distribution of medals, gorgets, and patents that signified rank and authority.[18] These symbols of power, the Europeans hoped, would

Figure 21. Spanish medal with image of King Carlos III, presented to Quapaw chief in the eighteenth century. *Courtesy of Mr. and Mrs. Lawrence Supernaw*

make those who accepted them influential among the Quapaws; and their recipients, the theory went, would be grateful for the recognition and prestige that these insignia provided. Father Vitry maintained that a French medal "is for the Indians what the Cross of St. Louis is for the French; for the Indians have been made to understand that it is the reward for conspicuous and faithful service."[19]

The considerations that led commandants to recommend insignia for a particular Quapaw are revealed in a 1785 letter from Captain DuBreuil: He recommended a Quapaw named Thagesideska for a small medal because he "has given much evidence of being inclined to the Spanish and French nations, and he always gives good counsel to the young people and others of his nation." DuBreuil deemed it prudent to give Thagesideska a medal in order "to give him more authority and encourage him to keep his nation always quiet." DuBreuil reported that Thagesideska had assured him "that he wanted to sacrifice for Spain because he considers them to be brothers," and the commandant asked the governor to approve the appointment because the Quapaw was "an Indian of excellent conduct and much listened to in his nation."[20]

Figure 22. Commission from Governor Carondelet of Louisiana, dated 7 July 1795, appointing a Kansas chief named Manchiamany as a gorget chief. Quapaw chiefs received similar commissions in the eighteenth century. *Courtesy of Mercantile Library of St. Louis*

It is, of course, quite possible that the concept or institution of "chief" was not itself an indigenous one; perhaps it evolved in response to European hierarchical assumptions about how polities necessarily had to be ordered. It is certain in any case that the distribution of medals could cause trouble in the Indian villages. In 1789, for instance, Captain Vallière reported that a Quapaw named Pasemony did not want to accept a medal that Vallière had offered to him. Though Pasemony had thanked Vallière profusely for the suggestion, he preferred instead to take a gorget. He wanted, he said, to avoid having disputes with other Quapaws who would be jealous if he got a medal, and nothing that Vallière could say could persuade him to take it.[21]

In addition to the great chief of the Quapaw nation, the records frequently speak of chiefs of the large and small medal in the individual villages. In 1784, for instance, Tourima had two chiefs of the large medal, Osotouy had two chiefs of the small medal, and Kappa one of each.[22] The lack of a chief of the large medal in Osotouy may have simply been due to a vacancy; perhaps, for instance, the headman of the village had died and a successor had not yet been qualified or installed. But there are other possibilities. It is possible that there had not been enough large medals to go around or that the Spanish wished to influence larger tribal politics by not giving a large medal to anyone in Osotouy at the time. Perhaps, too, they thought that the headman of the village (assuming that there was one) was not worthy of a premiere distinction. We simply do not know.

This is not the end of the mystery. In 1777, we hear of first, second, and even third chiefs in the individual Quapaw villages,[23] with no hint given as to the meaning of these distinctions, though it is a reasonable guess that these chiefs would have been decorated with a large medal, a small medal, and a gorget, respectively. An interesting letter from 1798 reveals that Caskai-haus-tonica, a Quapaw chief of the large medal, was going to New Orleans to extend his compliments to the governor and to request a small medal for his eldest son Tasconquisiguidai and a gorget for his son-in-law Orhan.[24] The governor granted his requests.[25] Which if any of these personages was the chief of the so-called *cabanne de valeur* (lodge of valor), which seems to have been at least partly a place of religious observance, we cannot tell.[26] We cannot even be sure that these chiefs had enjoyed any previous internal political significance that resonated with the European recognition given them. It may be that some of the secondary decorations had gone to heads of particularly influential clans.

The unfortunate truth is that we know next to nothing about Quapaw political organization, or, indeed, whether the Quapaws even had institutions that can fairly be described as governmental and regulatory in the modern sense. The records and contemporary histories are discouragingly silent on the question. A letter from Captain Orieta in 1776,[27] reporting that Angaska, chief of the Tourima village, was leading a convoy of fourteen boats containing Quapaw families bound for the winter hunt, provides no real hint as to what the chief's duties and powers might have been. In late March of 1778, Villiers wrote that "the Quapaws are returning [from the hunt] little by little and soon they will all be assembled." Villiers also revealed that the great chief had already returned, so it would appear that one of his obligations was not to see the entire hunting party safely back to the villages, though what his duties, if any, with respect to regulating and overseeing the hunt itself might have been we cannot tell.[28]

The Spanish could, of course, be expected to try to influence the Indians' governmental forms and their selection of chiefs in a way that would draw the Quapaws into a closer connection to them. The extent to which they were successful in these kinds of efforts is not altogether clear, but we do catch the Spanish in the attempt on more than one occasion. In about 1770, Captain Desmazellières reported to the governor that a Quapaw chief had threatened to strike him when the captain had refused to give him liquor, and that Desmazellières had thrown the chief out of his house, deprived him of his present, and given it to another important Quapaw who was a gorget chief whom he had had "received as chief" in the place of the offender. He also told the Quapaws that the *habitants* had complained about the frequent insults that the chief had offered them, and that it was the chief's fault that "the red man did not have drink as they did in the time of the French." The captain assured the governor, moreover, that "this man is no longer regarded in the nation" because of these actions, but whether that was true, or whether the Quapaws were simply telling the commandant what he wanted to hear, is the hardest kind of question to answer.[29]

There was another event at the Arkansas that might at first blush seem to reveal a successful attempt by the Spanish to influence the internal governmental affairs of the Quapaws, but on close examination that appears to have been only partly the case. On 25 May 1773, Captain Leyba wrote the governor that Cassenonpoint, the great chief of the Quapaw nation, had died only a few days before, and that the Quapaws intended to choose his son as his successor; but since the son was only nine or ten years old, the Quapaws had asked Leyba to select an "interim governor," that is, a person who could serve as chief until the boy achieved his majority. Leyba, however, did not want to make the choice: Instead, he asked all the chiefs and principal warriors to gather at the Post three days later to elect someone by a majority vote. He did promise the governor to try to get the Quapaws to elect "one of the better Indians."[30]

About a week later, according to Leyba, "all the chiefs, principal warriors, and the greater part of this nation of Indians" came together at his house to choose a great chief and "interim governor." They chose Cassenonpoint's young son as chief (this was no doubt only a formality) and then prevailed upon Leyba to choose the interim chief after all. Leyba confided to the governor that he had at first been very reluctant to make the selection because so many Quapaws had lobbied him for the job, but in order to please the Indians he had relented and had chosen Guatanika for the position. He had selected Guatanika, Leyba said, because he was the senior medal chief and was very attached to the Spanish. After making his selection, Leyba asked the Quapaws one by one if they were happy with it, and they all answered that they were. The interpreter thereupon proclaimed the election and there followed a three-gun salute, a feast, a distribution of some small presents—and an announcement by Leyba that he was lowering the prices on all his goods![31]

While it is possible to view this event as a foreign relations coup on Leyba's part,[32] and it is at the very least quite a remarkable example of interracial and international cooperation, it is probably also right to discern in it some rather astute political maneuvering on the part of the Quapaws. The selection of an interim great chief was bound to be controversial, especially, as Leyba noted, because a number of people had been clamoring for the position. By forcing Leyba to make the choice, the Quapaws had rather adroitly moved to reduce the amount of internal strife that the selection would have generated if they themselves had been obliged to make it. Competition among clans for the post, for instance, might well have been very intense.

But on one occasion at least, it appears that the Spanish were able to deflect the normal course of internal Quapaw affairs in a fundamental way. When the Spanish took the field in 1779 with the Americans in their revolt against the English, Arkansas Post found itself probably the most exposed of all the Louisiana settlements, and Captain Villiers realized that his best chance of avoiding the destruction of his little town and fort was a resolutely loyal Quapaw nation. His principal difficulty, as he saw it, was that although Cassenonpoint's son Ouhappatisay had come of age in 1779 and had therefore taken over from the interim great chief, Villiers judged him to be "without spirit (*esprit*) and too young to lead the nation, especially in the critical times that we are in." He therefore asked the governor to send him "a patent in favor of Chief Angaska," whom he intended to install as great chief of the Quapaws despite Ouhappatisay's hereditary right. "It is in him only," Villiers confided, "that I trust, and he is the only one capable of making himself listened to."

As far as Ouhappatisay was concerned, Villiers suggested to the governor that "you can put in [Angaska's] patent that on his death the office of great chief will revert to Ouhappatisay, Cassenonpoint's natural son." Villiers was so anxious to get this business concluded that he informed the governor that he "was counting so much on your approval of this plan, that when I assemble the Quapaws to give them their presents (which I presume will arrive soon), I will seize the opportunity to proclaim Angaska interim great chief." Villiers concluded with a defense of this audacious plan: "In view of the present circumstances and the need that I have of these people for scouting," he said, "I am forced to do this."[33]

Just exactly how Villiers achieved his extraordinary aim he does not reveal, but achieve it he evidently did, for very soon he is referring to Angaska as the great chief[34] and Villiers's successor is reporting to the governor on Angaska's frequent expeditions to reconnoiter in the area of Chickasaw Bluffs.[35]

II.

One important way in which the Spanish sought to retain the allegiance of the Quapaws was by providing them with a gunsmith to keep their weapons in good order. On 10 May 1771, Leyba reported to the governor that one Malibe, the gunsmith to the Quapaws, had quit the job because of low pay.[36] This had upset the Quapaws, who were of the view that it was the Spanish king's duty to provide them with a gunsmith. Leyba asked the governor to allow one of the soldiers at the Post to provide the service.[37] A month later, Leyba reported that the Quapaws were very angry because they had given their old guns to the Spanish to be repaired and the new ones that they had received in their annual present (more about these presents later) were totally useless. They accused the captain of deliberately disarming them to make it easy for the Spanish or an Indian enemy to destroy them.[38]

Some years later, Villiers informed Governor Gálvez that the Quapaws' gunsmith had died, and he asked the governor to appoint one Pierre Joseph Lambert, a young man of good conduct who was born at the Post but who was then living in New Orleans, to the vacancy.[39] The governor responded that the Quapaws who had recently visited him had asked him to name Antoine Lepine to the position and he had acquiesced in the request, but he directed Villiers to choose whichever of the two seemed more likely to please the Indians. Gálvez revealed that one reason he had chosen Lepine was that Lepine's brother (who was settled at the German Coast) had gone to a lot of trouble to act as the interpreter for the Quapaws during their recent visit, and appointing Lepine seemed a way of doing the brother a favor.[40] Villiers nevertheless appointed Lambert to the position because he had left his home in New Orleans in reliance on Villiers's assurance that he could have the job and had built a house and a forge at the

Post. Besides, Villiers said, Lepine had allied himself with the interpreter Lajeunesse, whom he regarded as "a bad subject if ever there was one," and who had lost the Quapaws' confidence and his. Lepine and Lajeunesse had advised the Quapaws not to come see the commandant and kept them at home by supplying them with liquor.[41]

Although Villiers appointed Lambert to the post, it appears that Lepine eventually succeeded him, because in August of 1783 Captain DuBreuil wrote that Lepine wanted to be relieved of his duties as gunsmith since he could not see well enough to do the work. DuBreuil had appointed a soldier of his garrison named Juan Coxeran as interim gunsmith at Lepine's salary of nine dollars a month until the governor could send someone else to fill the position.[42] But Coxeran had deserted only a month after he had assumed the post, and DuBreuil had searched without success for a year and a half for someone to fill the resulting vacancy. The Quapaws' guns were useless, and they asked the governor to send them a gunsmith.[43]

A few months later, however, DuBreuil wrote that Antoine Lepine had recovered his sight and wanted to be both gunsmith and interpreter. With both salaries, DuBreuil believed, Lepine could afford the very high prices that things fetched at the Post. Lepine knew the Quapaws' language perfectly and "the true way to move them." The Quapaws were all for it: They were very unhappy with their interpreter, Jean Baptiste Sossier, who, DuBreuil volunteered, behaved himself very badly with the Quapaws and the whites of the Post alike.[44] Governor Miró soon approved the consolidation of the two jobs.[45] But not long thereafter, DuBreuil wrote Governor Miró that the Quapaws were going to come to New Orleans to discuss a number of matters, including the appointment of a gunsmith for them.[46] The governor replied that he would send a gunsmith to the Post as soon as he found one who wanted to go there.[47] Whether the governor succeeded we cannot tell, and late in the colonial period the Quapaws complained again that they needed a gunsmith and that their arms were entirely useless.[48]

III.

The interpreter, another employee of the Spanish government at the Arkansas, served the alliance in an important way, because one of the most impressive and potentially illuminating facts that emerges from the commandants' letters of the later eighteenth century is the frequency and intensity with which the Europeans at the Post and the Quapaws spoke with each other. They were constantly talking in both formal and informal settings.

Frenchmen's efforts to learn the Quapaw language began with their very earliest visits. In 1673, Father Marquette lamented that the Quapaws' "language is extremely difficult and with all my efforts I could not succeed in pronouncing some words."[49] A few years later, Father Membré said that with a little trouble his party had "managed to make themselves understood in the [Quapaws'] language," and, with the help of sign language, he had taken occasion "to explain something of the truth of God, and the mysteries of our redemption."[50]

Father Du Poisson in 1727 described the way that Europeans attempted to improve their vocabulary and learn the Quapaw tongue. "The Quapaws visit me frequently," he revealed. "I ask them *Talon jajai?* 'What do you call that'?" Soon he was able to make himself "understood in the commonest things," but regretted that there were "no Frenchmen here who are thoroughly familiar with [the language], as they have learned, and that very superficially, what is necessary that they should know for trade." He knew the language as well as the local Frenchmen did, he said, "but I foresee that it will be very difficult for me to learn as much as will be necessary in order to speak to these Savages concerning religion."[51]

The most ceremonial of the communications between the two nations, probably, took place when the commandant gave the Quapaws their present, which was supposed to be delivered annually. This was obviously a good time to discuss pressing matters of mutual concern and for the commandant to extract, if he could, promises from the Quapaws with respect to their future behavior.[52] It also provided an opportunity for the Quapaws to register any complaints that they might have had about the Europeans' treatment of them.[53] The arrival of a new commandant was also often marked by exchanges of complimentary speeches,[54] as were the fairly numerous visits that the Quapaws paid to the governor in New Orleans to assure him of their attachment and to talk over matters of importance to both nations.[55]

Besides these rather formal occasions, there were numerous ad hoc meetings (variously styled as *assemblées, conseils, juntas, consultas, or conferencias*) at which the commandant, *habitants,* and Quapaws got together and discussed matters that needed airing. As we have seen, the change of sovereignty from France to Spain, and the revolution in New Orleans that temporarily interrupted it, greatly disquieted the Quapaws, and there were quite naturally a number of anxious meetings that attended it.[56] War, too, generated a lot of discussion;[57] and the Quapaws not infrequently took the opportunity to unburden themselves of a speech (*harenga*) when they presented Osage heads to the commandant.[58] The very occasional breach of the peace by the Quapaws caused some discussion,[59] as did the Quapaws' complaints about prices being too high and other matters.[60]

The ability to speak with and persuade the Quapaws was a quality that the Arkansas commandant therefore indispensably required, and meetings with the Quapaws were so important that an officer's failure to attend them was a serious offense in the mind of the commandant.[61] The governor told Captain DeClouet, for instance, that he had "to use good arguments [*bonnes raisons*] coupled with the regular annual presents that are due them" to persuade the Quapaws to quit using alcohol.[62] Governor Unzaga directed Lieutenant Orieta to "influence the *habitants* and the Quapaws with smooth words, emphasizing the mildness of our government, its justice and equity," in order to convince them that "the sole object that it pursues [is] to do good to all."[63] Unzaga was evidently clear about the centrality of this aspect of the Arkansas commandant's job, for he instructed Desmazellières that a "commandant is supposed to use polish and affability with the Indians to whom we have given a beautiful present. This will always make a better impression than the vague and unfounded voices of either the English or Indians."[64]

Not every commandant thought that he was up to this part of the job. DeClouet, for instance, asserted that the Quapaws' resolve to trade with the English "will not be undermined by persuasion, and elegant speech is vainly wasted" on them. He also revealed his frustration with his inability to persuade the Quapaws to moderate their drinking. "Brilliant oratory, of which I am little capable," he lamented, "hardly serves to content people of this color."[65] Other commandants bridled at accusations that they did not speak frequently enough to the Quapaws. Captain Desmazellières wrote in response to the governor's complaint that he did "not do enough to publish to the Indians the goodness of the Spanish nation," that, to the contrary, he could assure the governor, without flattering himself, "that no one has more enthusiasm than I when it comes to nurturing good ideas in their minds."[66]

Captain Leyba was so enamored of his technique with the Quapaws that he was eager to share its secrets with his superiors in New Orleans. He told Governor Unzaga that when a Quapaw chief had refused a medal because it was too small, he had had "to puff his head up with wind" to get him to accept it. He revealed that "by nature and disposition, and because of my troubles, most of the time I seem more melancholy than happy. I have told this to the Indians several times, so that they wouldn't believe that their petitions and visits are the cause of my frowns."[67]

On another occasion, Leyba described what he thought were his extraordinary diplomatic skills in a detail that is quite instructive:

> I confess to your lordship that if I had more troops I would have less patience with these Indians and I believe that they would behave better. But for the moment I am a Job: I not only speak with them with affability, but I also try to compose my expression to show great happiness in their presence. Without betraying the least sign of disgust, I allow them, when they are drunk and slobber is falling all around, to kiss me on the mouth, for this is how they show affection to their loved ones. This is because, for all their savageness to all those whom they kill, there is no people more attractive than they are. I listen to all their tales of woe and demonstrate a great compassion; and I try to supply all their unreasonable demands, extending myself more than I can afford.[68]

Leyba believed that his persuasive powers were in fact so good that he had been able to overcome the Quapaws' initial dislike of him. Leyba claimed toward the end of his command that whenever the Quapaw chief came to speak with him "he was very shamefaced . . . for the evil with which he had repaid the favors that I continually did him." The chief allowed that Leyba was getting better and better every day. "Others," he said, "recite panegyrics in praise of me."[69] In fact, he ventured to think that he had charmed them, though he expressed his satisfaction that he derived from this a little cynically. The great chief "visits me very pleasantly," he claimed: "He has the kindness to tell the *habitants* that no finer commandant than I has ever come to the Post. While the brandy lasts, we are friends, since there is no equal in the nation to the great chief at drinking."[70]

It is therefore apparent that the *habitants* and the Quapaws had conversations on a regular basis, on matters that were important to their continued solidarity, although, in the nature of things, this kind of interaction will not often have left its trace in the written record. But in 1775, Lieutenant Orieta asserted that the Quapaws told "everyone whenever they came to town and to the fort . . . in small groups that they want to die on the land where they were born as their ancestors did."[71] Two years earlier Orieta had complained that whenever the Quapaws returned from striking the Osages, the *habitants* and hunters "without a single exception . . . give them many congratulations, embraces, and thanks, calling them their protectors and the avengers of their attackers." These manifestations of thanks and affection pleased "the Quapaws a great deal, and they see themselves as obligated to keep it up."[72] Even the weather was the subject of conversation. In 1780, Villiers reported that the month of January had been so cold that the Arkansas River had twice frozen over, which few of the Indians remembered ever having seen.[73]

It is plain from all this that it was absolutely crucial for the commandant to have a ready way to communicate with the Quapaws in order to maintain their affection for the Spanish and to learn what they were doing and thinking. (The French had had interpreters attached to their garrison as early as 1758, and no doubt much earlier.)[74] Many of the denizens of the Post spoke Quapaw, but since most commandants did not reside there for an extended period, and thus ordinarily would not acquire a facility with the Quapaw language, a commandant necessarily spoke to the Quapaws, and they to him, through an interpreter. The interpreter, an employee of the garrison, was however a good deal more than a casual facilitator of genial or even official conversation: He acted as a kind of deputy Indian agent and his loyalty and skill were crucial to the alliance and thus ultimately to the security of the Post.[75]

In 1770, Orieta reported that Montcharvaux the interpreter had gone to Pointe Coupée to marry a *métis* Indian girl who was a resident of the Post.[76] A few months later, Orieta reported that Montcharvaux was not fit for the job, because he was very arrogant and disaffected from Spain. Orieta indicated that a replacement should not be difficult to find since there were people who had been living at the Post for more than twenty years, some even who knew four Indian languages in addition to Quapaw.[77] Montcharvaux soon quit his post, and Leyba asked the governor to appoint Joseph Landroni in his place: He had been a soldier in the French garrison as early as 1758, and the *habitants* of the Post had recommended him for the job. Landroni wanted ten pesos a month, along with a soldier's ration, as a salary.[78]

Three months later, Leyba reported that Landroni had quieted the

Quapaws' anxieties considerably: They were not, he said, nearly as furious with Spain as they had been on his arrival; in fact, they seemed very pleased and reconciled with her. Landroni nevertheless proved in the event to have been a very bad choice. It developed that "he was a subject very disaffected from the Spanish nation" who was not telling the commandant the truth about what the Quapaws were saying and thinking, and was even mistranslating Leyba's words to the Quapaws and theirs to him.[79] Leyba appointed Nicolas Labuxière, a former soldier of the garrison, to fill the vacancy.[80]

This was another choice that Leyba very soon came to regret, because Labuxière proved to be entirely unsuited for the position (worse, even, than Landroni), and he came close to causing a genuine calamity at the Post. Leyba reported that Labuxière always reviled the Quapaws whenever they were spoken of at the Post, and he never revealed any secret information to the commandant. (This is proof of what we would anyway have had to guess, namely, that the interpreter was expected to act as the eyes and ears of the Spanish government in the Indian villages.) Leyba wrote that he had therefore been obliged to hire Anselme Lajeunesse as interpreter. Lajeunesse, Leyba said, had been a sergeant in the French garrison before the Spanish takeover, had settled at the Post, and possessed, Leyba believed, all the qualities necessary in a successful interpreter: He was truthful, obedient, and respected by the Indians.

Before Labuxière had been made interpreter, Leyba had had to arrest him and put him in irons with the intention of sending him to New Orleans, but Leyba had later felt obliged to free him because the Quapaws had threatened to break him out of jail.[81] In 1772, Leyba informed the governor that he now felt it absolutely imperative to get Labuxière away from Arkansas Post because of his seditious activities. Leyba said that he would have to smuggle him out under cover of darkness, since, given the opportunity, Labuxière would seek refuge among the Quapaws and they would give it to him.[82] The English at Manchac wanted Labuxière to desert and become their interpreter for the Quapaws, and it was a favorite object of Lieutenant John Thomas, the English deputy Indian agent at Manchac, to establish close ties with the Quapaws and to undermine their allegiance to the Spanish.[83]

Soon thereafter, Leyba again reported that he was going to send Labuxière down to New Orleans.[84] But the very day after Leyba had

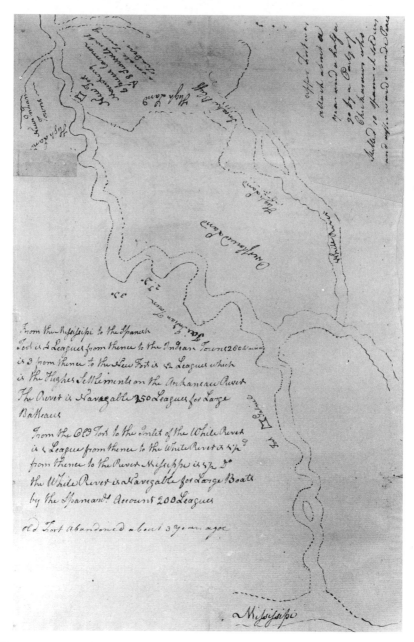

Figure 23. Map by Thomas Hutchins, 1784, showing the former location of
Arkansas Post (wrongly named Fort Gabriel here), the "New
Fort," and the old and new positions of the Quapaw villages.
Courtesy of Historical Society of Pennsylvania

written the governor to this effect, Labuxière told the Quapaw great chief and five of his warriors that he wanted them to gather all their tribesmen together in the woods to await his signal to attack the Post, because Leyba wanted to arrest him. He urged the Quapaws to reduce the Post and its inhabitants to ashes. He said that the garrison was so weak that it would hardly make any difference whether they waited for his signal to attack or not: Any time at all would do. The attack on the Post was evidently a very near thing indeed. Lieutenant Thomas's superiors had sent Henry Lefleur to the Quapaw villages to indicate that all of Thomas's overtures to them had been unauthorized, and Lefleur reported to the English Indian superintendent that he had delivered his message just as the Quapaws were preparing an attack.[85]

Leyba ultimately effected Labuxière's arrest in the dead of night, a time when there were no Indians on the Post. Though it was only a four-minute walk from the interpreter's house to the fort, on the way to the jail the party that took Labuxière into custody unluckily encountered a Quapaw in a canoe. Labuxière called out to the Indian to "tell my father the great chief the state that I am in so he can come to my aid." The Quapaw thereupon went to the Post, took a horse, and hurried to the Quapaw villages to give the news.[86]

Labuxière's reference to the Quapaw chief as "father," which Leyba let slip more or less by the way, lets us in on something of extreme importance, something that everybody in eighteenth-century Louisiana probably knew and accepted matter-of-factly, but that might otherwise have remained entirely hidden from our view. This chance remark opens a considerable window on Quapaw family law and on the strategies that the Europeans employed to turn Indian customs to their advantage. If the Quapaw chief was Labuxière's "father," it is probable that the Quapaws had adopted him and even that he had married the chief's daughter. (As we shall see, English traders did this in Arkansas to insinuate themselves into the Quapaws' governmental structure and to undermine Spanish influence.) His status as what we would call the chief's son-in-law would, in a patrilineal tribe like the Quapaws, give Labuxière not only considerable prestige in the abstract, but even actual "authority," though one needs to remember that Quapaw society was far from hierarchical.

Bossu's observations about eighteenth-century Quapaws need to be sifted through with a great deal of caution. Still, what he says about adoption by the Quapaws not only has about it a certain ring of truth, it also, if one judiciously discounts portions of it, comports with what we would expect from the logic of Quapaw social arrangements and what we know of American Indian customs in general. Bossu makes a Quapaw chief allow that "[b]y choosing a daughter of the Cacique [i.e., chief] to be your wife you rightly will be master, the adopted war chief." In that event, the Indian continues, "our warriors will go to fight the common enemy in order to take prisoners to be your slaves. Hunters will kill small game for you and fishermen will take from lakes and rivers the daintiest fish for your nourishment. Boys will play games with the racket before you, and girls will dance and sing pleasant tunes to cheer you." All of this is attractive enough, and it explains the well-known lure of Indian life to many colonial white men, especially to those with only tenuous ties to their own cultural traditions. But for our purposes, the important consequence of Quapaw adoption practices was the obligation to defend that figured in them. "Whoever dares to make an attempt on your life," Bossu's Quapaw ominously intoned, "we shall beat to death with blows of a club, without mercy."[87]

Bossu has no doubt embellished the matter greatly, as he usually does, but if we take his observations as true on some essential level, as they seem to be, it immediately becomes clear why the arrest of Labuxière could be expected to exercise and agitate the Quapaws so greatly. It was not just a threat to a friend or family member in the European sense but a threat to the tribe itself (and especially, probably, to Labuxière's adoptive clan), a threat from another nation, a nation, of course, with whom they had friendly relations, but a nation of foreigners nevertheless.

Leyba knew very well that it was quite impossible to defend the Post with his tiny garrison against the entire Quapaw nation. He therefore freed Labuxière and sent for the great chief to come and have a parley in order to determine whether he could change the chief's mind. Leyba locked himself and the chief in his room along with an interpreter and eventually brought him around to his view of the matter. "We are friends and comrades as we were before," Leyba wrote with satisfaction. But the chief had warned that if Labuxière weren't back within three months he "would put the Post to the knife," and he was quite sure that the Spanish would not retaliate because the Osages frequently killed white hunters and the Spanish did absolutely nothing about it.

This uneasy armistice cost Leyba more than sixty pesos in goods. The chief left immediately and told his people to withdraw. But when the Quapaws were about a league from the Post, they sent an Indian with a barrel to be filled with brandy: The Quapaw emissary said that the great chief had told him to return with the brandy or Leyba's head. "These threats occur every day," Leyba wrote, "and this is the confidence that can be had in their friendship." He went on to lament that "my tight situation makes it impossible to guarantee the safety of the lives of my wife and daughters. I would send them to New Orleans if I could afford it."[88]

IV.

The centerpiece, the single most important manifestation by the Spanish of their allegiance to the Quapaws, was the present that the Europeans bound themselves to deliver every year to the tribe. Whether the French provided the Quapaws with an annual present is unclear, but a reference to a "general present" being delivered to them in 1758 makes it likely that they did.[89] Presents to provide inducements for specific kinds of activity were, in any case, rather common during the French period as, for instance, when in 1739 the French gave the Quapaws a present to encourage them to join the effort to destroy the Chickasaws—"so that you may become more and more loyal," as the French officer Coustilhas put it.[90]

The annual presents that the Spanish provided included an interesting variety of goods that the Indians evidently found quite useful. For hunting and making war, there were trade guns, powder, balls, gunflints, wadpullers, ramrods, butcher knives, folding knives, hatchets, tomahawks, axes, and kettles. For agriculture, the Spanish provided hoes. For clothing, the Quapaws received plain and decorated hats (some with feathers), handkerchiefs, frock coats, decorated coats, Limbourg shirts, striped shirts, loincloths, plain and decorated white shirts, an occasional dress, little bells, boots, blankets, woolen cloth, Limbourg cloth, calico, silk, scissors, awls, sewing needles, and sewing thread. For cooking they got salt, strike-a-lights, copper kettles, and copper pots with lids. Personal items included mirrors, combs, vermilion, brass wire (for bracelets and other jewelry, and perhaps for snares), tomahawk pipes, tobacco, brandy, and rum.[91] In 1775, a particularly fine present included a scarlet coat with silver braid and matching trousers and nine hats with silver embroidery.[92]

The Quapaws regarded the failure to provide the annual gift as a sure sign of faithlessness on the Europeans' part. As Alexandre DeClouet put it, "it is true that [the Quapaws] are faithful to Spain and to France; but deprived of strong liquor, bread, and their present, one cannot count on them in any way."[93] The Europeans shared the Quapaws' sense of the present's essentiality to the compact between them and refused to deliver it if the Quapaws gave out serious signals of infidelity. So in 1770, as we saw, Desmazellières had deprived a Quapaw chief of his present because the chief, while drunk, had tried to break Desmazellières head,[94] and years later Villiers withheld Chief Angaska's present to force him to relinquish a medal and a flag that he had taken from the English.[95]

It was the importance to the Quapaws of the annual gift that led the English to attempt to undermine the Quapaws' confidence in the Spanish by telling them that the Spanish would not give them any more presents. In 1768, DeClouet had written that the Quapaws were complaining about the lack of a present, and while the Spanish government responded that one was on the way,[96] there is no indication that a present was ever delivered until late in 1769, when a huge one worth more than 515 pesos (perhaps $20,000 in today's money), more than any other Louisiana tribe received by a factor of four, demonstrated how keen the Spanish were to reassure the Quapaws of their friendship.[97] Desmazellières brought another one with him when he assumed command in the spring of 1770, and he was quick to use it as evidence that "the English were liars" and to pledge to the Quapaws "that every year they would have one like it." He tried to convince the Indians that "the Spanish would be for them as the French were and that they should not listen to the English any more because they were liars."[98]

The next year, Fernando de Leyba, the new commandant of the Post, left us a detailed description of the events surrounding the presentation of the annual gift that quite clearly reveals the centrality of its delivery to the life at Arkansas Post. Three hundred and fifty-two Quapaw men, women, and children gathered at the fort early in June of 1771 to receive their present. They witnessed the raising of the Spanish flag accompanied by a salute from the fort's cannons, and Leyba personally hung the large medal around the neck of the great chief, who was then treated to a three-gun salute. Leyba invited the great chief and the other important Quapaws (*principales*) to dine at his table with some of the Post's inhabitants and the interpreter. Meanwhile, the rest of the Quapaws busied themselves consuming a cow, a 280-pound barrel of flour, and sixty-six bottles of brandy. Leyba proudly reported to the governor that "there was not the least disorder in the two days that they were in the post."[99]

A year later, the Quapaws became extremely impatient because the annual present had not arrived by June, and they had called Governor Unzaga a liar because he had promised that the first boat that came up to the Post would bring it.[100] The present did not finally arrive until October, and Leyba handed out lots of bread and stewed meats when he presented it. The Quapaws liked the guns, and the powder was of good quality, but the great chief made a big fuss about the present given to him.[101] It is little wonder that late in 1772 Leyba urged the governor to send the next year's present early "so we won't have so much unpleasantness about tardiness as we have before."[102] The government obliged, no doubt at least partly because of the disasters that had threatened the Post in 1772, and Leyba was able to distribute the present on 7 April 1773.[103]

Early April was the best possible time to effect a distribution of the present, because by this time all the hunters, Quapaw and French alike, would ordinarily have returned from the various rivers in the Arkansas district with their skins, tallow, bears' oil, and salted meats, and this provided an excellent occasion for a frolic, rendezvous, and convocation. Unfortunately, the Spanish were unable to achieve this timing with any regularity. During the first fifteen years of Spanish rule the present was habitually late, and not infrequently it was incomplete, or part of it was damaged or of low quality. For instance, though Villiers was able to distribute a present not too tardily on 28 May 1777, the Quapaws refused the guns (they were English) because they were no good.[104] And the 1779 and 1780 presents were not even sent until 1781.[105] Their eventual shipment, along with the present of 1781, in the spring of 1781, was no doubt partly due to the fact that the Spanish badly needed the Quapaws to defend the Post during the American Revolution. Presents seem to have been delivered with some regularity after 1781.[106]

V

Competing Fathers and Quapaw European Policy

Despite all the very extensive efforts on the part of the Spanish to ingratiate themselves with the Quapaws, which, as we saw, included providing them with gunsmiths, interpreters, and elaborate presents, the Quapaws never became as attached to the Spanish as they had been to the French. Initial distrust of the Spanish caused things to reach such a desperate pass at the Spanish post of Los Arcos that the Quapaws and *habitants* were even giving serious thought to forsaking their settlements altogether. In 1770, Desmazellières wrote that "the *habitants* and Quapaws speak of nothing but abandoning the Post."[1] He informed the governor that "all the chiefs of the Quapaw nation tell me every day that they want to go . . . to settle on the Red River." Desmazellières even claimed that "the Quapaws and *habitants* were talking of going to settle with the Osages,"[2] at best a very odd ambition, given the long-standing enmity between the two Indian tribes. Desmazellières blamed Lieutenant Orieta, a Spaniard, for the desire to move: He claimed that Orieta wanted to be commandant and that this prospect had so greatly alarmed everyone at the Post that they wanted to leave.[3]

I.

A more serious threat to the stability of the settlement was the constant importuning of the English, who were virtually unceasing in their attempts to seduce the Quapaws away from the Spanish alliance. In the summer of 1770, Desmazellières reported that five or six Quapaw families had settled on the English side of the Mississippi. "Their huts were built about a month ago," he said, but he could not tell "if they mean to stay there or just spend the winter." He had done his best to discover their intentions, but so far, he said, "no one knows exactly what the Quapaws are thinking on the subject."[4] The next year, the Quapaw great chief had traveled to Pensacola to treat with the English, and Leyba had learned of "his intention to abandon his homeland" and that "he had pledged his word to the English" to join them. For their part, the English had "given him, among other things, portraits of the king and queen [of England]," "had loaded him up with a barrel of brandy," and had given "three or four bottles to each of the eighteen men who accompanied him."[5] Two years later, the great chief was still "threatening to cross over to the English side with his family [*sus parientes*]."[6]

Two years later still, the governor wrote to Orieta agitated by yet another report that the Quapaws were of a mind to move across the Mississippi into English territory. "I do not doubt," he told Orieta, rather icily, "that your prudence and zeal will dissuade them from the error into which they have fallen in wanting to abandon the territory where they were born and where they have been appreciated . . . and well regaled by us."[7] Orieta was glad to be able to report to the governor a few months later that "the Quapaws not only do not think of abandoning their villages" any longer, "but in the private councils that they hold every month, the only speech is to urge those present not to forsake either their homeland or the land of their birth, in which so much blood of their ancestors is buried." Orieta also said that the Quapaws gave "proof of this [resolve] whenever they came to town; they speak in small groups about how they want to die in the land where they were born as their ancestors did."[8]

One of the means to which the English made immediate resort in their effort to drive a wedge between the Spanish and the Quapaws was offering liquor in return for the Quapaws' peltries. At first, this commodity, in the form of cheap rum (*tafia*) and brandy (*eau de vie*), was available from the English only at some distance from the Quapaw villages—at Natchez[9] and at "the Tunicas."[10] But in the summer of 1768, Captain DeClouet learned that a Natchez merchant had promised to build a fort on the English side of the Mississippi opposite the mouth of the White River, "where the Quapaws will find all their needs in abundance and [will be able to do] all their shopping."[11]

There is no indication that the projected fort ever materialized, but the English did begin forming a settlement that same summer in the promised location. DeClouet wrote that "the major part of the Quapaws seem satisfied with this plan, which could only have been executed at their request." He said that Charles Stuart, the English Indian agent, was behind the scheme, and had left two men at the site who had begun clearing a plaza. Stuart himself had departed to fetch liquor and other merchandise for the Quapaw trade.[12] (By 1775, this establishment contained eighteen huts, gave shelter to five English traders, and had acquired the name of Concordia.)[13] In 1770, Captain Desmazellières reported that John Bradley, the Natchez merchant, had been undermining the Quapaws' confidence in the Spanish, but it is not clear whether he was at Concordia or Natchez at the time.[14] The same year, the captain reported that another Englishman, whom he called Mr. Feveham, had decided to abandon his store at Concordia and retreat to Natchez. Desmazellières, to get the man out of his hair, had sold him some horses so he could pack his goods across country.[15]

Two years later, Leyba reported that the Quapaw chief "sends a canoe every day to the other side of the river [i.e., the Mississippi] to see if the Messiah whom they are eagerly awaiting has come yet." Leyba proceeded to predict that if "this happens, many evils will occur, [since] the traders settled on the other side are used to sending a lot of liquor to this post."[16] This "Messiah," a new trader, was an agent of Lieutenant John Thomas, the English Deputy Indian Superintendent who lived at Manchac.[17] A month later, he had not yet arrived, but another trader had, "one who came from Mobile to try his luck in this location." The Quapaw great chief had even helped him build his house. "Neither my brotherly coaxing," an exasperated Leyba wrote, "nor my threats as a judge could restrain him; the more I ordered him, the less he said to me." Leyba added that "the other chiefs haven't been there, but the only reason is that there is no brandy there."[18]

The English were not content merely to sit passively on their side of the Mississippi and wait for the Quapaws to come to them to trade. In 1769, a barge associated with a store at Concordia, with a crew of ten Englishmen,

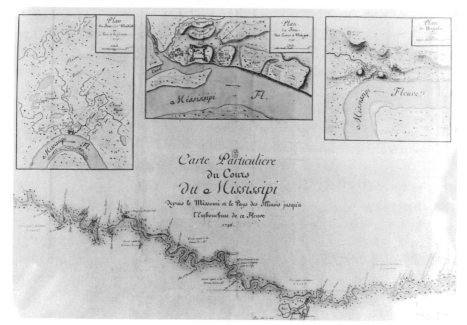

Figure 24. Detail from 1796 map, probably by Charles Warin, showing the Mississippi River and the Arkansas Region. *Courtesy of Bibliothèque Nationale, Paris*

entered the Arkansas River to visit the Quapaw villages. Their camp, DeClouet said, was "going to become a canteen for the Quapaws." An Englishwoman, the wife of a Canadian named Charpentier who headed up an establishment at Concordia, seems to have been in charge.[19] (DeClouet accused her of being a "Magdelen"—a prostitute—but surely he was only being polemical.)[20] By the next year, an Englishman had actually settled in one of the Quapaw villages and was "learning the language of the nation."[21]

Matters shortly became a good deal worse. In 1773, Captain Leyba reported that the English trader from Mobile had so ingratiated himself with the Quapaw great chief that the trader had been the chief's companion and interpreter on the trips that he had made to Pensacola in years past. In fact, the great chief had given the Englishman his daughter in marriage and had adopted him as a son, whereupon the trader had "abandoned the dress of an Englishman and adopted the look of an Indian by making a tuft of his hair like theirs." He had built a hut next to the chief's house, which served, interestingly, as both a store and a "little mosque," where he preached incessantly against the Spanish nation. He regularly denounced the Spanish as "tyrants who do not and will not have any fabrics for [the Quapaws'] clothes." He assured the Quapaws that "the king of Great Britain had wept many tears for them, and, in order to avoid their ruin, he had determined to chase the Spanish from Louisiana." The trader even claimed to have seen written orders to this effect in Virginia. His fervent wish was that they could "all become vassals of the same king and thereafter regard themselves as brothers."

Leyba reported that the great chief came to see him less and less, partly because Leyba did not want to speak with him about anything but the great chief's English son-in-law: Leyba constantly upbraided the Quapaw chief for being ungrateful for the medal that the Spanish had given him. The great chief customarily left Leyba's house immediately after the troublesome subject was broached, grumbling that Leyba did not want to do anything but argue. The other chiefs, according to Leyba, would not allow English goods in their villages. In fact, they promised Leyba to arrest the Englishman and bring him to the Post. Leyba opined, however, that they probably would not do so because they believed that if anyone killed the interloper "he would return from the other world to avenge his injury." Leyba was much affronted by the Englishman's daring defiance of Spanish trade and immigration laws, and he was particularly insulted because the trader had entered Leyba's room several times "with some Quapaws, dressed and painted the same as they." He could only promise "to try to persuade the Quapaws of their errors in falling in with these vagabonds" because his "forces [were] inadequate to take the Englishman against the Quapaws' will."[22]

The Englishmen's presence and the seditious sentiments that they were sowing among the Quapaws at last became intolerable to the Spanish. "They have not ceased to seduce this nation," Orieta declaimed, "in order to be able to draw them to their side, suggesting incredible things, telling them that this land will not belong to our monarch." Orieta continued: "As proof that it will be so, they point to the condition into which the stockade has fallen (the enclosure being totally in ruins), and to the fact that we have not made any repairs. For this reason, they have made these Indians believe that it is certain that this neighborhood will be English and that in a short time they will come to take possession of it." The Englishmen also poked fun at the fort's artillery, which, they claimed, was not in a serviceable condition.

Orieta, however, soon very effectively refuted these calumnies by repairing the fort and firing three successive salvos from the fort's cannons and swivel guns. The salvos, he said, had proved especially impressive: They were timed so that they were fired when Leyba was dining with the chiefs, and the noise was so thunderous that it caused the commandant's dining room to shake and the glassware hanging on its walls to crash to the floor. This created a great stir, Orieta said, and the Quapaws allowed that the English had lied to them and then drank the health of the governor. They left content and happy after yet another salvo from the guns. Perhaps they also expelled the English intruders, because we hear no more serious complaints about any Englishmen inhabiting the Quapaws' villages.[23]

While resident English traders apparently ceased thereafter to be a threat, English hunters nevertheless trespassed into the Arkansas country in worrisome numbers. "The English infest the White River," Lieutenant Orieta lamented in 1774, displacing the French hunters who wanted "to kill buffalo, cows, and bears, which are necessary to provide salted meats, tallow, and oil." Although the English were principally interested in deerskins, their activities in the region were scaring off the bears and the buffaloes. Orieta had tried to recruit a Quapaw war party to arrest the trespassers, but they were willing to set out only if he would send the interpreter and some soldiers with them.[24]

Two years later, when the Quapaws came to dance the calumet to welcome Captain Villiers and receive their present from him, they "promised not to allow the English either in their villages or in the rivers of this dependency."[25] Shortly thereafter, Villiers dispatched a party of twenty Quapaws, four soldiers, and the interpreter Lajeunesse to "pillage all the Englishmen that they find on the lands and rivers of the king's domain." But Villiers believed that the Quapaws' heart wasn't really in it. "They want us to start it," he wrote, "and above all they always want to have soldiers with them." Villiers could spare only four soldiers for this important undertaking, "and yet," he lamented, "I expose myself" by doing so. "I might get attacked if those rogues get together," he said, speaking of the English hunters. "I can't guarantee against a surprise attack."[26]

When this detachment was about one hundred fifty miles from the Post

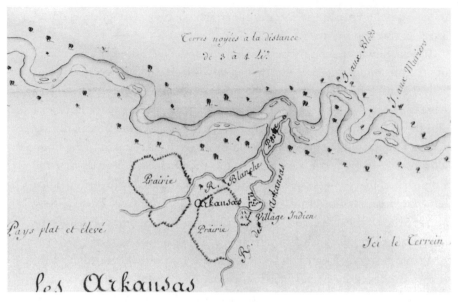

Pos Arkansas

Figure 25.   Detail from 1796 map, probably by Charles Warin, showing
Arkansas Post and an associated Quapaw village. *Courtesy of
Bibliothèque Nationale, Paris*

on the Arkansas River, it encountered two Quapaws who warned that
about forty Englishmen, having got wind of the plan to attack them, had
assembled farther upriver and were planning an ambush. They also asserted
that two boats full of people were coming to reinforce the English. The
Quapaws therefore resolved to abandon the project, though they did manage to pillage two Englishmen who were going to hunt on the White River.[27]

A few weeks later, Villiers reported that an English *métis* who was
settled among the Quapaws and had taken a Quapaw wife had decamped
and had not returned, along with another Englishman who frequented
the Indian villages. But thirty more Englishmen had introduced themselves into the Arkansas River region by land. Villiers predicted to the governor that "the number will certainly increase, which could be dangerous,
as you know, because this river connects with provinces dependent on
Mexico [i.e., New Mexico]." Almost all the Quapaws, Villiers lamented,
had departed for the winter hunt, which would "give every opportunity to
the English to take their skins out by the rivers in the months of January
and February."[28] In 1777, Captain Villiers recorded a similar complaint
against trespassing Englishmen: He wrote that the French hunters' "peace
is disturbed and their hunt is made more difficult by the great number of

Englishmen who hunt only for deer and beaver and who penetrate into our lands, starting all the animals and startling them to the point that one will have to regard the damage that they are causing the king's subjects as irreparable if one does not find the means to dislodge them."²⁹

The Quapaws' general attitude toward Englishmen did not please Villiers, and it caused him to doubt their commitment to expelling them from the neighborhood. Early in 1778, he had granted asylum to a number of Anglo-Americans who had fled the American Revolution, and he confessed to the governor that it pained him to see how the Quapaws "attach themselves and give more strokes [*caresses*] to the Englishmen to whom I have given refuge than to us." The Quapaws' behavior worried him greatly because he did not "need competition for authority here," and he urged the governor not to "give passports to English merchants to come" to Arkansas because it "would upset the balance" at the Post.³⁰ He had, however, indicated his approval of the Natchez merchant Jean Blommart, who, he said, had "seconded my peaceful intentions" and thus "ought not to be confused with that bunch of vagabonds who are capable of anything."³¹

English intrusions into Arkansas were hardly limited to hunting parties and relatively peaceful efforts to establish trade relations with the Quapaws. The English were barely in place at Concordia before they began leading and encouraging Chickasaw war parties who harried and looted the beleaguered hunters of the Arkansas. The year 1769 had only just begun when DeClouet reported that Frenchmen hunting on the Arkansas River had been plundered by Chickasaws led by two Englishmen and the Canadian named Charpentier, a man, DeClouet opined, "who ought not to be tolerated by any government in this region, so covered is he with crimes."³² A month later DeClouet confided to the governor that he had had "to sweat blood to get the Quapaw couriers to depart [for New Orleans because] the Chickasaws have been prowling for a long time in this region." He was trying to restrain the Quapaws from raiding the Chickasaws in retaliation.³³

In the summer of 1770, Desmazellières received a party of ten Chickasaw warriors and complained about the raids. They claimed rather vaguely that the Chickasaw great chief had daily tried to persuade "the young people" to desist, "but that in their village there were young people who were crazy." The Chickasaw delegation assured the commandant that they were going to do everything possible to curtail the raids. But in the same letter the captain reported that some Chickasaw war parties had just crossed the Mississippi to the St. Francis River and the Arkansas River to pillage the

French hunters of their powder and guns. One party had twenty-six men and another seventy-three.[34] Desmazellières was quite clear that it was the English who were inciting the Chickasaws to make the attacks, because the Chickasaws had told him so.[35]

In June of 1770, fifteen Quapaws journeyed to the Chickasaw villages to conclude a peace.[36] This peace was evidently achieved, for the following fall the Quapaw great chief Cassenonpoint sent a letter to Governor O'Reilly asking permission to join with the Caddos and the Chickasaws in an effort to destroy the Osages,[37] and we hear no more of English or Chickasaw war parties in Arkansas until the time of the American Revolution. In fact, in 1775 thirty Chickasaws joined with the Quapaws to set out against the Osages, and there were reports that the Caddos and Wichitas were going to join in the effort.[38]

II.

Much has been written, and rightly so, about European Indian policy. What we have only recently begun dimly to comprehend is what an Indian European policy might have looked like. Though such a policy is admittedly a good deal more difficult to reconstruct, partly because North American Indians had no written language, we get important glimpses of one in the letters from Spanish commandants at Arkansas Post, enough to allow us to be relatively confident of its main outlines.

Perhaps the most important clue, if we can only learn to read it properly, to the manner in which the Quapaws viewed their alliances first with the French, and then with the Spanish, lies in their habit of addressing European leaders as "father." A good example comes from 1770 in a letter from Cassenonpoint, great chief of the Quapaw nation, to Governor Unzaga in New Orleans. He was complaining that his "father" (that is, the Arkansas commandant) would not allow him to retaliate against the Osages who "have attacked and pillaged the hunters of my river." He asked permission to avenge these raids "as a favor that I ask from you my father."[39]

To us, and presumably to eighteenth-century Louisiana colonists as well, the word "father" comes laden with patriarchal and hierarchical assumptions the root of which no doubt lie deep in Roman ideas about paternal power. But while white Louisianians assumed (or at least hoped) that the term carried with it a right to demand obedience and to discipline, to the Quapaws the term connoted, if not primarily at least in important part, a parental duty to protect and provide for them. To them, the alliance was definitely a bilateral arrangement and their performance was, moreover, contingent on the Europeans' performance of the duties to feed and defend them.

Proof of this comes in a number of contexts that illuminate the Quapaws' appreciation of the arrangement that they had with their European visitors. In 1769, for instance, when the Englishwoman already alluded to set up store on the Arkansas side of the Mississippi, and the commandant complained about the Quapaws frequenting "this shack which is going to become a saloon for the red men," the Quapaws had a ready answer: The Spanish would not supply the goods, in this instance partly liquor, that the Quapaws wanted, so the Spanish were not holding up their end of the bargain. They told Chevalier DeClouet rather bluntly that if he continued "to be poor they will be forced to love the one more opulent than [he], and that this new father [i.e., the Spanish] proposes to cut his children off from their milk and their usual provisions [*douceurs ordinaires*]."

DeClouet assured them that the governor's "affection for them will support those who listen to me." The Quapaws' unanimous response was that "compensation for [their] loyalty had been deferred for a long time," so the credibility of the Spanish "remained to be seen."[40] What the Quapaws had reference to, no doubt, was the lateness of the annual present that was, as we have seen, the very cornerstone of the alliance. The intimate connection between the Quapaws' annual present and the duties of the Spanish as "father" is made explicit a few years later when Lieutenant Orieta had asked the interpreter why the Quapaws were upset, and the interpreter had responded that "the Quapaws said that their father had abandoned them because he hadn't sent them the customary present." They were unable to hunt for lack of powder and balls.[41]

Though the Quapaws usually conceptualized European officials as occupying a "father" role in their mutual alliance, they frequently also had resort to a mother-figure metaphor in their discussions with colonial leaders. They often described the duty of the Europeans in terms of providing "milk," a shorthand for nurturing. "Milk," it is true, was sometimes used as a kind of slang word for brandy. For instance, some Canadian Indians engaged in the Second Chickasaw War once greeted a French officer by saying that it was "a long time, father, since you have seen your children; your milk must hurt you, we would like to relieve you," meaning that they wanted brandy. After the brandy was drunk, the Indians' speaker allowed to the same officer, "Your milk is gone, father, but we only drank it on one side, we do not know how it tastes on the other side," a speech that cost the Frenchman a few more bottles.[42]

But the word "milk" had a broader, more metaphorical meaning as well. For instance, in 1769, in a discussion with DeClouet, the Quapaws assured him that they "preferred the natural father arrived in town [New Orleans] to an adopted one [i.e., the English], in whose house the milk could dry up."[43] And in trying to convince the Quapaws that the newly arrived Spanish deserved the same affection that the Quapaws had had for the French, Commandant La Grandcour assured them that the Spanish nation was "one in the same milk and one in the same breast [*mamelle*] as the French."[44]

At times, the Quapaws seem to have pushed the father-provider metaphor to unsupportable limits. In 1771, after Captain Leyba had given the Quapaws an elaborate feast in connection with the distribution of a present that had finally arrived, the great chief and some of his retinue regularly "did me the favor," as Leyba sarcastically put it, "of joining me at my table, always ten or twelve of them, . . . to whom it is necessary to give something." Leyba reported that, "If nothing is given, the chief takes it from the table and divides it up." When Leyba tried to deflect this demand for hospitality by pointing out to the Quapaws that "the king doesn't provide anything for them in his budget except the annual present," they simply responded "that their father is rich." Leyba said that it was not necessary to invite the Quapaws to eat, since "when they see the table set they pull up a chair and sit down." It was with only the greatest difficulty that Leyba was able to wean the Quapaws away from this incipient habit, and then in circumstances that so angered the great chief that, Leyba said, the chief "sailed off without saying anything or giving me his hand."[45]

The Quapaws were never of the view that choosing the Spanish as a "father" precluded trade with other nations. In 1769, a Quapaw party traveled to Illinois to sell horses to the *habitants* in the vicinity of Fort de Chartres. While in the neighborhood, the Quapaw chief decided to pay a call on the fort itself, "in imitation," as DeClouet put it, "of all men of his color, to demand from the commandant some mark of his good heart." When entry into the fort was denied him, the chief angrily avenged the rebuff by having his party board two English barges that he encountered at the mouth of the Ohio, rehearsing to the crew the affront that he had received, and taking flour and clothing from them in retaliation. When DeClouet remonstrated with the chief, indicating "that it would be advantageous for us not to disturb the peace reigning on the Mississippi," the chief was incredulous. He "responded quite dryly," DeClouet recorded, "that all the French hunters had been pillaged last year on the Mississippi" by Chickasaws incited by the English, and that "it was surprising that the Quapaws had waited so long, they being so poor, to do something about it." He further indicated his disdain for imaginary European boundaries by saying that "an Indian makes everything that he wants one land by calumet."[46]

It seems relatively clear that the Quapaws were seeking, despite the international border of the Europeans, to make their neighborhood "one land" by dancing the calumet in all the nearby English settlements that would receive them, thereby establishing a separate peace with them. The Quapaws, after all, had not been a party to the treaties that had ended the Seven Years' War, and although they had reached an understanding with their new benefactors, the Spanish, they sought finally to make up with the English as well. For instance, in 1768 Aubry learned that the Quapaws had "sung the calumet at the English fort at Natchez," and then had "crossed over to our side and professed all sorts of affection for us," whereupon "they went back to the English fort and made them the same protestations."

Aubry affected to regard this as perfidiousness on the Quapaws' part. "This shows," he complained, "how little one ought to count on them. They appear only for the moment to attach themselves to those who give them the most rum."[47] He seems to have been oblivious (perhaps deliberately so) to what surely was the Quapaws' attitude toward the alliance: As far as they were concerned, it did not carry with it a duty to eschew relations with other European nations or to obey Spanish trading laws, especially since the French of Louisiana themselves did not pay any attention to those laws.[48] In 1770, one of the Quapaw village chiefs went to Mobile on a trade mission, and Desmazellières lamented that "this Quapaw is entirely carried away with the English."[49] Soon thereafter, a Quapaw received a letter inviting him to Mobile to receive a present, entertainment, and a large medal.[50]

To the Spanish, the acceptance of a medal by a Quapaw chief was meant to signify an undertaking to support their king and country in their imperial ambitions. In particular, of course, they took it as a sign that the Quapaws would side with them in their contest with the English and the Americans for control of the Mississippi Valley. It was a matter of great concern therefore if one of the Quapaws, especially one who had accepted a Spanish medal, accepted a medal from the English. Such an event occurred in 1776. Angaska, the chief of the Tourima village, called at "the Tunicas" (Manchac) where Lieutenant Thomas, the British Indian agent, privately presented him with a medal and a flag, which Angaska had brought back to his village.

When Orieta confronted him about this, Angaska asserted that the whole matter was of some indifference to him and that he had not believed that accepting the insignia would upset the Spanish nation or separate his people from it. Orieta persuaded him to return the insignia to one of the Englishmen settled at Concordia. According to Orieta, the three villages were angry at Angaska for accepting the English insignia, and the chiefs and the other significant figures in them had joined in a determination to expel him if he had not complied with Orieta's request to give up the English insignia.[51] But about a year later, Villiers deprived Angaska of his annual present because he had taken yet another English medal and had hoisted the English flag anew in his village.[52]

Shortly thereafter, Villiers wrote an interesting evaluation of this chief and his adroitness. "Chief Angaska," Villiers reported, "is a shrewd [spirituel] man who took an English medal from the English agent at the Tunicas two years ago. He told me that he had given it up, mostly influenced by my strokes and presents. I flattered myself that I had reclaimed him; but our neighbors the English were so intent on importuning him, in order to have a patron in his nation, that the brandy that they plied him with persuaded him to hoist their flag anew and take another medal." Villiers went on to opine that Angaska was "not to be feared because he is not listened to in his nation, which scorns him."[53] Villiers also claimed that "the other chiefs approved" of him withholding Angaska's present.[54] Villiers said that the present was "deposited at the post where [Angaska] will not enter until he has surrendered his flag and his medal."[55] Two weeks later, Villiers wrote that he had finally "persuaded Chief Angaska to surrender . . . the English medal and flag." Since Angaska had "lost" his Spanish medal some time before, Villiers gave him a new one. Villiers personally hung it around Angaska's neck in an assembly of the chiefs, restored him to his office, and gave him his present.[56]

Although, as we saw, Commandant Villiers expressed confidence in Angaska's enthusiasm for Spain, and Angaska did lead numerous scouting expeditions to the Chickasaw Bluffs to determine what the English were up to there,[57] Villiers was afraid that the Quapaws' attachment to the Americans' War of Independence had very definite limits indeed. Villiers in fact warned Governor Gálvez in 1780 that he ought not to rely on any "aid that I might draw from the Arkansas in case of attack." He admonished that "this is something which one must not count on in any way." The Quapaws, he said, were good only for scouting: "If I were attacked they would perhaps appear on the other bank but in accordance with the attitude [esprit] of savages in general they would await the outcome in order to throw in with the stronger side."[58] Villiers may well have had in mind the behavior of the Choctaws, who had waited until they saw that the British had lost Manchac before they joined in the plundering and burning of the royalists' houses.[59]

The very next year, however, Angaska had Villiers eating out of his hand. He was advising Villiers on the best way to deal with the Chickasaws, telling him not to be constantly sending embassies to inquire of their intentions. The Chickasaws, Angaska said, were sure to read this as a sign of weakness. Villiers gratefully took the advice and wrote to the governor that he would "never cease, Sir, recommending to you this brave and faithful nation," and he requested "above all that you should send a commission of great chief and a standard with the coat of arms to Chief Angalska who is most useful to me."[60]

To show how quickly things could change, however, in the summer of 1782, Villiers's successor charged that Angaska was always looking for a way to avoid doing anything for the Spanish,[61] and Villiers's original prediction of 1780 proved all too prophetic. When the British attack on Arkansas Post finally came in April of 1783, Angaska failed to warn the commandant that a party of Chickasaws (who proved to be the advance of the main British force) was coming to the Post. Angaska's excuse was that these Chickasaws had deceived him by "telling him that they were coming with twelve Americans to give [the commandant] their hand," and he maintained that he had planned to tell the commandant the next morning that they were on the way to see him. The boat with the main force, he said, had slipped past his village without being detected "because it had had its oars and tholepins wrapped with leather."[62]

After the attack, Angaska did indeed set out in a successful effort to overtake the fleeing British expeditionaries, but the Spanish suspected that he had somehow connived in the original attack. Captain DuBreuil, speaking of the Quapaws' behavior, cautioned Governor Miró that "their conduct is very suspicious": They did not advise him of the attack, they only reluctantly accompanied a convoy that set out in pursuit of the attackers and their prisoners, and even that small escort had returned early. DuBreuil concluded rather bluntly that he could not "help but think that [the Quapaws] are capable of agreeing to a treason."[63] Governor Miró, who had other sources of information in addition to reports from DuBreuil, agreed with this assessment. "We have too many reasons to show [the Quapaws] some aloofness," he said, because they "seem to have concealed the plans of Colbert and his party to destroy [the Post] thus facilitating the attack on our fort, for the vile price of a barrel of brandy."[64] This was a hyperbole that even the governor could not have believed. If Angaska was cool to the American project, it was because, from the perspective of Quapaw national interest, he saw little to distinguish the imperial ambitions of the Spanish from those of the English.

Angaska died soon thereafter, and DuBreuil told the Quapaws that their present for 1784 had been made deliberately small "in order to punish them," and that when they gave "better evidence of their loyalty they [would] be treated better." The Quapaws appeared chastened, "laid all the blame on the deceased Angaska," and asked for "an opportunity to erase the stain that they had."[65]

Though the Spanish and the Quapaws made a lasting peace with the Chickasaws in the wake of the American Revolution, the Osages proved to be a considerable obstacle to stability and European expansion in the Arkansas region throughout the colonial period. The deaths, some gruesome beyond measure, of more than fifty European hunters at Osage hands during the Spanish period alone are discernable in the records,[66] and there were no doubt many others that went unreported or even undetected. As late as 1802, Captain Caso y Luengo, commanding at the Arkansas, could still write that "Indian warfare caused the deaths of several hunters every year."[67] When one recalls that Arkansas Post had only thirty-nine adult white males in residence in 1791,[68] and that there were usually no more than one hundred to one hundred fifty hunters on the Arkansas rivers during the hunting season, one can begin to appreciate the homicide rate for which Osage attacks were responsible. No modern American inner city could come even close to it.

Quapaws and Osages did not clash as frequently, partly because the Quapaws did not often venture into territory that the Osages claimed, but they did have their hostile encounters;[69] and in the early Spanish period the Quapaws often sought permission to avenge the deaths of French hunters,[70] perhaps because those hunters had some Quapaw blood in their veins. The Quapaws, in fact, were at first more keen on revenge than the Spanish, who wanted to bring the Osages to terms without bloodshed if at all possible. The Quapaws, whose international law demanded either blood vengeance or compensation for homicides, regarded the Spanish policy of peace as pusillanimous, and sometimes sent out war parties to avenge deaths despite the Arkansas commandant's very explicit animadversions to the contrary.

In 1773, for instance, the Quapaws had taken five Osage scalps and Captain Leyba had found it necessary to reward them. "Telling them not to wage war against the Osages," Leyba said, "is like talking to the deaf." The Quapaws were encouraged in their retributive inclination by the French residents of the Post, who congratulated them roundly and called them their saviors when the Quapaws returned from raids. The Quapaws rebuked Leyba, saying that his unwillingness to avenge the deaths of his own people made it seem as though he was glad that Osages took French lives. Some of the Osage scalps were sent to the governor in New Orleans so that he could see what good use the Quapaws had made of his recent gift to them.[71]

In 1774, the Quapaws killed three more Osages in a dispute over hunting territory;[72] and although Captain Villiers worried that the Quapaws, due to English influence, seemed reluctant to engage the Osages, in 1780 two separate Quapaw war parties killed twelve Osages and captured twenty-four horses.[73] There is evidence, however, that the Quapaws' anti-Osage ardor cooled considerably thereafter, perhaps, as Villiers feared, because of British influence among them during the American Revolution. While in 1787 the Quapaws took an Osage scalp, contrary to their promise not to attack Osages until the French hunters had returned from the rivers,[74] other war parties of theirs frequently sallied forth and returned without encountering the enemy; and in 1789 Vallière declined to arm any further parties after three consecutive ones had come back without success, a circumstance that has led one observer reasonably to believe that the Quapaws were at this time merely feigning attachment to the Spanish war effort against the Osages.[75]

VI

Whose Law, Whose Religion?

Some of the current literature on the subject of European law and native Americans adopts a polemical tone and structure virtually caricaturing the valuable interpretive constructs of anthropology that emphasize "encounters" and cultural contests between Europeans and "the Other." This recent work is, moreover, frequently characterized by talk of invasion, racism, and genocide.[1] The following discussion will attempt to describe and to analyze, critically and objectively, while relying on solid archival evidence, some episodes in Louisiana's colonial period that illuminate the question of whether, how, and to what extent, Europeans sought to apply their law to Indians.

It will help to understand and elucidate the significance of the situation in Louisiana if we begin with a look at relevant legal practices in other colonies in America. Colonists in Massachusetts were probably more successful than any other English colonists in incorporating Indians into their legal system. Indians living in Massachusetts towns were simply subject to the law of the colony in the same way and to the same extent as Europeans, unless some special law applicable to Indians was of relevance. These English courts were, of course, staffed entirely by Englishmen. On the other hand, the so-called plantation Indians, the ones who lived in the voluntary "praying towns" that were established to convert Indians to Christianity, were subject to courts staffed by native justices assisted by a white magistrate. Despite the existence of Indian judges, these courts applied the white man's law, not Indian law. Last, the Indians who lived in independent tribes were subject to European legal doctrine only to the extent, if any, that some relevant treaty so provided.[2] Law made by Puritan colonists penetrated so deeply into some parts of Indian society that as early as 1705 (only six years after Louisiana was founded) the Bay Colony had already published a book, printed in both the English and Massachusett (i.e., Algonquian) languages, that contained laws applicable to Indians.[3]

In Plymouth Colony, a similar precociousness is evident. By 1675, this government had already established a special tribunal to deal with disputes between Indians and whites; and in 1682 it placed an overseer in every Indian town to enforce a special code of conduct regulating the activities of the native peoples.[4] In seventeenth- and eighteenth-century Virginia, an arrangement roughly similar to the tripartite one in force in Massachusetts seems to have obtained, though the Virginians were not nearly so successful in subjecting the native peoples to their legal system in a systematic way, due partly to the pattern of settlement in their colony and to the large number of Indians living there.[5]

Because the Spanish ruled Louisiana from 1766 to 1803, the juridical situation in New Spain is more directly relevant to a consideration of the legal status of indigenous peoples in Louisiana. In Mexico, the absorption of the indigenous population into the Spanish legal system became an object of intense interest and elaborate effort very soon after the conquest, and by the late sixteenth century the General Indian Court in Mexico City had acquired a concurrent original jurisdiction over suits between Indians and over suits in which Spaniards sued Indians, though not over suits in which Indians complained against Spaniards.[6] In addition, local *cabildos* (city councils) staffed by Indians, including Indian judges, were chartered in the Indian towns. In fact, by the 1580s, Indian notaries were practicing their craft and drafting instruments conforming at least partly to Spanish peninsular legal form.[7] Although, as time went on, indigenous legal principles became more and more subverted to Spanish rules of decision, the native legal cultures in Mexico exhibited a surprisingly robust resistance to change, and were, in some particulars, able to prevent themselves from being subverted by Spanish substantive law.[8] In general, however, Hispanicization in Mexico proceeded rapidly and reached deeply into the aboriginal culture. But in the borderlands of New Spain—that is, in New Mexico and Texas—where the Spanish population was sparse, and hegemony correspondingly more difficult to achieve, cases involving Indians were evidently the exclusive domain of the governors.[9]

If we turn from the English colonies and Mexico and examine the situation in New France, probably the most relevant for our purposes of other colonial experiences, we find a strikingly different state of affairs. Although the French claimed technical sovereignty over Indian territory and over Indians in Canada, they usually found themselves unable to absorb them effectively into the legal system.[10] An early edict of the Sovereign Council in Canada purported to extend "the penalties prescribed by French law for murder and rape" to native offenders, but in most instances Indian defendants were not prosecuted, proceedings against them were dismissed, or they were pardoned, in order to accommodate important native allies.[11] Attempts to enforce laws against drunkenness were even less successful because of Indian resistance to the imposition of European law.[12] Canadian Indians simply took the view that they were beyond the reach of French law, and many French citizens were aware of this attitude: In 1721, for example, one Marguerite Chapel revealed that she had assumed that French law had nothing to do with the natives and so had not attempted to press a legal grievance against Indians in the courts.[13] The few instances in which the French were successful in imposing their law on natives resident in Canada involved Indians whose ties with their original cultures were extremely weak, as when in 1756 Sieur Douville's Montagnait maidservant was hanged for theft: Because she had been assimilated into French society "she had forfeited the protection of kin groups and native councils."[14] The French were also forced to admit that they could not effectively prohibit Indians from trading with the British, and thus allowed them to import British goods for their personal use.[15] Outside the Canadian administrative centers, in the west where the French population was smaller and could wield even less power, French influence was so weak that successful criminal prosecutions of Indians were extremely rare indeed.[16]

I.

When the French moved from Canada into Louisiana, there is evidence that their original aspiration, as in New France generally, was to "Frenchify" the Indians, that is, to make Frenchmen of them in every sense. La Salle's notary claimed that in 1682 the Quapaw Indians of Arkansas formally accepted Louis XIV as "master" of their lands;[17] and it is probable that "master" was employed as a term of art, implying that the Quapaws had taken an oath of allegiance recognizing French sovereignty. Interestingly, as we have already seen, when the Spanish acquired Louisiana from France, they extracted an oath of allegiance from the Quapaw Great Chief Cassenonpoint, by which he promised to recognize the Spanish governor as his "father."[18] Of course the Quapaw side of these events is completely absent, so we cannot be sure what they made of them.[19] In any case, if the French view of the matter had prevailed, the Europeans would have exercised both legislative and judicial jurisdiction over the Quapaws and the other Indians of the Arkansas region—that is, they would have passed laws binding on Indians and tried cases involving Quapaws in French courts. But the reality, as we shall see, was entirely otherwise.

The interesting truth is that the French were not always successful in applying their law even to Frenchmen, much less to Indians, when that law conflicted with an applicable Quapaw custom. For instance, the Quapaws successfully trumped French law with one of their cherished legal institutions when, on 20 June 1756, a meeting was held in the Government House in New Orleans to hear an extraordinary request from Guedetonguay, the medal chief of the Quapaws. His tribe had surrendered to the French three deserters from the Illinois garrison along with Jean-Baptiste Bernard, who had killed his corporal Jean Nicolet within the precincts of the fort at Arkansas Post. The chief had nevertheless come to the capital on behalf of his nation to ask Governor Kerlérec to pardon the soldiers. Guedetonguay, obviously a great orator, began his plea by saying that he had come a long distance to plead for the soldiers' lives despite the heat and the demands of the harvest; and he remarked that his head hung low, his eyes were fixed to the ground, and his heart wept for these men. He knew, he explained, that if he had not come they would have been executed, and this was intolerable to him because he regarded them as his own children.

Guedetonguay recited many friendly acts of the Quapaws to prove the fidelity of his people to the French. Among them was the release of six slaves (perhaps Chickasaws captured by the Quapaws) "who would have been burned" otherwise, and the recent capture of five Choctaws and two trespassing Englishmen. He himself, he related, had lost one son and had had a daughter wounded in the wars against the Chickasaws, which he counted "a mark of affection for the French." In recompense he asked for the pardon of the soldiers. The chief added that this was the only such pardon his nation had thus far requested,[20] and he promised never to ask again. He did not doubt that Kerlérec, "the great chief of the French, father of the red men," charged to govern them on behalf of the "great chief of all the French who lived in the great town on the other side of the great lake," would listen and do the just thing.

Guedetonguay left his best argument for last. He maintained vigorously that under his law, any criminal who managed to reach the refuge of the *cabanne de valeur* where the Quapaws practiced their religious rites was absolved of his crime. It was their custom that the chief of the *cabanne de valeur* "would sooner lose his life than suffer the refugee to undergo punishment for his crime." The soldiers were claiming this right, and Quyayonsas, the chief of the *cabanne de valeur*, was there to back them up. This last argument was an excellent one because it called upon the French to recognize an established Indian usage not dissimilar from the European custom of sanctuary. And the argument carried with it a threat of violent reaction if the custom were not allowed.

Kerlérec answered the chief that he was not unmindful of the past services of the Quapaws, nor was he ungrateful for them. "But," he said, "I cannot change the words declared by the great chief of all the French against such crimes, and . . . it would be a great abuse for the future" to pardon the soldiers. "So," he continued, "despite all the friendship that the French have for you and your nation, these men deserve death." The great chief stood for a long time with his head down and finally answered ominously that he could not be responsible for the upheavals that the chief of the privileged house might stir up—upheavals that he said "would not fail to occur." The argument continued and the governor offered to grant the chief "anything else except these four pardons." But Guedetonguay stubbornly maintained that "the sole purpose of his journey was to obtain the pardon of the four men," and that was his last word. In the end the governor extracted from the Quapaw chiefs "publicly and formally their word

. . . that they would in the future deliver up all deserting solders or mal-efactors or other guilty persons without any restriction or condition what-soever, and that [henceforth] pardons would be accorded at the sole discretion of the French."

The governor did not reach an immediate decision but later that day some of his advisors, having reflected on what they had heard, opined "that a refusal of the obstinate demands of these chiefs . . . the faithful allies of the French, would only involve the colony in troublesome upheavals on the part of the said nations who have otherwise up to the present served very faithfully." They concluded that "saving a better idea by *Monsieur le Gouverneur* it would be dangerous, under all the present circumstances, not to satisfy the Indians" by granting the pardons that they demanded.[21]

The governor took the advice but evidently did not write of the event to Berryer, the French Minister of the Marine, for some time. From the comfort of Versailles, it was easy for Berryer to pick at Kerlérec's decision. In responding to Kerlérec, Berryer first made the point that Bernard's case was different from that of the other captured soldiers since he stood accused of homicide. Then, too, the minister had a lot of questions: Couldn't the difference in Bernard's case have been urged on the Arkansas chiefs to get them to relent in his case? And where was the record of the legal pro-ceedings that should have been conducted relative to the killing? If this was a willful murder, the pardon had been conceded too easily. "It would be dangerous," the minister warned, "to leave such a subject in the colony, not only because he would be an example of impunity, but also because of new crimes that he might commit." (The arguments of general and speci-fic deterrence are not very recent inventions.) Finally, the governor was sternly admonished "not to surrender easily to demands of this sort on the part of the savages . . . If on the one hand it is necessary, considering all the present circumstances, to humor the savages, it is also necessary to be care-ful of letting them set a tone that accords neither with the king's author-ity nor the good of the colony." Nevertheless, the minister had talked with Louis XV, and the king ratified the governor's decision. Writs of pardon were therefore issued under the king's name for each of the Arkansas sol-diers.[22] The desire to accommodate an important ally meant that faithful adherence to legal principles had to yield to the more compelling demands of politics.

Whatever may have been the original French ambition in Louisiana

Figure 26. Captain Joseph Bernard Vallière d'Hauterive, commandant of
Arkansas Post from 1787 to 1790. *Courtesy of Arkansas Territorial
Restoration*

with respect to applying their law to Indians, the fact is that Europeans
attempted to extend their legal system to the Indians in Arkansas only
when an Indian killed a European. A particularly interesting (though
tragic) example of this kind of case occurred at Arkansas Post in 1788,
when Captain Joseph Vallière was commandant there. Andrés Lopez, a

merchant and farmer at the Post, and practically the only Spaniard (outside the garrison) who was living there at the time, got into an altercation late one summer night with some Choctaw Indians who came to his house in search of liquor. When Lopez retreated into his house and locked his door, the Indians battered it down. Before the night was over, a brawl had ensued in Lopez's back yard that involved the whole neighborhood: The participants had pulled up pickets from Lopez's garden fence and had had lustily at each other. Lopez himself was badly wounded, but that was hardly the worst of it: One of the Choctaws died from the beating that he received. Not being able to get any satisfaction from Captain Vallière (who said that the Indians were the aggressors and that the killing was not malicious), the Choctaws applied their own law of vengeance to the event and took the life of an eighteen-year-old Spanish boy named Pedro Serrano in retaliation. The choice of a Spaniard as the object of vengeance may well not have been accidental: A Spaniard had killed a Choctaw, and under the Choctaw law of vengeance it is possible that only a Spaniard would have been liable, as a member of the manslayer's "nation."[23] (More about this later.) To make matters worse, a soldier of the garrison, sent by Captain Vallière to prevent the Choctaws from scalping the white boy, somehow managed to set his gunpowder and then himself on fire, and he died from the burns a few days later.

The commandant and the governor were unable to do anything about the murder[24] of young Pedro Serrano, or the consequent death of the soldier, because the perpetrators fled and the pursuing Creoles were unable to catch up with them.[25] A treaty executed between the Spanish and the Choctaw nation four years before these events provided that if any Choctaw "committed the detestable crime of homicide against any vassal of our Catholic Monarch," the Choctaws were obligated "to deliver up the head of the aggressor,"[26] but whether the Spanish ever attempted to invoke the provisions of this treaty in this instance the record does not reveal. Such an attempt might well have proven rather sticky, since a Choctaw had been killed in the altercation, and in the same treaty the Spanish had promised to punish white people who murdered Choctaws. It is true that the treaty provided that white perpetrators' guilt would be determined under Spanish, not Indian law; but even so, a dispute as to whether the Choctaw had been killed in self-defense would almost certainly have arisen, if the Choctaw's death had been made an issue of under the treaty provision.

In any case, what the Arkansas commandant would have done, if he had had the opportunity, is perhaps revealed in another Arkansas case that occurred in the same year as the altercation with the Choctaws. It furnishes the only example of a successful attempt to impose penal sanctions on Indians in Arkansas that I have encountered in the entire eighteenth century, and it had to do with a homicide committed by two Quapaws.[27] According to Captain Vallière, these Quapaws were guilty of an unprovoked attack on an American hunter named Robert Wilson, who was on his way back to Arkansas Post to collect his wife and children after the Osages had robbed him and his three comrades. Vallière called a council of the Quapaw chiefs and told them that the two guilty parties deserved swift punishment. The chiefs apologized profusely for the crime, but said that they would have to hold a council on the matter in their villages and promised a response within three days. The answer, when it came, did not please Vallière: The Quapaws did not want the two responsible parties punished. In the first place, the Quapaws pointed out (rightly) that the Osages were always killing Europeans and were never punished for it. In the second place, the Quapaws observed that the guilty parties belonged to "a big family." Though the record does not say so, the reference to the perpetrators' "big family" probably indicates that the Quapaws were afraid of vengeance by the perpetrators' clan (family) if an execution were carried out, not that they were reluctant to execute a person because of his social status. In any case, the Quapaw chiefs' response angered Vallière, who railed that the Quapaws had to do as he said or Governor Miró might well order the destruction of their entire nation. Vallière told the Quapaws that the governor was already very angry with them because they had been behaving badly for a long time, and he had the means to cut them down as easily as if they were a sapling an inch thick![28]

This outburst must at the least have impressed the Quapaws with Vallière's implacability on the subject, but it is not easy to believe that it frightened them very much. The Spanish fort on the Arkansas was forever in a pitiably dilapidated condition, its garrison was always tiny, and it is doubtful that the militia (such as it was) could have been counted on to attack its Quapaw neighbors. The Quapaws, moreover, at this time outnumbered the local Europeans by a ratio of at least five to one, and there is good reason to believe that the Quapaws had more firepower.

But, for whatever the reason, Vallière's wishes ultimately prevailed, though only partly. On 28 April 1789, some Quapaws executed a member of their tribe in front of the fort and in the presence of the garrison, the townspeople of the Post, and a party of Abenaki Indians who were temporarily in the environs.[29] The executioners, along with a young chief, then went to New Orleans to report the deed to the governor and, not incidentally, to receive a present for doing it. The governor gave Vallière his laconic approval: "This appears quite good to me," he wrote, "and in consequence I have rewarded the chief and those who accompanied him, for which they left satisfied."[30]

This series of events is rich with interesting characteristics. First of all, we need to notice that the facts of the case seem not to have been in dispute. That is, it seems to have been agreed that two Quapaws had killed Robert Wilson. Without this agreed-upon state of facts, it is doubtful that the matter could have been settled, because there was no institution—that is, no court—to whom both nations could have looked for a resolution of disputed matter. The Quapaws would nevertheless have had, from the standpoint of their legal assumptions, some large and legitimate objections to Vallière's request. Under Quapaw law, we may presume, the culprits would not have been punished, at least not in a formal way. That is because the Quapaws had no abstract state whose job it was to punish offenses against what we glibly and quite unthinkingly call "society." It is even possible that the Quapaws believed that compensation to "cover" the dead was all that was due, especially since they were allied with the Spanish, and, if so, taking a Quapaw life was simply out of the question.[31] But the evidence points to the conclusion that for the Quapaws an international homicide was ordinarily a wrong to be avenged by the clan of the deceased victim taking a life in retaliation. In 1768, for instance, Alexandre DeClouet, commandant of Arkansas Post, wrote that a Quapaw chief wanted to go to war against the Choctaws "to avenge, according to him, a man of his family [i.e., clan] who had been killed by them."[32]

There is evidence, as we have already seen, that some Indians regarded European nations as separate tribes,[33] so perhaps the Quapaws might have reasoned that the Americans, not the Spanish government, had a *duty* of retaliation under American law. However that may be, the Quapaws probably would not have thought that anyone had a *right* to vengeance, since the deceased was not a member of their tribe. Executing one of their own for killing someone who was not a member of their tribe therefore would ordinarily be significantly contrary to their customs.[34] Besides, how could the executioners be shielded from the vengeance of the clan of the man-slayers? Perhaps in this kind of exigent circumstance the Quapaws could draw on a custom similar to the one practiced by their kinsmen the Osages that allowed their chiefs "in extreme instances" to execute a particularly recalcitrant tribal member without fear of retaliation from the clan of the person executed.[35] But in circumstances similar to the ones presented in this case, a civil war may have been touched off when the Choctaws had executed Choctaws who had murdered Frenchmen.[36]

Under the Quapaws' law, more importantly, what we call the *lex talionis,* the law of an eye for an eye, only one life could be forfeited as satisfaction for the life (Robert Wilson's) that had been taken. The Quapaws were therefore no doubt horrified by the Spanish demand that two lives be for-feited. Thomas Jefferson, incidentally, understood and respected this native legal principle, because in 1808 he cautioned Meriwether Lewis, the gov-ernor of Louisiana Territory, to execute only one of three Indian murder-ers because only one white man had been killed.[37] (It is interesting, is it not, that in this instance the *lex talionis,* so reviled by many for its severity and its focus on vengeance, is actually more merciful than our European law? That is because European law focuses on the guilty minds of all perpetra-tors, so that many can suffer though only one has perished.)

While the sources do not say so directly, what seems to have happened here is that Indians and Europeans reached a compromise: The Indians would violate their customs and execute one of their own, but the Spanish had to be satisfied even though one of the guilty would go unpunished. Both sides gave up a part of their principles. But notice this: The Quapaws did not submit so far to European norms as to allow Europeans to execute an Indian. They did the job themselves. Most important, we need to see that the improvised solution in this case occupied a kind of uneasy "middle ground"[38] that drew on the legal assumptions of both nations but did not actually conform to either. The event demonstrates neither the imposition of cultural norms by the Europeans nor a successful resistance by the native peoples. The Indians are not the rock, the Europeans are not the sea, the storm has not dissolved the rock, nor has the rock endured.[39] What has been produced is a third thing, a *tertium quid,* that is not quite either sea or rock, but a little bit of both. The solution ultimately agreed to was an adaptation made necessary because there were dual sovereigns who badly needed an accommodation in the middle ground.

II.

The Arkansas commandants never sought to apply their law to any other dispute involving Indians, even when they committed a crime against a European. An event that occurred in 1771 reveals quite clearly the reason for their reluctance. In that year, Captain Fernando de Leyba, commanding at the Arkansas, wrote the governor in an illuminating detail that is worth quoting at some length:[40]

> On 26 September [1771] an Indian of this nation [i.e., Quapaw] inflicted three stabwounds on an inhabitant of this post named Bartholome, who took flight with the Indian in pursuit. The Indian had a horse tied up in his village, and, having noticed the horse's absence, he went to the middle of the plaza of the village and announced the theft in a loud voice to all his countrymen. When no one came out to his complaint, he then said in an equally aggressive way that "since no one admits the theft of my horse, I am going to kill a Spaniard," and set out immediately for this post. The first man that he encountered was the said Bartholome who was making a pirogue on the river bank, and, without saying a word, he attacked Bartholome with a knife and inflicted three wounds on him. Of those, only the one that Bartholome received in the neck was of any consequence, the other two being only slight. We are exposed to these and more serious assaults because of our lack of forces.

From the foregoing, it is plain that sheer impotence had to serve as Leyba's excuse for inaction.

This was not by any means an isolated event. In the summer of 1771, Captain Leyba had a contretemps with a drunken Quapaw, who, he said, was "completely set on cutting down one of the columns of the gallery of my house with a hatchet." "When I stopped him (although pleasantly)," Leyba reported, "the Indian threatened to hit me with the hatchet." A punishment swift and condign, we can be sure, would have awaited any European who would have dared to offer such an affront to a Spanish commandant, but the Indian evidently did so with impunity. Leyba wrote that liquor caused Indians to "commit a thousand disorders against the *habitants,* who ceaselessly complain to me about these prejudices."[41]

This kind of powerlessness in the face of illegal activity by the Quapaws manifested itself on two occasions in 1785 alone. On one of these, Captain DuBreuil had to hurry a soldier named Joseph Grillo off to New Orleans because the Quapaws had twice tried to kill him "by treachery." It seems that Grillo had caught a Quapaw attempting to steal one of his chickens and had given him quite a thrashing. The captain could think of no response to the situation except to get the soldier out of harm's way. There was no question, evidently, of formal proceedings against Indians who had attempted to murder a Spanish soldier.[42] Later the same year, DuBreuil had to send another soldier (this one named Bernardo Madrigal) to the capital, because the captain feared that some Quapaws were going to kill him. This time, the Quapaws' sense of honor had been engaged because Madrigal was on guard duty one night when he fired at (but missed) a Quapaw who was passing near the fort and who had refused to identify himself despite the fact that Madrigal had shouted "Who goes there?" three times. DuBreuil wrote the governor that the Quapaws knew Madrigal's identity (either because the Quapaw fired on had recognized the soldier's voice, or because someone had revealed who had shot at him), and the offended Quapaw and his clan [*parientes*] had determined to kill Madrigal if they could catch him outside the fort.[43]

Members of the Quapaw tribe were hardly the only Indians who committed acts that were contrary to European legal norms. In the 1790s, the scarcity of game, the frequency of crop failures in their ancient homelands, and pressures from an expanding American frontier periodically caused various Indian groups to cross the Mississippi to hunt, and Chickasaw bands were prominent among them. Whether from poverty or from other motives, some of their parties robbed the hunters and *habitants* of Arkansas Post of their horses and killed their livestock.[44] They also occasionally pillaged the camps of Arkansas hunters, robbing them of their arms, munitions, and other supplies, even threatening to kill them instantly if they ever returned.[45]

These kinds of activities could cause severe hardships at the Post. In 1793 Captain Delinó reported that a party of eight Chickasaws had stolen ten horses from three *habitants* who were settled two miles from his fort, making it impossible for those *habitants* to do their planting. They were understandably so demoralized that Delinó thought it likely that they would soon seek a more peaceful place to live.[46]

The Arkansas commandants repeatedly asked the governor for permission to use armed force against these depredations (or at least to send armed parties to retrieve the stolen animals),[47] but the governor was at first inclined to respond in less violent ways. In accordance with a provision of a treaty executed between the Chickasaws and the Spanish in 1784,[48] he sought compensation for the thefts from the Chickasaw nation,[49] or threatened to deduct the value of stolen horses from the Chickasaws' annual present if stolen livestock was not returned.[50]

It is not clear whether these methods were successful, but in 1796 the governor told the commandant that whenever the Chickasaws committed an offense against one of his *habitants,* he should try to arrest the two or three most culpable and send them to New Orleans for punishment. Failing that, he should report the name of the chief of any offending party of Chickasaws to him, so that compensation could be demanded.[51] There is no evidence that an Arkansas commandant was ever successful in apprehending any Chickasaw who committed an offense in his bailiwick, or, indeed, ever attempted to do so. Finally, Governor Carondelet gave the harried *habitants* of the Arkansas permission to fire on Indians who were attempting to steal their horses.[52] It appears that this desperate self-help measure may have worked some success, but the complaints about marauding Chickasaws did not entirely cease.[53]

The Chickasaws were not the only tribe that disturbed the peace of the Arkansas region. Late in the colonial period, Choctaw bands likewise began to pass over the great river to hunt and trade in the environs of the Post because of crop failures and the depletion of game in their own territory.[54] In 1794, Captain Vilemont wrote that twenty-two Choctaws, thirty Loups, and twelve Chickasaws had paid a call on him, apparently without incident.[55] But these visits did not always prove to be peaceful. In the summer of 1795, for instance, a party of thirty Choctaws threatened to raise a party of four hundred warriors to attack the Post and destroy the Quapaw villages, in retaliation for some fights that had erupted between the tribes because, the Quapaws said, the Choctaws had violated some Quapaw women. The Choctaw party, on leaving the Post, had stolen eight horses from various *habitants.*[56] A few years later, Vilemont reported a rumor that a considerable party of Choctaws and Alabamans had joined forces to destroy the Caddos and the Quapaws.[57] No Choctaw attacks ever materialized, however, and in 1798 the Choctaws, in accordance with their treaty obligations of 1784,[58] even returned some carbines that they had taken from white hunters on the Arkansas.[59]

It would seem, then, that about the only relief that *habitants* of Arkansas

Post who were aggrieved by Indian thefts might expect to receive was restitution of the stolen goods, but even this evidently did not occur with any frequency. The only example that reveals the process in any detail occurred in 1771, when two Quapaws stole seven horses from *habitants* at Natchitoches. As soon as Captain Desmazellières learned about the theft, he summoned the Quapaw great chief and accused the Quapaws. The chief immediately admitted the misdeed, but answered that the perpetrators had "lost their minds and that at the first demand they would return the horses."[60]

That opportunity came soon enough. Lieutenant Governor DeMézières of Natchitoches sent a party of fourteen Natchitoches Indians and a courier to the Arkansas Post to demand satisfaction. When they arrived, Desmazellières caused the return of the horses that the Quapaws had stolen and "in the presence of the party vigorously reprimanded the two rogues who committed the offense." The miscreants, he maintained, promised not to do it again. But they claimed that it was the expensiveness of blankets that had caused the disorders. "It used to be," the commandant said, "that they would have a blanket of Limbourg for eight deerskins and today Tounoir had raised it to twenty before his departure" for New Orleans.[61] A few weeks later, the commandant asked the governor to set a tariff on blankets at the Arkansas because it was high prices, according to the Quapaws, "that caused their young people to do wicked things."[62] Consequently, when a merchant named Juan Diard ascended to the Arkansas in December of 1770, the governor directed the Arkansas commandant to "make sure that Diard sells the goods in accordance with the tariff that I have sent you."[63]

Captain Vilemont knew that he and his soldiers were all but powerless to curtail the harm done by Indian miscreants. He wrote that Indians of various nations gathered near his fort and committed "offenses and robberies without any fear because of the small garrison and because there are so few men here during the hunting season—all of them are hunters." In addition, he pointed to "the ruinous condition of the artillery": He had only three cannons, and they were "full of holes and irregularities, and the touchholes are so large that the charge runs through them; for they are very old and entirely eaten up by rust." And of his seven swivel guns, he said, "only one can be fired without risk." Completing this picture of utterly laughable impotence was the fact that the stockade of the fort was so rotten

Figure 27. Captain Charles Melchior Gérard de Vilemont, commandant of
Arkansas Post from 1794 to 1802. *Courtesy of Arkansas Territorial
Restoration*

"that the least gust of wind would blow it to the ground."[64] Vilemont's
lamentations confirm Victor Collot's observation that in 1796 the settlers
of Arkansas Post, "having no means of defense against the Indians, who
are continually pillaging their cattle and robbing them of the fruits of their
industry, are in general poor and miserable."[65]

III.

When Indians committed crimes against Indians, the Spanish would naturally have been even more reluctant to attempt to impose the kind of punishment that European law demanded. For instance, in 1781 Captain

Balthazar de Villiers wrote that some Houmas had killed a Quapaw in lower Louisiana and that the Quapaws had demanded as satisfaction either the scalp of the murderer or a large compensatory payment. Villiers stopped an incipient war by promising to write the governor to urge him to intervene with the Houmas and persuade them to compose the quarrel.[66] The governor, in response, promised Villiers to order the appropriate commandants to see to it that, "one way or another, the Houmas give complete satisfaction to the Arkansas."[67]

The same relative hands-off attitude prevailed when the Quapaws were the accused instead of the accuser. In 1791, some Quapaws, without any apparent justification, lifted two Abenaki scalps on the White River, and the governor ordered Captain Delinó, who was commanding at Arkansas Post, to tell the Quapaws in no uncertain terms how disgraceful this incident was and "how necessary it is that they immediately make the proposed satisfaction"—that is, provide compensation for the deaths.[68] A similar event occurred in 1796, when Captain Charles de Vilemont reported to the governor that some Alabamans had wanted to kill a Quapaw because they thought that the Quapaws had connived in the murder of an Alabaman by the Chickasaws at Arkansas Post. The Quapaws had wanted the governor to tell the Alabamans that "their intentions were to live with the Alabamans amicably and that they were provoked with the Chickasaws" to the point that "they would not allow them to dance the scalp dance in their village."[69] The same year, a party of Choctaws killed a Calolacho Indian at the Post with perfect impunity.[70]

Nor did the Spanish intervene even when Quapaw killed Quapaw. In 1787 Captain Vallière reported that some Quapaws of the Kappa village had killed a chief of the Osotouy village at Arkansas Post during a drunken brawl and had thrown his body into the river. This quarrel the Spanish left entirely to the internal law of the Quapaws to settle, though Vallière did suggest to the governor that he prohibit the sale of liquor to Quapaws at the Post. In the three months that he had been there, Vallière asserted, five Quapaws had been killed by Quapaws, and it was all because of liquor.[71]

In all of these last cases, the most that the Spanish could do was act as mediators between the disputants and force a composition of the quarrel if possible. They never sought to punish any of the wrongdoers by exercising judicial jurisdiction over the parties themselves. In 1796, Victor Collot, the French spy, observed two Chickasaws attack a Mascouten Indian within sight of the fort at Arkansas Post, killing and scalping him under the very eyes of the commandant. Collot observed to the unnamed commandant (he would have been Charles de Vilemont) that this was a violation of His Catholic Majesty's territory and an affront to his sovereignty. Vilemont merely replied that "he had express orders not to mingle in any quarrel which the Indians might have with each other; that the Chickasaws were a very powerful nation; and that if he prevented the murder, perhaps in a fortnight the Post and all the Whites would have been destroyed." Collot chose not to believe this explanation, preferring, instead, to lay Vilemont's inactivity to the commandant's desire not to annoy potential customers; that is, in Collot's words, Vilemont chose not to act because "these Indians would keep off from their counters, and would carry elsewhere the produce of their hunting," if commandants meddled in Indian affairs.[72]

But Collot is surely wrong here. The commandant's explanation is entirely credible. Almost certainly, this French commandant, acting on behalf of a Spanish king, was moved neither by direct commercial concerns nor by what Francis Parkman supposed was the Frenchman's inclination to embrace and cherish the Indian.[73] The commandant was attempting to maintain his delicate position in a country in which he was so far outnumbered that he was forced as a practical matter to recognize the Indians as equal sovereigns beyond the reach of his legal authority. In situations like this, all the governor could do was to exhort the Arkansas commandant to try to compose quarrels so that friendly nations could be held to allegiance and the peace maintained.[74]

There is good evidence that during the colonial period the Arkansas commandant commanded enough respect from the Quapaws that they would be likely to seek and take his advice on how to compose quarrels that arose between them and other Indian nations. John B. Treat, the head of the United States government factory (trading post) at the Arkansas, wrote in 1807 that the Quapaws were "the mildest of any of the Red Brethren" and had "long been accustomed to ask advice of their White neighbors" when they got involved in serious altercations with another tribe.[75] But this kind of deferential consultation could not be regularly expected from any tribe other than the Quapaws, and even with respect to them there was no effective legal mechanism that could force their compliance with a commandant's wishes or advice, or compel them to conform to the European legal norms that would be brought to bear if the same quarrels had arisen between Europeans.

IV.

From a lawyer's standpoint, what is perhaps most noticeable about the situation in Arkansas is the kinds of cases that are completely missing from the adjudicatory record. While the archives of Arkansas Post have been lost, an inventory of what was in them has survived. There are no Indian criminal cases recorded there whatsoever: No cases involving murder, rape, robbery, burglary, larceny, or any other crime involving Indians, either as defendant or victim.[76] But there is more. While lay people, when they think of courts at all, may well tend to think of the criminal law, that is really only a relatively small and frequently minor part of what most courts do. Courts mostly concern themselves with the law of obligations, that is, with compensating for breaches of contract and injuries to persons and property, and with domestic relations and the transmission of wealth. All of this, in other words the entire civil law, the law that governs most relations between people, was evidently excluded from the purview of the adjudicatory process in Arkansas if one of the parties was an Indian.

More startling perhaps, it appears that Arkansas was not atypical in this respect in the province of Louisiana. Though I cannot pretend to have looked at all of the surviving Louisiana judicial records from the eighteenth century, I can claim to have looked at large numbers of them, and not a single one involves an identifiable Indian as a party. I have looked at the records of the Louisiana Superior Council of the French period[77] and the records of Natchez[78] and St. Louis[79] for the entire eighteenth century. The story is the same: The Indians are simply absent. Most remarkably, a recent study of all the criminal cases in the New Orleans courts during the Spanish period also reveals no cases against Indians.[80] The aloofness of the Louisiana legal system from Indian affairs is all the more noticeable when one compares the legal arrangements there with those in place in the English colonies and in Mexico, where, as we saw, there was a considerable legal assimilation of the indigenous population.

This aloofness will require some explanation, because it can hardly be that Indians always adhered to European legal norms, or never broke their engagements or committed wrongs, or, for that matter, were themselves never wronged or disappointed with respect to their undertakings. What seems most likely is that the French made a deliberate decision not to incorporate the Indians into the regular legal system for practical reasons, and the Spanish simply continued this policy as they did, for fairly well known causes, with respect to most of the other aspects of French Indian policy that they found in place when they purchased and took possession of Louisiana.[81] Besides, as we have already noticed, relevant provisions of the Laws of the Indies mirrored the previous French practice by committing Indian causes, not to the regular courts, but to the governors of borderland provinces, and it is probable that they dealt with them by negotiating with relevant parties or appropriate chiefs in some informal way that did not leave a trace in the legal records. These cases were no doubt considered a part of the governor's political and administrative duties rather than his strictly judicial ones.[82]

In a remote outpost like Arkansas Post, it would seem right to guess that the local commandant was expected to adjust difficulties between natives and Europeans as best he could. How an informal method of adjustment of this sort might have worked in practice will be hard to document because by hypothesis it will not have precipitated the paper record that a regular application for judicial relief almost always does. In fact, we have no reason whatever to anticipate that we would ever get even a glimpse of such a process. But as luck would have it, a document that Captain Joseph Vallière set his hand to in 1789 quite unexpectedly allows us a very detailed look at one.

It seems that in 1789 one Pedro Nitar, a merchant of long standing at Arkansas Post, had complained to Governor Miró that Captain Vallière had refused to order an Abenaki Indian to perform a contract that Nitar had made with the Indian. Vallière, full of outrage and injured innocence, filed a six-page answer to Nitar's allegations. He maintained that the Abenaki had come to see him on another matter, whereupon Nitar had appeared and demanded that the captain make the Indian hand over twenty-five pounds of beaver skins that Nitar had bought from him. When Vallière told the Indian to deliver the skins, he replied that Nitar had cheated him, and effectively wanted to steal the skins from him, because Nitar had given him only ten musket balls for each pound of beaver, and that it would therefore be unjust to enforce the agreement.

At this juncture, Nitar protested that he had given the Indian a great deal of brandy in addition to the musket balls. When Vallière pointed out that Nitar had just admitted to a crime since the law prohibited trading liquor to Indians, Nitar was left, as Vallière put it, "without an argument" and thus offered him no rejoinder. But Nitar told the Indian that he should pay him nevertheless because he had given the Indian something valuable, and it was irrelevant whether this benefit was received legally or not. At that point, the Abenaki proposed giving Nitar twelve pounds of beaver skins, about half of the original debt, but only, he said, because the captain had ordered it, not because Nitar deserved it. Nitar, according to Vallière, capitulated and accepted the offer.[83]

This event does not involve an exercise of judicial jurisdiction in the usual sense. The captain had not, in fact, despite what the Indian had said, ordered him to give Nitar twelve pounds of skins. There was no hint of the promise of coercion that usually characterizes a citizen's contact with the state as authoritative arbiter of disputes. Vallière would never have risked seizing the Abenaki's property or person in execution of any judgment that he might have rendered, especially since the Abenakis were camped just across the river from the fort, a fact that Vallière himself noted in a different part of his extensive answer to Nitar's complaint. What Vallière's papers allow us to see is a process of negotiation, persuasion, mediation, conciliation, and compromise, all shaped by a little bullying from the commandant. Along the way there were appeals to a sense of fair play and natural justice by both sides, in the course of which a number of interesting ethical quandaries were mooted, including whether, as modern lawyers would say, a court ought to enforce bargains that are based on inadequate consideration and whether quasi-contractual obligations can arise from bargains that fail for illegality. On some level, then, there is a lot of law here: But there is no court. Vallière facilitated a settlement, nothing more. Indeed, the essence of Nitar's complaint against Vallière might well have been Vallière's refusal to enforce the agreement against the Abenaki in the same way that Vallière would have against a European.

V.

If the French and the Spanish had enjoyed only a very limited success in incorporating the Quapaws into their legal system,[84] it appears that their sporadic efforts at Christianizing them were even less fruitful. While the matter is not completely free from doubt, it appears reasonably certain that the Quapaws entered the nineteenth century with their religious traditions almost entirely intact.

The Quapaws' religious traditions, practices, and beliefs have not come down to us outfitted with the kind of reliability that will allow us to describe them with any real confidence. We do know that, in common with their Osage kinsmen, they believed in a life force called *Wah-kon-tah* that was present in every animate and inanimate thing and thus operated to unify all creation.[85] The Quapaws' religious ideas, therefore, in a rather remarkable way, mirrored their notions of government: Neither was hierarchical and each emphasized a kind of equality among persons. Governor Bienville has left us what is probably a somewhat garbled description of the Quapaws' belief in *Wah-kon-tah* when he remarked that "it is true that [the Quapaws] have an idea of a supreme being who is a spirit." He also claimed that they believed that that "same force was the author of all the evil that they have [and] of all the unhappiness that happens to them."[86] This last, we can believe, must have been true in a sense, because *Wah-kon-tah* permeated everything, including forces that were capable of doing harm.

Some French observers claimed that the Quapaws had no religion,[87] but it is clear that what they meant was that the Quapaws had no liturgy, theology, religious edifices, or formal kinds of worship, not that they did not have a spiritual life. One version of Tonty's memoirs makes him say that the Quapaws "adore all sorts of animals, or rather they worship but one divinity, which discovers itself in a certain animal, such as it shall please their 'juggler' or priest to pitch upon; so that it will be sometimes an ox, sometimes a dog, or some other."[88] This seemingly indicates that the Quapaws possessed manitous that they regarded as the locus of spiritual powers. When La Harpe remarked in 1722 of the Quapaws that "the serpent is their principal divinity,"[89] he was probably describing a manitou in a mistaken way: The serpent was not a divinity, it was instead the residence of certain special powers on which the Quapaws were keen to draw. Bossu reports, in this case rather reliably, that the Quapaws never went "off to war without consulting their 'manitou.' They attribute both their good and bad fortune to it" (echoes of Bienville here) and "if the manitou is not good to them," he claimed, "they abandon it unceremoniously and take another."[90] The manitou, he reported, could be "a dried crow, snake, amphibian, or quadruped."[91] Thomas Nuttall, in describing the Quapaws, confirms these observations: "Every family," he tells us (meaning every clan), "chooses its *penates,* or guardian spirit, from among those various objects of creation which are remarkable for their sagacity, their utility, or power."

Figure 28.   Fanciful representation of Bossu destroying a supposed Quapaw
idol. Jean-Bernard Bossu, *Nouveaux voyages dans l'Amérique
septentrionale* (Amsterdam: 1777), 162.

Thus, he said, "some will perhaps choose a snake, a buffaloe, an owl, or a raven."[92]

The Quapaws may have believed in an afterlife, because in 1721 Father Charlevoix observed a woman pouring *sagamité* over her son's grave, perhaps as food for his journey to the spirit world.[93] Another female mourner had lit a fire next to a tomb, "probably," the good father reasonably guessed (we cannot know) "in order to warm the deceased person."[94] Governor Bienville reported that the Arkansas Indians "have for their dead a veneration altogether peculiar,"[95] a cultural characteristic that, as we saw, the Spanish learned to exploit in trying to persuade the Quapaws not to abandon their homeland when the government of Louisiana passed to Spain later in the century.

Further details of Quapaw spiritual life that have come down to us are both meager and difficult properly to evaluate. Diron d'Artaguiette said that the Quapaws "believe in metempsychosis," that is, presumably, in the transfer of human souls to animals. But he said that their attachment to this idea had "this reservation: that they believe that the soul of their relatives does not take up its abode in the wild animals that they kill or in their enemies." He claimed further that he had seen a Quapaw kill a buffalo and warn the Frenchmen in his company to keep off "until he had given numerous yells and had spoken some words which we did not understand, after which he told us that it was an enemy, who was in the body of this animal."[96] Diron's meaning is difficult to divine here, but it might be right to guess that the Quapaw whom he described had engaged in a ceremony that included incantations aimed at ensuring that the slain buffalo's relatives would not seek to avenge the killing. Descriptions of Quapaw religious practices are sometimes unfathomable and often unreliable because of most Europeans' rather superficial interest in comprehending them and, possibly, because the Quapaws would have been chary of revealing their religious ideas to foreigners.[97]

Although, as we have seen, some of the seventeenth-century French priests expressed optimism about converting the Quapaws to their religion, the missionaries never spent enough time in the Arkansas region to allow us to believe that they accomplished more than a very superficial Christianization of the Quapaws at most. Indeed, the Quapaws showed an occasional hostility to early missionaries. In 1702, Father Nicolas Foucault abandoned his mission at the Arkansas because, he said, the Indians had mistreated him in some unspecified way. On his way down the Mississippi, his Koroa escorts murdered him, and some of the French religious were of the view that the Quapaws had connived in the killing.[98] It would not be cause for wonder if Father Foucault had clashed with an Indian shaman, precipitating Foucault's departure, and one is entitled to wonder too whether intriguing Englishmen did not have a hand in the good father's death.

It is true that, according to Father Le Petit, immediately after Father Du Poisson was killed at Natchez in 1729, Quapaw warriors encountered some Frenchmen on the Mississippi and "passed their hands over them from head to foot, according to their custom, in testifying to their sorrow for the death . . . of their father in Jesus Christ"; and Le Petit also wrote that "the faithful *Akensas* mourned every day in their Village the death of Father Du Poisson, and with the most earnest entreaties, demanded another Missionary."[99] But, in the first place, it was Father Du Poisson himself who, as we saw, had been quite pessimistic about converting the Quapaws only the year before his death. Le Petit, it also needs noticing, makes no claim that conversions were taking place; and it is probably significant that the Quapaws were mourning Du Poisson's death in accordance with their own religious customs. There is no doubt that Quapaws frequently venerated the Roman Catholic priests who came among them because these priests were spiritual people; in fact, the Quapaws sometimes referred to them as "spirits." But the Indians' vow to avenge Du Poisson's death is perhaps evidence only that they had finally succeeded in incorporating him into their tribe, thus giving rise to a duty of vengeance under Quapaw law; it does not provide much evidence of spiritual conversion. In fact, late in the French period, a Jesuit, speaking of the Arkansas, lamented that there was "little hope . . . of leading the savages of the place to Christianity."[100] After Du Poisson's death, moreover, priests were present only intermittently at the Arkansas, and there was no resident priest at all from 1758 to the 1790s.[101] And the Spanish did not provide any missionaries to the Indians of Louisiana.

It is true that full-blood Indians were occasionally baptized at Arkansas Post, but they were frequently identified as the slaves of Europeans[102] or as the wives of Europeans.[103] Indian women sometimes received baptism simultaneously with their children, with no mention of the husband and father;[104] but, without more, it would be hazardous to guess whether their offspring were full-bloods or half-bloods. And while three Indian women were baptized without their children, if any, being mentioned,[105] it would be wrong simply to assume that they did not have European husbands. Only five children who one can be reasonably sure were full-blood, free Indians without some close European family connection were baptized during Arkansas's entire colonial period; and only three of these were Quapaws.[106] All of this provides ample indication that no significant Christian influence was brought to bear on the region's indigenous population during Arkansas's colonial epoch. It seems right to conclude, therefore, as Professor Baird has, that the missionary efforts of the Europeans among the Quapaws "resulted in friends rather than converts," and that "the inability to sustain a mission" at the Arkansas may well have "reflected the continued allegiance of the tribe to traditional gods."[107]

VII

Fin de Siècle/Fin del Siglo/
End of an Era

What first struck many visitors to the old Post of Arkansas in the early nineteenth century, though they would not have said so in terms, was the remarkable symbiosis that Indians and whites had achieved in the five or six generations that they had been thrown together in the Arkansas country. To the travelers who sojourned there, the result of this protracted elbow-rubbing was both visible and audible: The residents in and around the creaky creole village were overwhelmingly of mixed blood (the best possible proof of decades of congenial interaction), and some of them at least even spoke a French-Quapaw patois.

François Marie Perrin du Lac, a French visitor to the Post in 1802, marveled at the extent to which "French emigrants from Canada" had been Indianized by their long association with the native people of the Arkansas country. "More than half the year," he remarked, "one finds in this village only women, children, and old people. The men go hunting for deer (the skins of which are valued less than those from the northern country), for buffalo, which they salt for their use, and for a few beaver, which they still find at some distance. On their return home, they pass their time playing games, dancing, drinking, or doing nothing, similar in this as in other things to the savage peoples with whom they pass the greater part of their lives, and whose habits and customs they acquire."[1] But the extent to which the white people of Arkansas Post had been acculturated to Indian ways had run deeper even than the lifeways of the resident population. It had also included the governmental forms that the commandants at the Post had adopted as a way of trying to influence Quapaw politics.

An appreciation of this fact follows from a careful evaluation of the document to which the Quapaw great chief Cassenonpoint set his hand in 1769 as evidence of his respect for Carlos III, the Spanish king who had just claimed sway over Louisiana. In this document,[2] as we saw, the chief "of the large medal and grand chief of all the warriors of the three Arkansas villages" promised Governor O'Reilly only "to recognize him as my father and to listen to all that my father DeClouet tells me on his behalf." What is immediately noticeable about the chief's undertaking is that he does not by any means pledge allegiance to Carlos III or promise an undying attachment to him. He promises merely to "listen to" Governor O'Reilly and Captain DeClouet, the King's agents; he does not promise necessarily to heed or obey them. What the chief undertakes, at bottom, is to attend carefully to, to consider, and to weigh the words of the Spanish, just as any *consideré* would do with respect to the chief's own words. In other words, the governor would be received into the tribal environment as an important and wise person, but not as anything remotely resembling a European sovereign. The phrase "listened to" was most likely adopted from the Quapaw idiom used to describe an important Indian leader (a "chief" in European parlance), for in describing influential Quapaw chiefs to others, Arkansas commandants would often say that they were "much listened to" in their villages.

What European leaders could aspire to, in other words, under the arrangement that Cassenonpoint endorsed, was to be Indian "chiefs," not European rulers. The contrast provided by the oath of allegiance that the Frenchmen of Arkansas Post subscribed on the same day that Cassenonpoint signed his, drives this point home with a vivid and unmistakable clarity. The Post *habitants* of their "own free will swore an oath of fidelity to the Catholic King between the hands of Mons. le Chevalier DeClouet," and "from this moment" recognized "this monarch as master of our lives and goods, which we dedicate to his superior royal will."[3] The sheer abjectivity of this undertaking serves to differentiate it quite obvi-

Figure 29. Jefferson peace medal presented to Quapaw chief in the early nineteenth century. *Courtesy of Mr. and Mrs. Lawrence Supernaw*

ously from the more communitarian tone of the promise to which Cassenonpoint had put his mark. Indeed, a comparison of the two oaths pointedly exposes to view important differences between European and Quapaw social and governmental structures. Commandants and governors became, at best, Indian chiefs, not European sovereigns, and thus themselves, like the lower orders, had become Indianized by their contact with the Quapaws.

What early nineteenth-century visitors to the Post certainly could not have discerned, at least not immediately, were the conditions that had made the symbiosis that they observed possible and even inevitable: The French, and then the Spanish, neither of them ever very numerous, had found it imperative to attract the Quapaws as allies to effect their imperial plans; and the Quapaws, much diminished by disease, were in need of European goods, and especially guns and munitions, to support and protect themselves. Nor could these post-colonial newcomers have seen the ways in which this symbiosis had been achieved and maintained. The French and the Spanish had frequently been obliged to accommodate both the legal and religious values of the Quapaws, and on occasion the two parties succeeded in creating cultural artifacts occupying a middle ground with which both could live, if grudgingly. Sometimes, however, the two groups had saluted each other across the cultural gap, each in its own way faithful to internal custom. For instance, when Commandant Orieta died at the Post in 1776, three Quapaw chiefs appeared at the fort to perform a mourning rite for the deceased captain;[4] and twelve years later, when Chief Tagin Degeska passed away, the Spanish garrison accorded him what the commandant described as "due honors."[5]

There can be no doubt that interracial relations at the Post were complex, and racial attitudes no doubt varied with economic class. Colonial commandants and European visitors, for instance, sometimes spoke deprecatingly of the mixed-blood denizens of the Post,[6] which can only create a curiosity about how deep that kind of racial condescension may have run, along with a doubt whether, in the end, the racial amalgamation for which the region became famous was not sometimes as much the cause of division as it was of unity. The gentry of the Post, it is true, fathered some of these mixed-blood creoles, and they even occasionally provided well for them; but the Post's social structure was very much like that of more familiar Latin republics to the south of us, with the very interesting difference that in Arkansas the mestizo peasant component of the society were hunters rather than subsistence farmers. These societies are not famous for racial tolerance on the part of the upper classes.[7]

While the current literature on the lives of colonial *métis* in Louisiana and elsewhere contains some brave talk about mixed-blood French-Indians as mediators between white and native cultures, the sad truth is that these "people in between," as they have been very aptly dubbed,[8] must surely have often found themselves caught in perilous circumstances that divided their loyalties and pulled them in opposite directions. The experience of one such person, a Quapaw named Saracen, though his life was hardly typical, may be instructive on the point.

From his name, it seems right to guess that Saracen was the son of one François Sarazin, who was a cadet soldier at Arkansas Post as early as 1744 and was the Quapaw interpreter there by 1752. François was eventually promoted to the rank of lieutenant and was killed by the Chickasaws in 1763.[9] Saracen was reported to have been about ninety years old when he died around 1840, so he would have been born squarely in the period during which François Sarazin served as interpreter to the French garrison; and interpreters, as we have seen, were among the most dependable and consistent progenitors of mixed-blood Quapaws. A tombstone carrying Saracen's name in St. Joseph's Catholic Cemetery in Pine Bluff marks a

grave that may or may not contain his remains, and it informs passersby
that he was "friend of the missionaries" and "rescuer of captive children,"
echoing the words of the dedicatory panel of a church window, now evidently lost, that once graced St. Joseph's Church.[10]

It appears altogether probable that Saracen was a hero of the Revolutionary War battle of 1783 at Arkansas Post. Commandant DuBreuil's letter of that year, written to the governor and describing the battle and its
aftermath, speaks of an unnamed Quapaw who threw a tomahawk into
the midst of Colbert's band at the time that Colbert released the women
and children whom he had captured during the raid.[11] By the late colonial
period a Spanish commandant is already referring to Saracen as "famous,"
and in 1824 the Protestant missionary Timothy Flint reported seeing "a
noble looking Quawpaw chief, rather advanced in age" who, according to

universally accepted local lore, had rescued a Post commandant's child from marauding Indians (Flint identified them as Creeks) by throwing a spear into their midst and frightening them away.[12] The similarity between this tale and the event recorded in DuBreuil's 1783 letter is obvious. By 1895, the story had changed somewhat, but according to it a Quapaw, now identified as Saracen, is credited with having rescued two children, this time from Chickasaws, though the locus of the kidnapping had somehow magically been transferred to "a few miles below Pine Bluff," and the children were said to have belonged to "a trapper's family."[13]

While Saracen was adulated by his white neighbors and beatified by them as a protector of their children (and, in fact, the people of Pine Bluff once contemplated erecting a monument to his memory),[14] his reputation did not fare nearly so well among many of the Quapaws. He found himself truly a "person in between." During the 1820s and 1830s, when the American government was treating the Quapaw tribe with a cavalier inhumanity, the Quapaws, now evidently numbering fewer than five hundred souls, became split into two groups, the one under the leadership of the traditional chief Heckaton, the other under Saracen, whom Governor James Miller of the Arkansas Territory had elevated to the position of "chief," despite his lack of hereditary right.[15] In 1827, Saracen, some of his family having actually starved to death, and he himself being reduced by extreme poverty to begging the federal government for help, found it necessary to abase himself by assuring Governor Izard "that he himself was half a white man by Birth and entirely white in Affections & Inclination."[16] This kind of behavior must surely have caused great resentment among Heckaton's followers, and one chronicler of the Quapaws has suggested that Saracen does not deserve to be remembered today only as a selfless friend of women and children.[17]

Saracen, then, had found his *métis* status useful, at least in the short term, but the use to which he had put it had generated dissension in the tribe. Other mixed-blood Arkansans acted in ways that indicated their desire to hide from their Indian connections, no doubt in order to shield themselves from condescension. In 1799, when Constance Menard, the natural daughter of François Menard and a *métis* Quapaw woman, married herself in New Orleans to a Spanish native of Havana, the cathedral's record solemnly asserted that she was the daughter of François Menard and his lawful wife, Magdelene Lajeunesse.[18] Constance had distanced herself from her Quapaw kin and was trying to "pass" as white.

The Arkansas *métis,* it appears, was sometimes romanticized by upperclass nineteenth-century Arkansans. J. W. Bocage, for instance, a judge and local antiquary, who settled at Pine Bluff in 1836, was acquainted with the French-Quapaw Joseph Bonne, himself a relative (a brother?) of Constance Menard's mother. Judge Bocage described Bonne as "a halfbreed native, his tawney limbs covered with dressed buck-skins, . . . looking toward the setting sun, at the retreating forms of his red brothers; then turning to the east, with hand extended, he welcomed his white brother as he came to seek a home at his side." Bonne was, Bocage rhapsodized, "a double picture of melancholy parting and joyful greeting." A few days before Bonne died, the good judge claimed to have seen him "gazing upon a steamboat loading with cotton, the product of the white man's industry, seemingly the last link between barbarism and civilization."[19] Judge Bocage was thus evidently quite fascinated by Bonne, and even expressed a kind of admiration for him, but this is a long way from accepting him as a social equal. Indeed, Judge Bocage conceptualized him simply as an inevitable if regrettable casualty to the progress of civilization.

Judge Bocage's offhand romanticization of the destruction of the Quapaws' way of life, and the near destruction of the tribe itself, though it was perhaps typical of his generation, is likely to offend modern sensibilities. But it is also true that our own generation may be falling victim to another form of romanticism, this one oddly similar to the kind practiced by a few eighteenth-century French *philosophes.* Some modern social critics, employing a trick as old as Tacitus, seem bent on investing Indians with all the qualities that they regard as lamentably missing from modern Americans, and the temptation to lapse into a kind of reductionist Garden-of-Eden reverie when contemplating the life of native Americans is not one that all historians, even sophisticated ones, have been able to resist. It needs saying, therefore, that there is not the first indication in the mass of surviving letters and other primary sources that bear on the history of colonial Arkansas that the Quapaws were environmentalists or conservationists, or that they lived in some magically balanced communion with nature before the arrival of Europeans somehow upset the delicate prelapsarian harmony.

It is certainly true that the Europeans introduced some goods into the Arkansas region that caused serious social dislocation, and liquor was the most notorious of these. We have noticed, in fact, that the Quapaws had become very fond of raw brandy and rum by the time that the English had set up their trading post at Concordia in the 1760s, and that by the 1780s liquor was causing violence, perhaps routinely, and even a number of deaths, in the Quapaw villages. Captain Villiers remarked to the governor several times on the Quapaws' dependence on alcohol. "The passion for drink," he said, "is incurable among these savages" and "causes the tribe to degenerate."[20] In 1786, Quapaw chiefs, who had earlier complained that the regulation of the Indian liquor traffic was an irritating discrimination (since anyone could freely trade liquor to whites), had implored the governor to prohibit the trade of liquor to Quapaws altogether because of widespread drunkenness and addiction to alcohol among the members of the tribe.[21]

But to lay these tragic occurrences at the door of "the market," as some would do,[22] serves only to obscure the vexing moral and ethical questions that underlie this kind of exchange. Should we, for instance, blame the ruinous passion of the Choctaws for drink, or the avaricious demand of Englishmen for deerskins, for the depletion of the game east of the Mississippi? What is the ethical force, if any, of the fact that both parties to these exchanges got exactly what they asked for? What, exactly, is the objection to depleting game, anyway, and what duty, if any, does one generation owe to another to sustain a renewable resource? Is the fact that liquor is "addictive," and both parties to the transactions knew it, entitled to any weight? If it is true, as a rather huge literature would have it,[23] that resources that are not individually owned are likely to be overexploited and undermaintained, what impact did this economic fact of life have on the depletion of game herds that had no owner? Markets, in any event, were not European inventions: The Quapaws, or their progenitors, had no doubt been participating in them a long time before white people ever set foot in America.[24]

However all this may be, for almost one hundred twenty-five years the Quapaw Indians had been consumed with devising strategies to deal with individual Old World newcomers from various countries, as well as with the frequently competing imperial pretensions of the French, English, and Spanish nations. Though the Quapaws had been perhaps eight to ten thousand strong when their French visitors had arrived in the seventeenth century, epidemics in 1690, 1699, 1721, 1748, 1752, 1777, and 1781 (and probably others as well), coupled with losses due to war and alcohol, had reduced them to a nation of perhaps only seven hundred or eight hundred persons by the end of the eighteenth century.[25] In losing upwards of 90 percent of their population due to white contact, the Quapaws shared the experience of large numbers of other Indian tribes in North America. But the Quapaws, again in common with other native groups, developed and pursued strategies to survive the onslaught of what we may appropriately call storms brewed in other men's worlds.[26]

In contriving and fashioning the means of survival, the Quapaws quite naturally drew on available native cultural institutions (what else?) with which they were familiar. Calumet rituals of adoption and international alliance provided basic frameworks for dealing with the exigencies caused by European expansionist ambitions, and a trading prowess, a facility probably developed long before the arrival of the French, stood them in good stead as well. The Quapaws, after all, were participating in market networks that extended to New Mexico, Florida, and New England when white people first established a connection with them. Their own marriage customs, their law of domestic relations, and their law of retaliation were also more than adequate to the task of shaping the ways in which they would deal with European friend and foe alike.

But what emerges from their story is not simply the enduring character and responsive capacity of Quapaw cultural institutions: To see only that would surely be to miss out on a more informative lesson. There are certain things that transcend culture in the sterile, static sense: Logic and basic human psychology are two such things, but the greatest and most insistent of them is the human inclination to pursue happiness, especially when survival is at stake. Whether or not that urge has a biological and genetic origin,[27] it lies at the core of what made Europeans and Indians know that they were both human. Both were forced to recognize the power and authority of the other, and sometimes to seek an accommodation in the middle ground.

There is a curious reluctance in the current literature of Indian-white relations to recognize what was surely the case, namely, that native American peoples were rational economic actors.[28] To conclude otherwise, it seems, is not merely a significant mistake of fact, but an oddly atavistic return to the time when the question of whether Indian people were, in the scholastic phrase, capable of reason, was much mooted. To posit what seems to be the plain truth, that the Quapaws were rational economic actors, is not, of course, to intimate that they thought only (or even mostly) of money. It would, indeed, not be surprising if they never thought of money, given the fact that there was so little specie available at any time during Arkansas's colonial epoch.

It bears emphasizing that economics is not, or at least not usually, about money at all. It is about rational choice and exchange, and exchange not just in the sense of swapping "physical goods," but broadly defined to encompass any volitional change of condition. Money merely facilitates these changes, and then only at times. All lawyers and economists, moreover, know that property and goods are not things but in things, that property is valued for its usefulness in promoting human happiness, and that that is what determines its price. An exchange of material objects between people, in common with any other change of position that people choose for themselves, is therefore aimed at increasing human satisfaction; and since satisfaction exists only in the mind, an exchange at bottom never has anything at all to do with "materialism." The peculiar urge in popular philosophical thought to separate the physical from the mental is impossible to justify. One's welfare, one's sense of well-being, exists in the mind and nowhere else. All income is therefore psychic. It may not be derived from intellectual or spiritual rumination, but it is mental.

Self-interest should not be confused with selfishness, and the fact that the Quapaws' traditions and customs frequently imposed a duty to share material goods with each other does not mean that they were not rational economic actors. Altruism is just as rational as selfishness and, indeed, it can often promote one's self-interest. Nor does the duty to share indicate that the Quapaws had no sense of private property. In many instances when a duty to share arose, it is probable that no particular individual could lay claim to goods acquired by another; and sharers often gained prestige and authority by distributing goods to others, something that seems difficult to explain if those others were taking as a matter of right. The Quapaw who resolved to kill the first Spaniard whom he saw, because he thought that a Spaniard had stolen his horse, was not, moreover, a person who did not have a well developed sense of what belonged to him.

In maximizing their welfare, the Quapaws, as this book has shown, sought to influence not only the governmental forms of the Europeans who claimed sovereignty over them, but even the appointments of the individual commandants and interpreters at Arkansas Post. The Quapaws resisted the English takeover of the Illinois region, and when that resistance failed they sought to make peace with the English and to use them effectively as foils against the Spanish, partly to maximize the amount of goods that could be derived from European sources. When war came between the Spanish and the English over the unexpected question of whether there would be a country called the United States of America, the Quapaws rather adroitly refused to take an active role in the matter, if they did not also connive, at least passively, in the British attack on the Post. When the Spanish emerged victorious in that battle, the Quapaws affected to blame their original lack of enthusiasm for the Spanish project on the great chief Angaska, now conveniently expired. All of these actions are the acts of rational economic actors, because they involved a calculation of costs and benefits and aimed to maximize the benefits, or minimize the costs, of events that were likely to affect the Quapaws' welfare.

The Quapaws' cultural forms were well adapted to the advancement of their national interests, as one can see from the tribe's responses to what their European neighbors were doing. Their adoptive Spanish "father," for example, was not holding up his end of the bargain, or their law of retaliation was not being observed in the so-called war with the Osages, or their own governmental forms were not sufficiently hierarchical to compel obedience to a chief's word. All of these responses were seriously grounded in cultural assumptions about how a moral world was ordered, assumptions to which the Quapaws were sincerely attached. But when cultural norms proved too burdensome, the Quapaws, like the Europeans with whom they lived, did not scruple to abandon them. For instance, when their interpreter Labuxière, probably a chief's adopted son, was arrested by the Spanish, this was a kidnapping that under Quapaw law demanded immediate and swift retaliatory action; and, indeed, the Quapaws did threaten to reduce the Post to ashes and to cut every European throat in it if the Spanish did not release Labuxière unharmed. But the threats came to nothing, and Labuxière ended up in a Spanish prison in North Africa.[29] Not too many years later, and perhaps even more remarkably, the Quapaws executed one of their own for the murder of an American, an action that was quite significantly contrary to their customs.

That the Quapaws survived, therefore, was not simply because of the resilience and adaptiveness of their cultural traditions (though perhaps they could not otherwise have done so), but also because their will to survive was sometimes greater than their attachment to their culture. That the Quapaws took this path is hardly a pejorative observation: On the contrary, the desire to survive is among the most important things that connect them to us, and both them and us to every living creature.

Abbreviations

ADM	Herbert Eugene Bolton, ed., *Athanase de Mézières and the Louisiana Frontier, 1768–1780,* 2 vols. (Cleveland, Ohio: Arthur H. Clark Company, 1914).
AGI, PC	Archivo General de Indias, Seville, Papeles Procedentes de Cuba. Various *legajos* (bundles, abbreviated *leg.*) are cited.
AHQ	*Arkansas Historical Quarterly.*
ANC, C¹³ᴬ	Archives Nationales, Paris, Archives Coloniales, *sous-série* (sub-series) C¹³ᴬ. Various other sub-series are cited.
APLB	*Letter Book of the Arkansas Trading House, 1805–1810,* National Archives, Washington, D.C.
BLC	A. P. Nasatir, ed., *Before Lewis and Clark: Documents Illustrating the History of Missouri, 1785–1804,* 2 vols. (St. Louis, Mo.: St. Louis Historical Documents Foundation, 1952).
GPHSB	*Grand Prairie Historical Society Bulletin.*
JR	Reuben Gold Thwaites, ed., *The Jesuit Relations and Allied Documents: Travels and Explorations of the Jesuit Missionaries in New France, 1610–1791,* 73 vols. (New York: Pageant Book Company, 1959).
LHQ	*Louisiana Historical Quarterly.*
Margry	Pierre Margry, *Découvertes et établissements des Français dans l'ouest et dans le sud de l'Amérique septentrionale,* 6 vols. (Paris: 1875–1885).
SMV	Lawrence Kinnaird, ed., *Spain in the Mississippi Valley, 1765–1794,* 3 vols. (Washington: Government Printing Office, 1949).
VP	Bill Baron, ed., *The Vaudreuil Papers* (New Orleans, La.: Polyanthos, 1975).

Appendix I

Quapaw Population, 1682–1805

Speaking perhaps of the time when he had first made contact with the Quapaws, Henri de Tonty wrote that the Quapaws at one time had had 1,500 warriors, indicating a total population of as many as 7,500 people. By 1700, however, according to Tonty, 80 percent of the Quapaw nation had perished from disease and war.[1] Father Montigny's 1699 estimate of the devastation was similar: He thought that disease and war had destroyed upwards of 85 percent of the Quapaws during the previous decade.[2]

One of the most destructive of the diseases that struck the Quapaws was smallpox. In December of 1699, Father St. Cosme related being "sensibly afflicted to see this Acansea nation once so numerous entirely destroyed by war and sickness." He said that it was "not a month since they got over the smallpox which carried off the greatest part of them. There was nothing to be seen in the village but graves." Two of the Quapaws' villages had combined, he reported, and he estimated that "there were not a hundred men; all the children and a great part of the women were dead."[3]

Just over twenty years later, Father Charlevoix observed the effects of yet another smallpox epidemic. A "Frenchman passing this way was taken ill of the disease," he said, and "the infection was first communicated to a few of the Indians, and soon after to the whole canton." Mass burials resulted, and Father Charlevoix remarked that "the burial-place appeared like a forest of stakes and posts newly erected, on which was suspended almost everything in use among" the Indians.[4]

Another epidemic occurred in 1748, but the disease is not indicated.[5] In 1752 Henri d'Orgon reported that in the preceding eighteen months unspecified diseases had carried off a third of the Quapaws' warriors, and hence they could field no more than one hundred and fifty men in time of war.[6] In 1777, twenty-eight Quapaws died in an epidemic which Villiers described as "une maladie espece d'esquinancie" (a kind of quinsy).[7] Four years later, a "rhume epidemique" (cold epidemic) carried off about twenty Quapaws and several European residents of Arkansas Post in a space of six weeks.[8]

Quapaw population estimates appear with some regularity in the colonial sources, but they are often quite obviously inaccurate; and since it is frequently the case that only the number of warriors is given, estimating Quapaw population reliably can be a very elusive enterprise indeed. In the material that follows, I have assumed that in the late seventeenth century the ratio of grown men (warriors) to total population was about 1 to 5, and that, due to disease, that ratio gradually declined during the course of the eighteenth century to about 1 to 3.[9]

🛡️

1. *1687.* Henri Joutel estimated in this year that the Quapaws could muster 700 warriors, which would indicate a total population of perhaps 3,500 people. Margry, 3:462.

2. *1699.* Father Montigny reported in 1699 that there were 200 Quapaw warriors, or perhaps a total of 800 people for the tribe. Less than ten years before, he said, there had been 1,200 warriors, perhaps about 6,000 people, but disease and war had taken a terrible toll. See Delanglez, ed., "Tonti Letters," 229 n. 35.

3. *1700.* Tonty estimated the number of Quapaw men at 300 in 1700, or a total population of perhaps 1,200. He said that 1,200 warriors had perished "by disease and war," which would indicate a previous population of around 7,500. Delanglez, ed., "Tonti Letters," 229.

4. *1702.* In this year, Iberville estimated the Quapaw tribe at about 200 families, or perhaps 800 people. *BLC,* 1:8 n. 15.

5. *1714.* Father Le Maire said that in 1714 there were 300 or 400 Quapaw warriors, indicating that there were around 1,200 to 1,500 people in the entire tribe. Jean Delanglez, "M. Le Maire on Louisiana," *Mid-America* 19 (1937): 124, 147.

6. *1722.* In this year, Bénard de La Harpe reported that the tribe had 730 people in all. Smith, "Exploration of the Arkansas River," 346, 350.

7. *1723.* Diron d'Artaguiette said that the Quapaws had "perhaps 300

warriors" in 1723, indicating a tribal population of about 1,200 people. Mereness, ed., *Travels,* 57.

8. *1726.* Bienville said that although there had formerly been 500 Quapaw warriors, the tribe could provide only 220 in 1726. This would make for an effective population of about 880. See ANC, C^{13C} 1:387.

9. *1727.* Father Du Poisson estimated the total Quapaw population at "1,200 souls" in 1727. *JR,* 67:319.

10. *1732.* A memoir of this year puts the Quapaw population at 300 families, or about 1,200 people. See ANC, C^{13A} 15:177.

11. *1739.* An estimate of this year put the Quapaw warrior strength at 400, so the total population was probably about 1,200. Shea, ed., *Journal de la guerre,* 34.

12. *Ca. 1740.* An undated memoir of around 1740 gives the Quapaw population as 220 warriors, indicating a population for the tribe of around 660 people. See ANC, C^{13C} 1:362.

13. *1750.* Father Vivier said that in 1750 the Quapaw tribe consisted of about 400 warriors, or around 1,200 people. *JR,* 69:217.

14. *1752.* The population estimate in 1752 put the number of Quapaw warriors at 150. This would make for a total population of about 450 people. Pease and Jenison, eds., *Illinois on the Eve of the Seven Years' War,* 739.

15. *1758.* The Quapaw tribe was said to be capable of producing 160 warriors in this year, indicating a total tribal population of perhaps 480. *BLC,* 1:53–55.

16. *1765.* Captain Philip Pittman said that the Quapaw tribe consisted of 600 warriors in 1765, indicating a total population of about 1,800. Pittman, *The Present State of the European Settlements on the Missisippi,* 40. This estimate seems to be rather high, to say the least.

17. *1769.* An estimate of about 300 warriors for the Quapaw tribe was made in this year, revealing that there were perhaps about 900 Quapaws at that time. See AGI, PC, *leg.* 107:23.

18. *1777.* A Spanish census of this year gave the Quapaw tribe a population of 509 people. See AGI, PC, *leg.* 190:111.

19. *1784.* A Spanish census of this year reported the Quapaw population at 708. See AGI, PC, *leg.* 107:510.

20. *1794.* A late eighteenth-century estimate put the number of Quapaw warriors at 200, for a total population of about 600. James Alexander

Robertson, ed., *Louisiana under the Rule of Spain, France, and the United States, 1785–1807* (Cleveland: Arthur H. Clark Company, 1911), 1:309.

21. *1804.* There were, according to one source, 130 warriors in the Quapaw tribe in 1804, making for a total population of perhaps 390 people. *BLC,* 2:759. This estimate is surely too low.

22. *1805.* The American Indian factor at Arkansas Post placed the number of Quapaw warriors at about 250 in 1805, indicating a total for the tribe of about 750 people. *APLB,* 24.

Appendix II

Arkansas Post Interpreters

The importance of the interpreters to maintaining the Quapaw alliance was adumbrated in chapter 4, where some information on the activities of interpreters named Montcharvaux, Landroni, and Labuxière is set out. There are many interesting details in the surviving record about the activities of later interpreters, but it seemed unnecessary to encumber the mainstream of the book with them. Since these details may however prove useful in the future for a number of purposes, I set them out here in an appendix.

In 1772, Leyba gave Labuxière's successor, Anselme Lajeunesse, leave to go to the Illinois to sell some horses, because he was poor and had a large family. Anselme's brother Baptiste was going to fill in during the absence.[1] Early the next year, Lajeunesse asked for a raise to ten dollars a month. Leyba supported the request because he thought it was clear "that [Lajeunesse] was poverty-stricken."[2] Unzaga gave him the raise.[3]

A few months later, however, Lajeunesse directed a petition to the governor complaining about the expenses associated with his job. He was, he said, forced to stay at home all year because the Quapaws expected him to put them up and feed them at his house when they came to the Post to trade. He claimed that these obligations consumed most of his salary, making it impossible for him to support his family of six children.[4] He therefore asked to be released from his commitment. Leyba told the governor that finding a qualified replacement would be difficult because, although there were a number of people at the Post who spoke Quapaw, the interpreter's pay was too low to make the job attractive. Leyba revealed that Lajeunesse had wanted to be relieved for some time, but Leyba had tried to dissuade him from this ambition because of his excellent qualifications.

Pierre Jardela wanted the post, Leyba believed, but Leyba considered him only a middling candidate. Nevertheless, Leyba said that he would offer Jardela the job as soon as Jardela returned from hunting.[5]

When Jardela returned, he rejected Leyba's offer, but Leyba soon found a replacement with whom he was delighted. He recommended Pierre Lajambri for the position. Leyba wrote the governor that he had not at first thought of Lajambri in this connection because Lajambri was reasonably well off and so Leyba had assumed that he would not be able to interest him in the job.[6] If Lajambri was in fact appointed to the job, Lajeunesse was evidently soon reengaged as interpreter, for in 1776 Villiers wrote that he was going to keep him on until he could find a replacement, something that he had not yet succeeded in doing.[7] The next year, Governor Gálvez promised that he would reimburse Lajeunesse for the expenses that he incurred in connection with visits from the Quapaws.[8]

A few years later, Villiers warned the governor that the Quapaws were going to come to New Orleans to try to persuade him to remove Lajeunesse from his job as interpreter and replace him with Antoine Lepine. Lepine, he said, was a wicked man who was plumping for the post. The Quapaws' real complaint against Lajeunesse, Villiers said, was that he would not supply them with liquor.[9] In his response to Villiers, Governor Miró said that one of the qualities that an Indian interpreter ought to have was the ability to keep the Indians happy and to reduce the complaints that they present to the governor. Angaska had complained that Lajeunesse did not give proper attention to giving the Quapaws their annual presents from the governor. Miró further indicated that if he had received Villiers's letter before he had made his representations to Angaska he might have made a different decision; but since he had not, he had promised Angaska to grant his request to have Lajeunesse relieved because of his great desire to keep the Quapaws happy. When Indians complain about a commandant, Miró explained, it had no effect on him, because Indians are difficult to keep happy; but when they complain about an interpreter, he said, it was different, because an interpreter's very first obligation was to keep the Indians happy.[10]

The next relevant communication came later the same year from Louis de Villars. He wrote to Miró that as a consequence of Miró's letter he had asked Lajeunesse to his quarters and told him of Angaska's complaint. According to Villars, Lajeunesse had protested that whenever a present came the commandant would speak to him and tell him to assemble the nation to receive it, and he would then comply; and after the nation was all assembled, the commandant would give them whatever there was. He also said that his only involvement in this process was to interpret, that is, to tell the Indians exactly what the commandant ordered him to tell them.[11]

In a memorial, evidently of the same date as Villars's letter, Lajeunesse explained to the governor that the commandant would give him two or three days' notice before he wanted to hand out presents to the Quapaws and would tell him to assemble the three villages and allot to them what the commandant indicated he should. Lajeunesse went on to say that he always did as he was told. The only explanation that he could think of for the Quapaws' complaint was that he always admonished them to listen to the governor's words and to those of the commandant, and to abstain from liquor, because otherwise they did not listen well, though they were quite tractable when not drinking.[12]

Soon thereafter, Miró wrote Villars that he was sending Jean Baptiste Sossier to the Post to serve as interpreter to the Quapaws to replace Lajeunesse because Lajeunesse could not keep the Quapaws happy.[13] Sossier arrived on 11 August 1782, and Villars put him in possession of his new position.[14] But only three years later, DuBreuil wrote to Navarro saying that Antoine Lepine wanted to be appointed both gunsmith and interpreter. DuBreuil revealed that he was very unhappy with Sossier, who was behaving badly with the Quapaws and the whites of the post alike.[15]

In 1786, DuBreuil wrote to Miró to say that despite the complaints that he had made against Sossier in a previous letter, the interpreter did know the Quapaw language perfectly, and his meager salary was the cause of his discontent. DuBreuil said, moreover, that if the interpreter quit, no one else would take the job because the salary was too low; and besides there was no one who could speak or understand the Quapaw language as well as Sossier could. DuBreuil revealed that the interpreter had twice given him petitions seeking a raise from the governor, but DuBreuil had not passed them along because he didn't think that a raise was in order. But now DuBreuil said that he was of the view that the interpreter's misdeeds were the result of a salary that was too low for a place where the cost of living was quite high.[16] Piernas wrote back about three weeks later, indicating that he would speak with the captain general about the requested raise, but he thought that there would likely be a difficulty about it because of the repeated orders from the court in Madrid to economize. Besides, Piernas said, it didn't seem to him that the interpreter had all that much work to do anyway.[17]

In 1789, Vallière transmitted to Miró a petition from the interpreter Jean Baptiste Sossier asking for a raise. Sossier's petition said that it was impossible for him to live on his salary of fourteen pesos a month. Miró gave him a raise of three pesos a month.[18] It seems quite likely that Sossier served the Spanish as interpreter until the colonial period ended, for the United States trading factory hired him as its interpreter, a position that he held until 31 December 1808.[19] It would appear, then, that Jean Baptiste Sossier was interpreter for the Quapaws for more than twenty-five years.

Notes

Introduction

1. Previous efforts of mine to uncover the history of colonial Arkansas are Morris S. Arnold, *Unequal Laws unto a Savage Race: European Legal Traditions in Arkansas, 1686–1804* (Fayetteville: University of Arkansas Press, 1985) and Morris S. Arnold, *Colonial Arkansas, 1686–1804: A Cultural and Social History* (Fayetteville: University of Arkansas Press, 1991). Morris S. Arnold and Dorothy Jones Core, eds., *Arkansas Colonials* (DeWitt, Ark.: Grand Prairie Historical Society, 1986) is a collection of censuses with some minor commentary interspersed.

2. William T. Hagan, *American Indians* (Chicago: University of Chicago Press, 1993), x.

3. "Sneak Preview: Fill 'er up with History," *Arkansas Democrat-Gazette,* 18 September 1997, page 12B.

Chapter I
Family Ties: Dalliances and Alliances

1. Louise Phelps Kellogg, ed., *Early Narratives of the Northwest, 1634–1699* (New York: Charles Scribner's Sons, 1917), 313; Thomas Falconer, ed., *On the Discovery of the Mississippi* (London: Samuel Clarke, 1844), 84.

2. See, e.g., John Gilmary Shea, ed., *Early Voyages up and down the Mississippi* (Albany, N.Y.: Joel Munsell, 1861), 125.

3. Shea, ed., *Early Voyages,* 127; John Gilmary Shea, ed., *Discovery and Exploration of the Mississippi Valley* (New York: Redfield, 1852), 47; *JR,* 59:155.

4. Shea, ed., *Discovery and Exploration,* 47.

5. Shea, ed., *Early Voyages,* 127.

6. *JR,* 67:253.

7. Margry, 3:453–54.

8. Ibid., 456.

9. Seymour Feiler, ed., *Jean-Bernard Bossu's Travels in the Interior of North America, 1751–1762* (Norman: University of Oklahoma Press, 1962), 65 n.10.

10. Melville B. Anderson, ed., *Relation of Henri de Tonty Concerning the Explorations of LaSalle from 1678 to 1683* (Chicago: The Caxton Club, 1898), 75.

11. Margry, 3:442.

12. Shea, ed., *Discovery and Exploration,* 169.

13. Margry, 2:208; Marion A. Habig, *The Franciscan Père Marquette: A Critical Biography of Father Zénobe Membré, O.F.M.* (New York: Joseph F. Wagner, 1934), 210.

14. Shea, ed., *Early Voyages,* 79.

15. Louise Phelps Kellogg, ed., *Journal of a Voyage to North America* (Chicago: The Caxton Club, 1923) 2:231. See also Feiler, ed., *Bossu's Travels,* 60, for the statement that the Quapaws were "tall, well-built, brave Indians."

16. Margry, 5:402.

17. Margry, 5:402 n.2. Early French travelers almost always described the physical appearance of American Indians in glowing terms. See generally, Laura Schrager Fishman, "How Noble the Savage?: The Image of the American Indian in French and English Travel Accounts, ca. 1550–1680," Ph.D. diss., City University of New York, 1979.

18. Shea, ed., *Early Voyages,* 77.

19. Margry, 2:208; Habig, *The Franciscan Père Marquette,* 210.

20. Antoine Simon Le Page du Pratz, *Histoire de la Louisiane* (Paris: 1758), 2:291.

21. Ralph A. Smith, "Exploration of the Arkansas River by Benard de la Harpe, 1721–22," *AHQ* 10 (Winter 1951): 339, 348.

22. Newton D. Mereness, ed., *Travels in the American Colonies* (New York: Macmillan Co., 1916), 57.

23. Shea, ed., *Early Voyages,* 76.

24. *JR,* 67:261–63.

25. Samuel Dorris Dickinson, ed., *New Travels in North America by Jean-Bernard Bossu, 1770–1771,* (Natchitoches: Northwestern Louisiana State University Press, 1982), 40.

26. For other early discussions of the Quapaws' religious beliefs and practices, see [Henri de Tonty], *An Account of Monsieur de la Salle's Last Expedition and Discoveries in North America* (London: 1698), 83; Falconer, ed., *On the Discovery of the Mississippi,* 64; Shea, ed., *Early Voyages,* 72; Margry, 5:402 n.2; Kellogg, ed., *Journal of a Voyage,* 2:231; Mereness, ed., *Travels,* 58; Smith, "Exploration," 350; Bienville's mémoire, ANC, C^{13C} 1:362; Feiler, ed., *Bossu's Travels,* 63–64; Dickinson, ed., *New Travels,* 39.

27. Melville B. Anderson, ed., *Relation of the Discovery of the Mississipi River, Written from the Narratives of Nicolas de La Salle* (Chicago: The Caxton Club, 1898), 19. See also, to the same effect, Shea, ed., *Discovery and Exploration,* 169.

28. Habig, *The Franciscan Père Marquette,* 209–10; Margry, 2:208; Shea, ed., *Discovery and Exploration,* 169.

29. See, e.g., Mereness, ed., *Travels,* 58; Margry, 5:402.

30. Dickinson, ed., *New Travels,* 42.

31. See, e.g., Father Marquette's observations in *JR,* 59:157.

32. Margry, 3:462.

33. Shea, ed., *Early Voyages,* 127.

34. Ibid.

35. Margry, 3:441.

36. Dickinson, ed., *New Travels,* 39.

37. Anderson, ed., *Relation of Henri de Tonty,* 75.

38. Kellogg, ed., *Early Narratives,* 298.

39. Mereness, ed., *Travels,* 58.

40. J. Leitch Wright Jr., *The Only Land They Knew: The Tragic Story of the American Indians in the Old South* (New York: Free Press, 1981), 8; Charles Hudson, *The Southeastern Indians* (Knoxville: University of Tennessee Press, 1976), 267–68.

41. Kellogg, ed., *Journal of a Voyage,* 2:231.

42. Savoie Lottinville, ed., *A Journal of Travels into the Arkansas Territory during the Year 1819* (Norman: University of Oklahoma Press, 1980), 97.

43. Shea, ed., *Early Voyages,* 72.

44. Mereness, ed., *Travels,* 73.

45. Ibid., 48.

46. Ibid., 58.

47. Le Page du Pratz, *Histoire,* 1:7.

48. Dickinson, ed., *New Travels,* 44.

49. Louis Dubroca, *L'Itinéraire des Français dans la Louisiane* (Paris: 1802), 78–79.

50. Letter from Father Du Poisson, 3 October 1727, *JR,* 67:285.

51. Ibid., 297. For more on French women in early colonial Louisiana, see Mathé Allain, *"Not Worth a Straw": French Colonial Policy in the Early Years of Louisiana* (Lafayette: Center for Louisiana Studies, 1988), 83–88; Vaughan B. Baker, *"Cherchez les Femmes*: Some Glimpses of Women in Early Eighteenth-Century Louisiana," *Louisiana History* 31 (Winter 1990): 21.

52. Dr. and Mrs. T. L. Hodges, "Possibilities for the Archaeologist and Historian in Eastern Arkansas, *AHQ* 2 (June 1943): 141, 156.

53. To take but one example not already alluded to, Dubroca's *Itinéraire* was condemned the very year that it appeared as "a book written in a public library, by a man who, not having been on the spot himself, has made only an unreliable synthesis." See Louis N. Baudry Des Lozieres, *Voyage a la Louisiane, et sur le continent de l'Amerique septentrionale* (Paris: 1802), 264 n.1.

54. But see Arnold, *Unequal Laws,* 80, 81, for some notice of the Francoeur brothers and their Indian wives.

55. Most of this genealogical work was done by Dorothy Jones Core and appeared in the *Grand Prairie Historical Society Bulletin* between 1974 and 1989. See, e.g., the following articles: "Pierre Lefevre of Arkansas," *GPHSB* 17 (April 1974): 14–17; "Pierre Lefevre of Arkansas (Part Two)," *GPHSB* 17 (October 1974): 9–14; "Pierre Lefevre of Arkansas (Part Three)," *GPHSB* 18 (April 1975): 17–20; "Canadian Baugis to Arkansas Bogy," *GPHSB* 18 (October 1975): 3–6; "Canadian Baugis to Arkansas Bogy (Part II)," *GPHSB* 19 (April 1976): 19–23; "Canadian Baugis to Arkansas Bogy

(Part III)," *GPHSB* 19 (October 1976): 36–38; "The Vaugine Arkansas Connection," *GPHSB* 21 (April 1978): 6–24; "Imbeau—A First Family of Arkansas," *GPHSB* 27 (October 1984): 5–12; "Imbeau—A First Family of Arkansas (Part II)," *GPHSB* 28 (October 1985): 2–8; "Valliere Documents," *GPHSB* 32 (April 1989): 2–9. See also Mary P. Fletcher, "A Sketch of Peter Le Fevre," *AHQ* 13 (Spring 1954): 86–89; Myra Vaughan, "Genealogical Notes of the Valliere-Vaugine Family," *AHQ* 15 (Winter 1956): 304–18.

56. See Dave Wallis and Frank Williamson, eds., *A Baptismal Record of the Parishes along the Arkansas River, August 5, 1796 to July 16, 1802* (Pine Bluff, Ark.: Jefferson County Historical Society, 1982).

57. For some information on the Imbeaus and their Quapaw connections, see Margaret Smith Ross, "Squatters Rights: Some Pulaski County Settlers Prior to 1814," *Pulaski County Historical Review* 4 (June 1956): 17, 18–20. For the Francoeurs and their Indian wives, see, e.g., Representation tres respecteuse a Monsieur Demazellieres Capitaine Commandant pour le Roy au Poste des Arques, 17 June 1770, AGI, PC, *leg.* 107:105.

58. W. David Baird, *The Quapaw Indians: A History of the Downstream People* (Norman: University of Oklahoma Press, 1980), 217.

59. Ibid., 217, 219.

60. See Dorothy Jones Core, "Testament François Menard," *GPHSB* 20 (April 1977): 23–24; Morris S. Arnold, "Testament II: François Menard," *GPHSB* 37 (April 1994): 23–26.

61. "An Early Letter from Arkansas Post," *Jefferson County Historical Quarterly* 4 (1973): 29, 30.

62. Amos Stoddard, *Sketches, Historical and Descriptive, of Louisiana* (Philadelphia: Mathew Carey, 1812), 206.

63. The French "poste" is infected with the same ambiguity as the English "post," and thus can be used to describe either a commercial or military outpost. But Joutel referred to Tonty's little settlement on the Arkansas as a "post" as early as 1687, only one year after its settlement, and long before any soldiers were posted there. See Margry, 3:439–40. It appears, therefore, that I erred in stating that "Arkansas Post . . . took its name . . . from the fact that it was a military establishment." See Arnold, *Colonial Arkansas,* 98.

64. For the activities of Couture and the Carolina traders, see Arnold, *Colonial Arkansas,* 7, and Patricia Galloway, "Couture, Tonti, and the English-Quapaw Connection: A Revision," in Hester A. Davis, ed., *Arkansas before the Americans* (Fayetteville: Arkansas Archeological Survey, 1991), 74–94. For Father Foucault, see Linda Carol Jones, "Conversion of the Tamaroas and the Quapaws: An Unlikely Outcome in the Missions of the Seminary of Québec," 56–76, M.A. thesis, University of Arkansas, 1997; Jean Delanglez, *The French Jesuits in Lower Louisiana (1700–1763)* (Washington: Catholic University of America, 1935), 33–35.

65. Verner W. Crane, *The Southern Frontier, 1670–1732* (Ann Arbor: University of Michigan Press, 1929), 90–91.

66. See generally Morris S. Arnold, "The Myth of John Law's German Colony on the Arkansas," *Louisiana History* 31 (Winter 1990): 83–88.

67. *JR,* 67:255.

68. See, e.g., Joan Cain, Virginia Koenig, and Glenn R. Conrad, eds., *The Historical Journal of the Establishment of the French in Louisiana* (Lafayette: Center for Louisiana Studies, 1971), 144, 147; Bougés, "Colonie de la Louisiane, journal historique," 7, 19. Tulane University Library, special collections, M 955.

69. *JR,* 67:261.

70. Jean Delanglez, ed., "Journal of Father Vitry of the Society of Jesus, Army Chaplain during the War against the Chickasaws," *Mid-America* 28 (1941): 30, 34.

71. See, e.g., Preston Holder, "The Fur Trade as Seen from the Indian Point of View," in John Francis McDermott, ed., *The Frontier Re-examined* (Urbana: University of Illinois Press, 1967), 129, 131; Willard H. Rollings, *The Osage: An Ethnohistorical Study of Hegemony on the Prairie-Plains* (Columbia: University of Missouri Press, 1992), 81.

72. *JR,* 67:255–57.

73. For an illuminating discussion of Father Du Poisson's encounter with the Quapaws, see George Sabo III, "Inconsistent Kin: French-Quapaw Relations at Arkansas Post," in Davis, ed., *Arkansas before the Americans,* 122–24. For explanations of the social and cultural meanings of the calumet ceremony that the Quapaws and Caddos employed in greeting Europeans, see George Sabo III, "Rituals of Encounter: Interpreting Native American Views of European Explorers," in Jeannie M. Whayne, ed., *Cultural Encounters in the Early South: Indians and Europeans in Arkansas* (Fayetteville: University of Arkansas Press, 1995), 76–87. See also, for much relevant matter, George Sabo III, "Encounters and Images: European Contact and the Caddo Indians," *Historical Reflections/Reflexions Historiques* 21 (Spring 1995): 217–42.

74. Shea, ed., *Discovery and Exploration,* 47.

75. Shea, ed., *Early Voyages,* 124.

76. In 1690, the Caddos had thirty horses, which they called *cavali,* a word manifestly derived from the Spanish, and which they no doubt acquired from New Mexico. See Falconer, ed., *Discovery of the Mississippi,* 88.

77. Shea, ed., *Discovery and Exploration,* 47. According to Joutel, the Quapaws' trade network also extended to tribes living near New England, from whom they drew "porcelain necklaces made of certain shells." Margry, 3:446.

78. Margry, 3:443.

79. Shea, ed., *Discovery and Exploration,* 47.

80. Margry, 3:460. Cf. ibid., 440–41.

81. Margry, 3:436, 452, 457.

82. Ibid., 452.

83. Margry, 3:451; Shea, ed., *Discovery and Exploration,* 220; Jean Delanglez, ed., *The Journal of Jean Cavelier* (Chicago: Institute of Jesuit History, 1938), 125.

84. Margry, 3:450.

85. ANC, C^{13A} 40:391v, 31 December 1758.

86. ANC, C^{13A} 40:387–91v, 31 December 1758.

87. Denombrement du Poste des Arkansas . . . , AGI, PC, *leg.* 190:111.

88. Gamon de Larochette to Duclos, 11 January 1758, ANC, C^{13A} 40:291.

89. See, e.g., Layssard to ?, 7 November 1758, ANC, C^{13A} 40:332.

90. See Devergès's certificate, dated 24 December 1758, ANC, C^{13A} 40:349.

91. DeClouet to Aubry, 6 December 1768, AGI, PC, *leg.* 107:51. Early in the American period, the head of the Arkansas trading factory reported that the Quapaws hunted only about six weeks a year, having decided to devote their efforts to raising corn and horses to trade with the whites at the Post and with visiting Indian tribes from across the Mississippi. *APLB,* 25, 57.

92. Cain, Koenig, and Conrad, eds., *Historical Journal,* 147.

93. Martha Royce Blaine, "French Efforts to Reach Santa Fe: André Fabry de la Bruyère's Voyage up the Canadian River in 1741–42," *Louisiana History* 20 (Spring 1979): 133, 142.

94. Ibid., 151–52.

95. Smith, "Exploration," 350.

96. Margry, 3:452.

97. Dickinson, ed., *New Travels,* 40.

98. Ibid., 75.

99. *JR,* 67:311–13. Cf. *A Full and Impartial Account of the Company of the Mississippi* (London: 1720), 63: "The *Natchés* have a Government peculiar to themselves, and are the only Nation among whom there is a perfect Submission to their Rulers and some sort of Religious Worship."

100. Delanglez, ed., "Journal of Father Vitry," 35.

101. Ibid.

102. Périer to the minister, 30 April 1727, ANC, C^{13A} 10:215.

103. Diron to the minister, 9 February 1730, ANC, C^{13A} 12:352.

104. Périer to the minister, 10 April 1730, ANC, C^{13A} 12:300.

105. *JR,* 68:217.

106. Périer to the minister, 10 December 1731, ANC, C^{13A} 13:57.

107. Feiler, ed., *Bossu's Travels,* 60–61.

108. Mémoire sur la Louisiane [after 1731], ANC, C^{13A} 13:231.

109. Diron d'Artaguette, 24 June 1731, ANC, C^{13A} 13:145.

110. Salmon to the minister, 21 July 1732, ANC, C^{13A} 15:177; Périer to the minister, 25 July 1732, ANC, C^{13A} 14:68.

111. Périer to the minister, 25 January 1733, ANC, C^{13A} 16:178.

112. Bienville to the minister, 22 April 1734, ANC, C^{13A} 18:153; abstract of Bienville's letters of 15 March and 23 April 1734, ANC, C^{13A} 18:217. Unfortunately, the Quapaws fell in with the Tunicas, who were on a similar mission to theirs, renewed an old quarrel with them, and almost came to blows. When the Tunicas retreated, the Quapaws resumed their search but without success.

113. Abstract of Bienville's letter of 29 May 1738, ANC, C¹³ᴬ 23:77.

114. See, e.g., Vergès's account in ANC, C¹³ᴬ 25:279, reporting on his trip to the Arkansas to reconnoiter a road to the Chickasaws in the fall of 1737; Delanglez, ed., "Journal of Father Vitry," 35; John Gilmary Shea, ed., *Journal de la guerre du Micissippi contre les chicashas* (New York: Cramoisy Press, 1859), 63.

115. Bienville to the minister, 6 May 1740, ANC, C¹³ᴬ 25:42.

116. Shea, ed., *Journal de la guerre,* 63.

117. Ibid., 72. For more information on the Second Chickasaw War, see Margaret Kimball Brown, *"Allons, Cowboys," Illinois Historical Journal* (1983): 273–82; Joseph L. Peyser, "The Chickasaw Wars of 1736 and 1740: French Military Drawings and Plans Document the Struggle for the Lower Mississippi," *Journal of Mississippi History* 44 (February 1982): 1–25.

118. Shea, ed., *Journal de la guerre,* 75.

119. Salmon to the minister, 21 July 1743, ANC, C¹³ᴬ 28:112 (attack on a man named Guillaume and his wife ascending the Mississippi to Arkansas Post); Loubourg to the minister, 30 July 1743, ANC, C¹³ᴬ 28:53 (attack on Arkansas Post *habitant* William Bienvenu).

120. Vaudreuil to La Houssaye, 2 November 1743, *VP,* 295; Vaudreuil to Louboey, 6 November 1743, *VP,* 297.

121. Vaudreuil to the minister, 24 December 1744, ANC, C¹³ᴬ 28:251; *VP,* 195.

122. Vaudreuil to the minister, 30 October 1745, ANC, C¹³ᴬ 29:57; *VP,* 208.

123. Vaudreuil to the minister, 20 March 1747, ANC, C¹³ᴬ 31:17. See also *VP,* 17.

124. Vaudreuil to the minister, 5 November 1748, ANC, C¹³ᴬ 32:122; *VP,* 41.

125. Vaudreuil to the minister, 24 June 1750, ANC, C¹³ᴬ 34:261. The Quapaws delivered some Chickasaw scalps to the governor in 1751 as well. See Vaudreuil to the minister, 10 May 1751, ANC, C¹³ᴬ 35:102.

126. For details of the attack and its aftermath, see Stanley Faye, "The Arkansas Post of Louisiana: French Domination," *LHQ* 26 (July 1943): 633, 684–86; Arnold, *Colonial Arkansas,* 105–7; Vaudreuil to the minister, 22 September 1749, ANC, C¹³ᴬ 33:79; Vaudreuil to Rouile, 22 September 1749, *VP,* 60, 66; Vaudreuil to the minister, 1 February 1750, ANC, C¹³ᴬ 34:251; Vaudreuil to the court, 24 June 1750, *VP,* 250.

127. This was a virtually uniform strategy pursued throughout the province by the French during the colonial Louisiana period. See Joseph Zitomersky, *French Americans—Native Americans in Eighteenth-Century French Colonial Louisiana* (Lund, Sweden: Lund University Press, 1994), 359–87; cf. Carl J. Ekberg, *French Roots in the Illinois Country: The Mississippi Frontier in Colonial Times* (Urbana: University of Illinois Press, 1998), 70.

128. Vaudreuil to the minister, 10 October 1751, ANC, C¹³ᴬ 35:167. See also Vaudreuil to Macarty, 9 September 1751, *VP,* 101; Macarty to Vaudreuil, 20 January 1752, *VP,* 110.

129. Kerlérec to the minister, 15 September 1754, ANC, C¹³ᴬ 38:95.

130. Kerlérec to d'Erneville, 12 September 1754, ANC, C¹³ᴬ 38:95.

Chapter II
An Animal and Human Refuge

1. Willard H. Rollings, "Living in a Graveyard: Native Americans in Colonial Arkansas," in Whayne, ed., *Cultural Encounters*, 38–60.

2. There is a great deal of interesting and useful matter touching on the importance of hunting and the Indian trade to the economy of colonial Arkansas in Gilbert C. Din, "Between a Rock and a Hard Place: The Indian Trade in Spanish Arkansas," in Whayne, ed., *Cultural Encounters*, 112. For discussions of the nature of the Arkansas colonial populace, see Arnold, *Colonial Arkansas*, 53–72, and Morris S. Arnold, "The Significance of Arkansas's Colonial Experience," in Whayne, ed., *Cultural Encounters*, 131.

3. It appears that buffaloes migrated into Arkansas from the Great Plains in the sixteenth and seventeenth centuries. See John H. House, "Buffalo Bones Identified at Lincoln County Archeological Site," *Field Notes*, Arkansas Archeological Survey, No. 248, September/October 1992, 3. See also Erhard Rostlund, "The Geographic Range of the Historic Bison in the Southeast," *Annals of the Association of American Geographers* 50 (June 1960): 395–407. There were, according to one account, still a few buffaloes in Arkansas as late as 1866. See Keith Sutton, ed., *Arkansas Wildlife: A History* (Fayetteville: University of Arkansas Press, 1998), 28.

4. Shea, ed., *Discovery and Exploration*, 44.

5. See Steven G. Platt and Christopher G. Brantley, "Canebrakes: An Ecological and Historical Perspective," *Castanea* 62 (March 1997): 8–21.

6. Ibid., 10.

7. Ibid., 12, 13.

8. Shea, ed., *Early Voyages*, 80.

9. Ibid., 58.

10. Ibid., 65.

11. *JR*, 67:321–23.

12. Anderson, ed., *Relation of Henri de Tonty*, 75.

13. Dickinson, ed., *New Travels*, 36; Shea, ed., *Journal de la guerre*, 24, 27; Mereness, ed., *Travels*, 45.

14. Cain, Koenig, and Conrad, eds., *Historical Journal*, 145.

15. Mereness, ed., *Travels*, 54.

16. Ibid., 85.

17. Ibid., 61, 62, 63, 64, 65, 66.

18. Ibid., 83.

19. Feiler, ed., *Bossu's Travels*, 68.

20. Margry, 3:443; Dickinson, ed., *New Travels*, 41–42, 62. The buffalo was still much in evidence on the Grand Prairie in 1809. In that year, an officer of the American garrison at the Post wrote that the prairie "produces annually a luscious growth of grass which gives pastures to immense droves of cattle . . . At its N.W. extremity it is covered with buffalo and wild horses for whose support it seems to have been

formed." "An Early Letter from Arkansas Post," *Jefferson County Historical Quarterly* 4 (1973): 29, 30.

21. Smith, "Exploration," 351.

22. Ibid., 354, 357, 358, 359, 361.

23. Blaine, "French Efforts to Reach Santa Fe," 133, 142.

24. Dickinson, ed., *New Travels,* 45.

25. S. D. Dickinson, "An Early View of the Ouachita Region," *The Old Time Chronicle* 3 (July 1990): 12, 15.

26. Delanglez, ed., "Journal of Father Vitry," 36.

27. *JR,* 67:285. Buffalo meat had become a staple of the French colonial diet by the 1720s, and no doubt even earlier. See Mereness, ed., *Travels,* 22.

28. *JR,* 67:285.

29. De La Houssaye to Vaudreuil, 22 December 1752, *VP,* 150.

30. Le Page du Pratz, *Histoire,* 1:319–20.

31. Gilbert C. Din, ed., *Louisiana in 1776: A Memoria of Francisco Bouligny* (New Orleans: 1977), 53.

32. Ibid., 46. Buffalo hunting remained good in parts of northeast Arkansas well into the nineteenth century. In 1840, a German hunter encountered a herd of sixteen buffaloes in the Cache River area, and shot one. See Frederick Gerstaeker, *Wild Sports in the Far West* (London and New York: Geo. Routledge & Co., 1854), 208–9. I owe this reference to the kindness of Lance Peacock.

33. François Benjamin Dumont de Montigny, *Mémoires historiques sur la Louisiane* (Paris: 1753), 1:75.

34. Le Page du Pratz, *Histoire,* 2:67–68.

35. Shea, ed., *Journal de la guerre,* 85. A *mémoire* on Louisiana, written about this time, describes Arkansas Post as a place where "the hunt for buffaloes useful to the colony is made." ANC, C^{13C} 1:112v.

36. See, e.g., Layssard to ?, 19 May 1758, ANC, C^{13A} 40:313.

37. For Governor Gálvez's tariff of 1777, reissuing Governor O'Reilly's tariff of 1769, which Gálvez notes has been ignored, see *SMV,* 1:239–40.

38. See Mereness, ed., *Travels,* 82, for a reference to careening a boat "to give it a coat of tallow."

39. Layssard to ?, 13 December 1758, ANC, C^{13A} 40:340.

40. Dickinson, ed., *New Travels,* 41, 42.

41. Le Page du Pratz, *Histoire,* 3:378.

42. Unzaga to Orieta, 22 April 1775, AGI, PC, *leg.* 107:221; Orieta to Unzaga, 12 June 1775, AGI, PC, *leg.* 107:228.

43. Villiers to Gálvez, 20 June 1780, AGI, PC, *leg.* 193:129.

44. Edmund Robert Murphy, *Henry de Tonty, Fur Trader of the Mississippi* (Baltimore: Johns Hopkins Press, 1941), 20.

45. Ibid., 38.

46. Ibid., 39–40.

47. Ibid., 86.

48. N. M. Miller Surrey, *The Commerce of Louisiana during the French Régime, 1699–1763* (New York: Columbia University Press, 1916), hardly ever mentions buffalo hides as an object of trade, though references are found on pages 345, 346 n. 3, and 357. But cf. Le Page du Pratz, *Histoire,* 3:378, where the claim is made that "dried buffalo skins are quite valuable." He also says that buffalo hides were "an object of consideration" because the Indians "prepare them with the wool on so well that they render them more supple than our buffalo," and also "paint them in different colors and wear them." He reported, too, that buffalo hides served the French "as the best blankets, being at one and the same time very warm and very light." Le Page du Pratz, *Histoire,* 2:68.

49. Mémoire sur la Louisiane, ANC, C^{13C} 1:90.

50. *ADM,* 2:121. Cf. Gilbert C. Din and A. P. Nasatir, *The Imperial Osages: Spanish-Indian Diplomacy in the Mississippi Valley* (Norman: University of Oklahoma Press, 1983), 110 n. 52, for a list of traders among the Osages and the amount of peltry that they traded for, all deerskins. See also François Marie Perrin du Lac, *Voyage dans les deux Louisianes* (Lyon: 1805), 226–27, where the author, in describing the peltries produced in the Missouri region, mentions only deerskins.

51. The Osages evidently decided in the eighteenth century that buffalo hides were simply too large and too bulky to transport economically, so they declined to produce them in any significant numbers. See Rollings, *The Osage,* 93.

52. For an account of Osage methods of buffalo hunting, see ibid., 73–78, 83. Tonty says that the Indians of lower Louisiana simply set fire to the canebrakes in which the buffaloes were foraging and shot at them with bows and guns when they emerged. See Henri de Tonty, *Dernieres decouvertes dans l'Amerique septentrionale de M. de la Sale* (Paris: 1697), 194–95.

53. [Baron de Lahontan], *Nouveaux voyages de mr le baron de Lahontan, dans l'Amerique septentrionale* (The Hague: 1709), 1:173–74; Baron Lahontan, *New Voyages to North-America* (London: 1735), 1:133; Reuben Gold Thwaites, ed., *New Voyages to North-America by the Baron de Lahontan* (Chicago: A. C. McClurg & Co., 1905), 1:203–4.

54. Le Page du Pratz, *Histoire,* 1:312–15.

55. Ibid., 2:67–68.

56. Smith, "Exploration," 358.

57. Father Du Poisson reports that, when coming to the Post, he and his company "made a *great kettle* of a bear" between the Yazoo and Arkansas Rivers. *JR,* 67:317. Du Pratz asserts that bear meat was "very good and very healthy." Le Page du Pratz, *Histoire,* 2:88.

58. Bear's oil was a staple of the French colonial diet in Louisiana by 1720. Mereness, ed., *Travels,* 22.

59. Description de La Louisianne dans l'Amérique septentrionalle [undated], ANC, C^1, 187; C. Fred Williams, "The Bear State Image: Arkansas in the Nineteenth Century," *AHQ* 39 (Summer 1980): 99–111.

60. Dumont de Montigny, *Mémoires,* 1:76–77.

61. C. C. Robin, *Voyages dans l'intérieur de la Louisiane* (Paris: 1807), 2:364. Southeastern Indians used bear's oil "as a condiment, a cooking oil, and even as a cosmetic. For use as a cosmetic, they mixed a red pigment into it and scented it with fragrant sassafras and wild cinnamon. They rubbed it into their hair and onto their bodies." They also slathered bear oil on to dried meat, "much as we add mayonnaise to dry luncheon meat." Hudson, *The Southeastern Indians,* 300–301, 302.

62. Le Page du Pratz, *Histoire,* 2:88–89. White settlers in Arkansas continued to use this Indian storage technique well into the nineteenth century. In 1818, Schoolcraft stayed with a family in northern Arkansas who had a "dressed deer-skin, served up much in the shape the animal originally possessed, and filled with bear's oil, and another filled with wild honey, hanging on opposite sides of the fire-place." Henry R. Schoolcraft, *Journal of a Tour into the Interior of Missouri and Arkansaw* (London: 1821), 30–31.

63. Le Page du Pratz, *Histoire,* 2:89–90. See also ibid., 3:385–86, where Du Pratz repeats the claim that bear lard was good for curing rheumatic pains. Du Pratz was quite fascinated by bears, and he devoted fourteen pages to discussing their habits and characteristics. See Le Page du Pratz, *Histoire,* 2:77–90.

64. ANC, C^{13C} 1:362.

65. See Daniel H. Usner Jr., *Indians, Settlers, and Slaves in a Frontier Exchange Economy: The Lower Mississippi Valley before 1783* (Chapel Hill: University of North Carolina Press, 1990), passim, and Daniel H. Usner Jr., "The Frontier Exchange Economy of the Lower Mississippi Valley in the Eighteenth Century," *William and Mary Quarterly* (April 1987), 3^d series, 44:165–92.

66. Orieta to Unzaga, 22 March 1776, AGI, PC, *leg.* 189B:43. See Villiers to Unzaga, 14 December 1776, AGI, PC, *leg.* 190:75 for a similar report.

67. Census of the Post of Arkansas, 7 June 1777, AGI, PC, *leg.* 190:111. Villiers also wrote twice to the governor to ask that a tariff be established for the Indian traders at the Post, a tariff that fixed the number of deerskins that it took to buy a blanket, "and so in proportion" for other goods. But this does not necessarily imply that deerskins, or many of them, were being traded at the Post, for a deerskin was a common unit of currency (money of account) in colonial Louisiana. See Villiers to Gálvez, 19 July 1779, AGI, PC, *leg.* 192:168; Villiers to Gálvez, 21 July 1779, AGI, PC, *leg.* 192:172.

68. *APLB,* 40, 53, 61.

69. Dumont de Montigny, *Mémoires,* 1:75. La Harpe noted that on his way up the Arkansas River his Indian hunter "killed two deer for dinner." Smith, "Exploration," 352.

70. Shea, ed., *Discovery and Exploration,* 48. Cf. Anderson, ed., *Relation of Nicolas de La Salle,* 21, where he reports that La Salle received fifty or sixty buffalo hides as a present from the Quapaws in 1682. See also Margry, 3:461, where Joutel reported that the Quapaws offered to trade some otter skins "and a few beaver" for European goods.

71. Shea, ed., *Discovery and Exploration,* 219.

72. Favrot's petition to Desmazellières, 27 June 1770, AGI, PC, *leg.* 107:109.

73. *APLB,* Treat to Davy, 15 April 1805, 63–64.

74. *APLB,* Treat to Davy, 27 February 1806, 53.

75. *APLB,* Treat to Davy, 15 April 1806, 61. In concluding that the denizens of Arkansas did not produce many deerskins and furs during most of the eighteenth century, I find myself in substantial disagreement with M. Carmen González López-Briones, "Spain in the Mississippi Valley: Spanish Arkansas, 1762–1804," 168–72, Ph.D. thesis, Purdue University, 1983.

76. ANC, C^{13A} 30:242, 250. See also ANC, C^{13C} 1:112, 113, a *mémoire* written before 1750, where the author remarks of the Arkansas country that "there is considerable buffalo hunting done there."

77. Philip Pittman, *The Present State of the European Settlements on the Missisippi* (London: 1770), 40.

78. Abraham P. Nasatir, *Spanish War Vessels on the Mississippi, 1792–1796* (New Haven, Conn.: Yale University Press, 1968), 155–56, 161–62.

79. Vaudreuil to Maurepas, 25 March 1748, *VP,* 25.

80. D'Orgon to Vaudreuil, 7 October 1752, *VP,* 136.

81. *Resancement General des habitants, voyageurs, femmes, enfans, esclaves, chevaux, beufs, vaches, cochons, etc. de Post des Akansa, 1749.* Vaudreuil Papers, LO. 200, Huntington Library, San Marino, California.

82. La Grandcour(?) to Governor [1766?], AGI, PC, *leg.* 107:605.

83. Bienville to Maurepas, 20 August 1735, ANC, C^{13A} 20:155v; Fontaine Martin, *A History of the Bouligny Family and Allied Families* (Lafayette: Center for Louisiana Studies, 1990), 30–31.

84. Michel to ?, 20 July 1751, ANC, C^{13A} 35:327. According to one authority, Delinó's successor, Captain La Houssaye, had a monopoly over trade with the Quapaws, a privilege from which he was supposed to repay himself for the expenses that he incurred in rebuilding the fort at Arkansas Post. See Faye, "The Arkansas Post of Louisiana: French Domination," 712.

85. Vaudreuil to ?, 12 May 1751, ANC, C^{13A} 35:117v.

86. DeClouet to Aubry, 6 December 1768, AGI, PC, *leg.* 107:51; Din and Nasatir, *Imperial Osages,* 67.

87. Leyba to Unzaga, 10 May 1771, AGI, PC, *leg.* 107:244. He repeated his request in Leyba to Unzaga, 6 June 1771, AGI, PC, *leg.* 107:247. Leyba's accounts, and some details of how he fared as a trader on the Arkansas, may be viewed in Leyba to Unzaga, 13 April 1772, AGI, PC, *leg.* 107:286; Leyba to Unzaga, 27 April 1772, AGI, PC, *leg.* 107:291; Unzaga to Leyba, 9 June 1772, AGI, PC, *leg.* 107:304; Leyba to Unzaga, 29 July 1772, AGI, PC, *leg.* 107:320; Leyba to Unzaga, 7 June 1775, AGI, PC, *leg.* 107:361; Leyba to Unzaga, 7 October 1773, AGI, PC, *leg.* 107:369; and Unzaga to Leyba, 26 December 1773, AGI, PC, *leg.* 107:370–71. In Leyba to Unzaga, 13 April 1772, AGI, PC, *leg.* 107:286, Leyba asks the governor for a monopoly on the sale of wine and brandy at the Post. He promised to keep alcohol out of the hands of the Indians, who commonly got drunk and did damage, and opined that his

monopoly would not simply redound to his own benefit but would serve the interests of the *habitants* as well.

88. Vigo's passport to go up the Arkansas River for three months, dated 20 July 1774, is in AGI, PC, *leg.* 107:199. See also Unzaga to Orieta, 9 August 1774, AGI, PC, *leg.* 107:97; Orieta to Unzaga, 17 October 1774, AGI, PC, *leg.* 107:200; Unzaga to Orieta, 23 February 1775, AGI, PC, *leg.* 107:218; and Menard's certificate stating that Vigo was unfit for service because of "seven ulcers in the left leg occasioned by a defect in the blood," 23 February 1775, AGI, PC, *leg.* 107:218. For a full-blown biography of Vigo (a Sardinian by birth), see Bruno Roselli, *Vigo: A Forgotten Builder of the American Republic* (Boston: Stratford Company, 1933).

89. DuBreuil to Miró, 4 February 1784, AGI, PC, *leg.* 107:490.

90. In 1777 there were only four merchants living at the Post in addition to Villiers. See Denombrement du Poste des Arkansas et de la Nation Sauvage de ce Nom, AGI, PC, *leg.* 190:111.

91. Desmazellières to Unzaga, 27 June 1770, AGI, PC, *leg.* 107:68 (extract); Desmazellières to Unzaga, 27 June 1770, AGI, PC, *leg.* 107:107 (full letter).

92. Villiers to Gálvez, 15 May 1780, AGI, PC, *leg.* 193A:143.

93. Villiers to Gálvez [1781?], AGI, PC, *leg.* 194:79.

94. Villiers to Gálvez, 5 December 1778, AGI, PC, *leg.* 192:112.

95. *ADM,* 1:166. On the character of many of the Arkansas hunters, see also Arnold, *Unequal Laws,* 37–38, 78–83.

96. LaGrandcour (?) to Governor [1766?], AGI, PC, *leg.* 107:605.

97. Desmazellières to Mon General, 15 July 1770, AGI, PC, *leg.* 107:111.

98. Cf. Peter Stern, "Marginals and Acculturation in Frontier Society," in Robert H. Jackson, ed., *New Views of Borderlands History* (Albuquerque: University of New Mexico Press, 1998), 157 at 166: "The protests of Spanish religious, civil, and military authorities, even taking into account exaggeration and racial prejudice, leave little doubt that the Borderlands were in a dangerous state of lawlessness."

99. For lists of deserters, libertines, tobacco smugglers, salt smugglers, and other exiles sent to Louisiana during Law's regime, see, e.g., Winston De Ville, *Louisiana Colonials: Soldiers and Vagabonds* (Baltimore: Genealogical Publishing Co., 1963); Glenn R. Conrad, *The First Families of Louisiana* (Baton Rouge, La.: Claitor's Publishing Division, 1970). Though in May of 1720 the king in council forbad the further forced immigration of criminals to Louisiana, see *Arrest du conseil déstat du Roy . . . du 9 May 1720,* the custom did not entirely cease, and the moral character of the colony continued to be affected by deportees. See Carl A. Brasseaux, "The Moral Climate of French Colonial Louisiana, 1699–1763," *Louisiana History* 27 (Winter 1986): 27–41. See also Gwendolyn Midlo Hall, *Africans in Colonial Louisiana: The Development of Afro-Creole Culture in the Eighteenth Century* (Baton Rouge: Louisiana State University Press, 1992), 5–8; Allain, *"Not Worth a Straw,"* 68, 84. Thomas N. Ingersoll, *Mammon and Manon in Early New Orleans* (Knoxville: University of Tennessee Press, 1999), 35 *et seq.* provides solid evidence that the lawlessness and immorality of French New Orleans has been greatly exaggerated, but, at

370 n.6, the author gives at least a qualified endorsement to my views on this matter with respect to Arkansas Post, citing Arnold, *Unequal Laws,* 203–8. For an extended treatment of the social structure of the Arkansas region in the colonial period, see Arnold, *Colonial Arkansas,* 53–72.

100. Villiers to Gálvez, 2 February 1779, AGI, PC, *leg.* 192:121. The same year, Athanase DeMézières complained that many Arkansas Post hunters were "introducing themselves among the Cadaudakioux [Caddos], to the prejudice of their creditors." *ADM,* 2:251.

101. Leyba to Unzaga, 25 March 1773, AGI, PC, *leg.* 107:344.

102. Gálvez to Villiers, 11 April 1777, AGI, PC, *leg.* 1:139.

103. Villiers to Gálvez, 28 May 1777, AGI, PC, *leg.* 190:101. Villiers's instructions to Lopez are dated 29 May 1777 and are in AGI, PC, *leg.* 190:109. Another reason that commandants hesitated to allow traders upriver was that they sometimes sold to the Osages, and the Quapaws complained that the Osages simply used these supplies to attack Quapaw and French hunters. See Leyba to Unzaga, 9 October 1772, AGI, PC, *leg.* 107:326.

104. Gálvez to Villiers, 6 June 1777, AGI, PC, *leg.* 1:156 (draft in AGI, PC, *leg.* 190:104).

105. Villiers to Gálvez, 9 June 1777, AGI, PC, *leg.* 190:110.

106. Gálvez to Villiers, 11 August 1777, AGI, PC, *leg.* 1:179.

107. Gálvez to Villiers, 10 August 1779, AGI, PC, *leg.* 112:161.

108. A partial copy of this ordinance is attached to Villiers to Gálvez, 25 February 1780, AGI, PC, *leg.* 193A:125. The governor acknowledged receipt of the ordinance and approved its application to Raymond Vassière, in Gálvez to Villiers, 7 May 1780, AGI, PC, *leg.* 193A:137 (draft). A seizure made pursuant to it is recorded in Villiers to Gálvez, 25 June 1780, AGI, PC, *leg.* 193A:151 and *SMV,* 1:379. For a similar proceeding, see Oath of Jacob Dortch, 29 January 1781, AGI, PC, *leg.* 194:47.

109. Gálvez to Villiers, 17 February 1778, AGI, PC, *leg.* 113:777.

110. Miró to Vallière, 6 March 1789, AGI, PC, *leg.* 6:334.

111. Vallière to Miró, 1 October 1789, AGI, PC, *leg.* 15:472.

112. Miró to DuBreuil, 30 April 1784, AGI, PC, *leg.* 3.

113. DuBreuil to Bouligny, 2 September 1784, AGI, PC, *leg.* 107:552.

114. Vallière to Miró, 1 October 1789, AGI, PC, *leg.* 15:473.

115. Miró to Vallière, 29 September 1789, AGI, PC, *leg.* 6:1233.

116. *SMV,* 2:184.

117. A copy of this agreement is attached to Vilemont to Gayoso, 31 March 1798, AGI, PC, *leg.* 215A:256.

118. Vilemont to Gayoso, 31 March 1798, AGI, PC, *leg.* 215A:258.

119. According to Captain Dubreuil, the *pro rata* rule for creditors other than the last outfitter was "a custom as old as the settlement of this Post." See DuBreuil to Miró, 1 June 1784, AGI, PC, *leg.* 107:539.

120. Gayoso to Vilemont, 24 April 1798, AGI, PC, *leg.* 215A:265. At about the same time, it developed that Louis Jardela, one of the very merchants who had

signed the agreement, had himself petitioned the governor for a license to go upriver to trade, a move that of course brought protestations from other Post merchants. See Petition of François Vaugine and Joseph Bougy, 19 April 1798, AGI, PC, *leg.* 215A:289. Gayoso made it clear that Jardela had an uncontestable right to hunt upriver, so long as he did no trading. See Gayoso to Vilemont, 24 April 1798, AGI, PC, *leg.* 215A:270 (draft). Vilemont therefore gave Jardela permission to hunt on the river. Vilemont to Gayoso, 15 June 1798, AGI, PC, *leg.* 215A:269.

121. Vilemont to Gayoso, 15 November 1798, AGI, PC, *leg.* 215A:81.

122. See, e.g., Governor (?) to Desmazellières, 19 December 1770, AGI, PC, *leg.* 107:135.

123. Lefevre to ?, 26 June 1796, AGI, PC, *leg.* 7:124; Carondelet to ?, 21 July 1786, AGI, PC, *leg.* ?:126.

124. Vallière to Miró, 31 December 1787, AGI, PC, *leg.* 13:872.

125. Miró to Vallière, 11 February 1788, AGI, PC, *leg.* 119:529.

126. Delinó to Miró, 18 December 1790, AGI, PC, *leg.* 16:1041.

127. ? to Delinó, 4 June 1791, AGI, PC, *leg.* 122A:232.

128. Caso to Salcedo, 6 August 1802, AGI, PC, *leg.* 77:13; Vilemont to Gayoso, 15 June 1798, AGI, PC, *leg.* 215A; Gayoso to Vilemont, 14 July 1798, AGI, PC, *leg.* 215A:268. See also Governor to Vilemont, 30 March 1801, AGI, PC, *leg.* 72:223 (draft), in which trading rights with the Abenakis and Cherokees in an amount of fifteen hundred pesos are granted to François Vaugine because Andrés Fagot did not have sufficient capital to finance it all.

129. Casa-Calvo to Vilemont, 19 March 1801, AGI, PC, *leg.* 70B:258.

130. Treat to Dearborn, 27 March 1806, *APLB,* 57.

131. Casa-Calvo to Vilemont, 27 March 1801, AGI, PC, *leg.* 70B:267. It is unclear whether the trade contemplated was with Indians, white hunters, or both.

132. Casa-Calvo to Vilemont, 20 March 1801, AGI, PC, *leg.* 70B:260.

133. DeClouet to Aubry, 6 December 1768, AGI, PC, *leg.* 107:51.

134. Desmazellières to Mon General, 7 October 1770, AGI, PC, *leg.* 107:134.

135. Desmazellières to Mon General, 18 August 1770, AGI, PC, *leg.* 107:124.

136. Unzaga to Desmazellières, 19 December 1770, AGI, PC, *leg.* 107:135.

137. Villiers to Gálvez, 15 September 1779, AGI, PC, *leg.* 192:182.

138. Desmazellières to Mon General, 7 August 1770, AGI, PC, *leg.* 107:121.

139. Leyba to Unzaga, 10 May 1771, AGI, PC, *leg.* 107:244.

140. Leyba to Unzaga, 25 March 1773, AGI, PC, *leg.* 107:344.

141. See Lefevre to ?, 26 June 1796, AGI, PC, *leg.* 7:124.

142. See Dorothy Jones Core, "First Bankruptcy in Arkansas County Records," *GPHSB* 16 (October 1973): 8, 11.

143. Treat to Davy, 15 November 1805, *APLB,* 33–34.

144. Treat to Davy, 1 September 1806, *APLB,* 124.

145. Pittman, *European Settlements,* 40.

146. Smith, "Exploration," 348.

147. Bougés, *Colonie de la Louisiane journal historique,* 11, 12.

148. Bienville's *mémoire* [undated], ANC, C¹³C 1:362.

149. See Mildred Mott Wedel, "Claude-Charles Dutisné: A Review of His 1719 Journeys," *Great Plains Journal* 12 (Fall 1972): 5–25 (Part I); Mildred Mott Wedel, "Claude-Charles Dutisné: A Review of His 1719 Journeys," *Great Plains Journal* 12 (Spring 1973): 147–73 (Part II).

150. See Mildred Mott Wedel, "J. B. Bénard, Sieur de La Harpe: Visitor to the Wichitas in 1719," *Great Plains Journal* 10 (Spring 1971): 37–70. But see George H. Odell, *Final Report on Archaeological Excavations Conducted between May and July, 1988, at the Lasley Vore Site (34TU-65), Jenks, Oklahoma* (1989), where the author posits that a site in present-day Tulsa is the place where La Harpe contacted the Tawakoni in 1719.

151. Blaine, "French Efforts to Reach Santa Fe," 133, 145.

152. See Mildred Mott Wedel, *The Deer Creek Site, Oklahoma: A Wichita Village Sometimes Called Ferdinandina, An Ethnohistorian's View* (Oklahoma City: Oklahoma Historical Society, 1981), 33.

153. Louisiana salted meats continued to find a market in the Islands until the very end of the colonial period. For instance, on 13 November 1802 the *Moniteur de la Louisiane* reported that the Spanish ship *Activa* had sailed for the Islands on 5 November "loaded with salted meats."

154. Wedel, *The Deer Creek Site,* 36–49.

155. Ibid., 45, 72.

156. Ibid., 44.

157. Michel to the minister, 20 July 1751, ANC, C¹³A 35:322.

158. Delanglez, ed., "Journal of Father Vitry," 34 n. 25.

159. Wedel, *The Deer Creek Site,* 45. Mrs. Wedel's translation of the census here is occasionally confused.

160. Ibid., 47–48.

161. Ibid., 49.

162. Arnold, *Unequal Laws,* 112.

163. Ibid., 91.

Chapter III
The French and Quapaw Alliance Illustrated

1. See *Robes of Splendor: Native American Painted Buffalo Hides* (New York: New Press, 1993), 28, 56–57, 91, and 136–37, for illustrations and discussion of this skin. There is another skin in the Musée de l'Homme, depicting hunters, animals, and dancers wearing buffalo heads (see Figure 8), that probably also has an Arkansas connection. See ibid., 65, 72, 73, 134–35. This skin may have captured the dance of the wild animal hunt described by Jean-Bernard Bossu or the buffalo dance described by Lahontan. For an account of these dances, see Samuel D. Dickinson, "Quapaw Indian Dances," *Pulaski County Historical Review* 32 (Fall 1984): 42, 46.

In the print department of the Bibliothèque Nationale in Paris, there are two volumes that include an engraving of the painted hide that is the subject of this chapter. See Of.4b tome I/folio and Of.4, Pet. fol. Neither volume, however, contains any indication of when the engravings were executed or of who executed them. They appear to belong to the last quarter of the eighteenth century.

2. Baird, *The Quapaw Indians*, 5.

3. See, e.g., ibid., 10–11. There was formerly a fourth village, Tonguinga, but it was consolidated with Tourima by 1727. See *JR*, 67:319. Father Charlevoix had reported this consolidation as early as 1720; but La Harpe, writing of conditions in 1722, said that the two villages still had a separate existence. Kellogg, ed., *Journal of a Voyage*, 2:230; Smith, "Exploration," 350.

4. See, e.g., the 1779 map of the Post of Arkansas in Arnold, *Colonial Arkansas*, 14–15, where the legend refers to *Akansas des 3 Villages*.

5. George P. Horse Capture, "From Museums to Indians: Native American Art in Context," in *Robes of Splendor*, 61, 91. In contrast, several earlier publications had identified the robe as Quapaw. See Anne Vitart, "Chronique d'une rencontre en terre de Canada," in Daniel Lévine, ed., *Amérique continent imprévu: la rencontre de deux mondes* (Paris: Bordas, 1992), 89, 106. See also, for what seems to be the earliest published picture of our painting, Manuel Ballesteros Gaibrois and Paul Kirchhoff, *Arte antiguo norteamericano: pieles de bisonte pintadas* (Madrid: Tipografía de Archivos, 1934), 6, where the authors attribute the robe to the Quapaws. Gordon Brotherston, *Book of the Fourth World: Reading the Native Americas through Their Literature* (Cambridge: Cambridge University Press, 1992), 26, 181–82, identifies the skin as Quapaw. But the author misreads one of the village names as "Cahokia," and my interpretation of the events portrayed on the skin differs considerably from his. See also Marius Barbeau, *Indian Days on the Western Prairies* (Ottawa: National Museum of Canada, 1960), 225–26, for a short notice of the skin that is the subject of this chapter.

6. Anne Vitart, "From Royal Cabinets to Museums: A Composite History," in *Robes of Splendor*, 27, 54. The hide was in the collection of the public library in Versailles by 1869; and if it was part of the collection of the Marquis de Sérent, from which much of this library's collection came, then it was in France by "about 1786" when the Marquis formed his collection. See *Cabinet de Curiosités et d'Objets d'Art de la Bibliothèque Publique de la Ville de Versailles, Catalogue* (Versailles: 1869), 1:21.

The suggestion made in Araceli Sánchez Garrido, "Plains Indian Collections of the Museo de América," *European Review of Native American Studies* 6 (1992): 21, 25, that the Musée de l'Homme robe collection antedates 1713 is not based on any evidence. Sánchez speculates that painted hides in the Museo de América in Madrid might at one time have been part of the same collection as the painted hides in the Musée de l'Homme, that the Madrid robes might have come from Cardinal Luis de Borbón, who might have inherited them from Felipe V, who came to Spain in 1713 and might have brought the hides with him because he might have inherited them from some supposed Dauphin of France. The difficulty with all this is that not a single one of the links in this fanciful chain has any support for it. There is no evidence even that the Madrid skins came from Luis de Borbón. See Paz Cabello Carro, *Coleccionismo americano indígena en la España del siglo xviii* (Madrid: Ediciones de Cultura Hispánica, 1989), 167–68. Sánchez relies for his views on a previous article (see Manuel Ballesteros Gaibrois, "Pieles de bisonte pintadas: tres ejemplares de Museo Arqueologico Nacional," *Tierra Firme* [1935], 65), but in that article Ballesteros simply made the reasonable suggestion that the Madrid hides and the Paris hides had been part of the same collection at one point and that the Madrid hides were sent from Paris because of the Bourbon family connection. He makes no suggestion about when that might have happened. The simple truth is that none of the Madrid robes "has any documented pre-1865 collection history." Sánchez Garrido, "Plains Indian Collections of the Museo de América," 29 n. 21.

7. Horse Capture, "Gallery of Hides," in *Robes of Splendor,* 136.

8. Margry, 1:599; Kellogg, ed., *Early Narratives,* 298.

9. See, e.g., Ann Linda Bell and Patricia Galloway, eds., "Voyage Made from Canada Inland Going Southward during the Year 1682," in Robert S. Weddle, ed., *La Salle, the Mississippi, and the Gulf: Three Primary Documents* (College Station: Texas A & M University Press, 1987), 29, 62; and Dumont de Montigny, *Mémoires historiques,* 1:142. On the general subject of the shape of Quapaw buildings, see Michael P. Hoffman, "Quapaw Structures, 1673–1834, and Their Comparative Significance," in Davis, ed., *Arkansas before the Americans,* 55–68.

10. Hoffman, "Quapaw Structures," 60; George Sabo III, *Paths of Our Children: Historic Indians of Arkansas* (Fayetteville: Arkansas Archeological Survey, 1992), 33–34.

11. Feiler, ed., *Bossu's Travels,* 62.

12. Dickinson, ed., *New Travels,* 39. For Quapaw council houses, see also Sabo, *Paths of Our Children,* 33. The sources also mention an important house of the Quapaws called the *cabanne de valeur* (house of valor) where religious ceremonies evidently took place. See Arnold, *Colonial Arkansas,* 132–33. Whether this building was different from the council house is not clear.

13. After I first came to this conclusion in Morris S. Arnold, "Eighteenth-Century Arkansas Illustrated," *AHQ* 53 (Summer 1994): 119, 122, I discovered that I was hardly the first to do so. The files in the Musée de l'Homme themselves contain notes made by Paul Kirschoff in 1934 that identify the European settlement depicted in our painting as "without doubt the French fort that was situated . . . on the lower course of the Arkansas River." Similarly, in 1948 an eminent architectural historian wrote of Arkansas Post that a "picturesque view of this little settlement, showing four French houses, may be seen in an Indian painting on deerskin [*sic*] still preserved in Paris." Charles E. Peterson, "French Landmarks Along the Mississippi," *Magazine Antiques* 53 (April 1948): 286.

14. Arnold, *Colonial Arkansas,* 31, 99–101.

15. Ibid., 31.

16. Ibid., 31, 105–6.

17. Mereness, ed., *Travels,* 72.

18. Vermilion pigment (mercuric sulfide) was one of the commonest items traded or given as presents to the Indians in French Louisiana. See Gregory Waselkov, "French Colonial Trade in the Upper Creek Country," in John A. Walthall and Thomas E. Emerson, eds., *Calumet & Fleur-de-Lys: Archaeology of Indian and French Contact in the Midcontinent* (Washington: Smithsonian Institution Press, 1992), 35, 40.

19. Henry Reed Stiles, ed., *Joutel's Journal of La Salle's Last Voyage, 1684–7* (Albany, N.Y.: Joseph McDonough, 1906), 182, 183.

20. Shea, ed., *Early Voyages,* 129.

21. John Pope, *A Tour through the Southern and Western Territories of the United States of North America; the Spanish Dominions on the River Mississippi, and the Floridas; the Countries of the Creek Nations; and Many Uninhabited Parts* (Richmond, Va.: John Dixon, 1792), 26.

22. Feiler, ed., *Bossu's Travels,* 63. To the same effect, see ibid., 65.

23. Jean Marie Shea, ed., *Relation de la Mission du Missisipi du Seminaire de Québec en 1700* (New York: Presse Cramoisy, 1861), 41.

24. Dickinson, ed., *New Travels,* 38 and n. 3; Feiler, ed., *Bossu's Travels,* 63 and n. 6.

25. See, e.g., Shea, ed., *Relation de la Mission du Missisipi,* 41 (drums) (per St. Cosme in 1699); Weddle, ed., *La Salle, the Mississippi, and the Gulf,* 47 (drums) (per Minet in 1682); Feiler, ed., *Bossu's Travels,* 63 and n. 6 (drums and bells) (per Bossu in 1751); Dickinson, ed., *New Travels,* 81 (drums and reed flutes) (per Bossu in 1770). The drums were clay pots over which a skin was stretched.

26. Lottinville, ed., *A Journal of Travels,* 97–98. Father Marquette had offered a similar observation almost one hundred fifty years earlier. See *JR,* 59:157.

27. Early accounts of the Quapaws' use of the calumet are extremely numerous. There is a detailed description of it in 1699 by Father St. Cosme in Shea, ed., *Relation de la Mission du Missisipi,* 40–42; Shea, ed., *Early Voyages,* 71–72; and Kellogg, ed., *Early Narratives,* 358–59. For an illuminating discussion of the meaning of the calumet and the various Quapaw ceremonies associated with it, see Sabo, "Inconsistent Kin," 105–12. There is an excellent reconstruction of a Quapaw calumet ceremony in Dickinson, "Quapaw Indian Dances," 42–44.

28. Shea, ed., *Early Voyages,* 130.

29. James Owen Dorsey, "Kwapa Folk-Lore," *Journal of American Folklore* 8 (January–March 1895): 130.

30. Henri Joutel, "Remarques de Joustel sur l'ouvrage de Tonty relatif à la Louisiane," Service Hydrographique Archives, Paris, 115–19, no. 12, f. 16.

31. Mereness, ed., *Travels,* 58. It appears from this passage that Quapaw painted skins were the object of trade. It is possible therefore that the hide with which this article deals was intended for export (i.e., for sale) at the time that it was painted. Whether the skin was intended to be worn is not altogether clear. Although it is perhaps not technically a robe because the hair has been removed, Indians used such skins as wrappers during warm weather. See John Canfield Ewers, *Plains Indian Painting: A Description of an Aboriginal Art* (Stanford University, Calif.: Stanford

University Press, 1939), 1. Among the Plains Indians, there is evidence that women produced the skins that exhibited geometric designs, while men produced those containing representative figures. Ewers, *Plains Indian Painting,* 7.

32. *JR,* 67:257–58. *Mataché* may derive from an Algonquian word that passed into Canadian French, whence it traveled to Louisiana in the eighteenth century. See William A. Read, *Louisiana-French* (Baton Rouge: Louisiana State University Press, 1931), 95–96. It survives in Louisiana French in such expressions as "un chien mataché" (a spotted dog) and in modern English in the word "matchcoat."

33. *JR,* 67:324–25.

34. Horse Capture, "From Museums to Indians: Native American Art in Context," 91.

35. The Quapaws and the Mitchegamea (an Illinois tribe) may have been at odds briefly in the late seventeenth century, see Samuel Dorris Dickinson, "Lake Mitchegamas and the St. Francis," *AHQ* 43 (Autumn 1984): 197, 203; but in general the Quapaws and the Illinois tribes were firmly allied in the French interest throughout the French colonial period as the text that follows demonstrates.

36. Margry, 2:96. Stanley Faye, "Indian Guests at the Spanish Arkansas Post," *AHQ* 4 (Summer 1945): 93.

37. For the parts played by the Illinois and the Quapaws in the First Chickasaw War, see Faye, "The Arkansas Post of Louisiana: French Domination," 633, 675; Clarence Walworth Alvord, *The Illinois Country, 1673–1818* (Urbana and Chicago: University of Illinois Press, 1987), 176–80. For the parts played by the Illinois and the Quapaws in the Second Chickasaw War, see Delanglez, ed., "Journal of Father Vitry"; Shea, ed., *Journal de la guerre;* Clarence Walworth Alvord, *The Illinois Country,* 182–83; Arnold, *Colonial Arkansas,* 101–4.

38. For more on this, see page 77–78 below.

39. Faye, "The Arkansas Post of Louisiana: Spanish Domination," 629, 643; Faye, "Indian Guests at the Spanish Arkansas Post," 93, 94–95; González López-Briones, "Spain in the Mississippi Valley: Spanish Arkansas, 1762–1804," 95, 123–24.

40. Arni Brownstone, *War Paint: Blackfoot and Sarcee Painted Buffalo Robes in the Royal Ontario Museum* (Toronto: Royal Ontario Museum, 1993), 11. See also Ewers, *Plains Indian Painting,* 17.

41. Since I first posited a Quapaw origin for this painting in Arnold, "Eighteenth-Century Arkansas Illustrated," other scholars have agreed with this attribution. See, e.g., G. Malcolm Lewis, "Hiatus Leading to a Renewed Encounter," in G. Malcolm Lewis, ed., *Cartographic Encounters: Perspectives on Native American Mapmaking and Map Use* (Chicago: University of Chicago Press, 1998), 55, 63; G. Malcolm Lewis, "Recent and Current Encounters," in ibid., 71, 86; Patricia Galloway, "Debriefing Explorers: Amerindian Information in the Delisles' Mapping of the Southeast," in ibid., 223, 228 ("apparently from a Quapaw Indian source").

42. Margry, 1:599.

43. See above, page 24. While it is probable that the hide was painted to commemorate and record a past raid against the Chickasaws, it is just possible that it

portrays a plan of action to be undertaken in the future. In fact, though this seems even less likely, it might have been executed to memorialize the making of a treaty and the obligations of the Quapaws under it. In that case, this buffalo skin would be both a work of art and a legal document.

44. W. H. Falconer, ed., "Arkansas and the Jesuits in 1727—A Translation," *Publications of the Arkansas Historical Association* 4 (1917): 352, 368–69; Delanglez, ed., "Journal of Father Vitry," 34.

45. See AGI, PC, *leg.* 190: 112–13, a census of the Quapaw nation that indicates the positions of the Indian villages relative to the Spanish fort.

46. This suggestion is made in Horse Capture, "Gallery of Hides," 136. The letters are of a color somewhat different from the black paint used elsewhere on the skin and may well have been drawn in ink.

47. Arnold, *Colonial Arkansas,* 105.

48. *VP,* 60.

49. Ibid., 250.

50. Patricia Galloway, ed., *Mississippi Provincial Archives: French Dominion, 1749–1763* (Baton Rouge: Louisiana State University Press, 1984), 5:76.

51. Baird, *The Quapaw Indians,* 28, 31.

52. Arnold, *Colonial Arkansas,* 27, 30–31, 180 n. 6.

53. Dunbar Rowland and A. G. Sanders, eds., *Mississippi Provincial Archives, 1729–1740: French Dominion* (Jackson: Mississippi Department of Archives and History, 1927), 1: 228, 367.

54. Rollings, *The Osage,* 118, 128.

55. Dickinson, ed., *New Travels,* 40.

56. Rochemore to the minister, 23 June 1760, ANC, C^{13A} 42:121.

57. Pittman reports "a barrack . . . , commanding officer's house, a powder magazine, and a magazine for provisions, and an apartment for the commissary." Pittman, *European Settlements,* 40. This might be read to mean that there were five buildings in the fort. But in a letter written on 17 December 1765, the magazine for provisions and the apartment for the commissary are not separated by a comma, indicating, perhaps, that the apartment was in the magazine. This would mean that the fort contained only four buildings. See John Francis McDermott, ed., *Captain Philip Pittman's The Present State of the European Settlements on the Missisippi* (Memphis, Tenn.: Memphis State University Press, 1977), LIV.

58. Perhaps some specialist may notice something in the design of the flintlocks, or the style of the painting, or the manner in which the enemy's hair is arranged, that will confirm my conclusions as to the date and content of this skin, or provide further clues with respect to these matters. Perhaps, too, a chemical and physical analysis might help fix the date that this work was executed and identify the kinds of paint that were employed. I would also welcome help on the identity of the extraordinary cross-like finials on the eaves of the French buildings!

59. For a synopsis of some of the Quapaw activities against the Osages, see Arnold, *Colonial Arkansas,* 112–24.

60. David I. Bushnell Jr., "Native Villages and Village Sites East of the Mississippi," *Bulletin of the Bureau of American Ethnology* (Washington: Government Printing Office, 1919), 69:68–69.

61. Mereness, ed., *Travels,* 57.

62. Feiler, ed., *Bossu's Travels,* 65.

63. Shea, ed., *Early Voyages,* 130. See also Samuel D. Dickinson, "Shamans, Priests, Preachers, and Pilgrims at Arkansas Post," in Davis, ed., *Arkansas before the Americans,* 95, 96.

64. Interestingly, in the cosmology of the Osages (Dhegihan Sioux cousins of the Quapaws), the sun represented the east and the moon the west. Garrick A. Bailey, ed., *The Osage and the Invisible World from the Works of Francis La Flesche* (Norman: University of Oklahoma Press, 1995), 33. The same was true of the Cherokees. See Hudson, *The Southeastern Indians,* 132.

65. For these activities, see Arnold, *Colonial Arkansas,* 101–2.

66. I am indebted to Malcolm Lewis for pointing this out to me.

67. For the diachronic character of much Indian art, see Arni Brownstone, *War Paint,* 26–30.

68. G. Malcolm Lewis, "The Indigenous Maps and Mapping of North American Indians," *Map Collector* 9 (1979): 25.

69. G. Malcolm Lewis, "Indicators of Unacknowledged Assimilations from Amerindian *Maps* on Euro-American Maps of North America: Some General Principles Arising from a Study of La Vérendrye's Composite Map, 1728–29," *Imago Mundi* 38 (1986): 9. On the matter of North American Indian maps, see also Gregory A. Waselkov, "Indian Maps of the Colonial Southeast," in Peter H. Wood, Gregory A. Waselkov, and M. Thomas Hatley, eds., *Powhatan's Mantle: Indians in the Colonial Southeast* (Lincoln: University of Nebraska Press, 1989), 292–343.

70. ANC, C^{13A} 25: 279, 288v.

71. Patricia Galloway doubts that the painting exhibits "significant French influence" or signs of "a *métis* provenience" because of "the elements shared with other 'event transcriptions' in the southeastern region." See Patricia Galloway, "Debriefing Explorers: Amerindian Information in the Delisles' Mapping of the Southeast," in G. Malcolm Lewis, ed., *Cartographic Encounters: Perspectives on Native American Mapmaking* (Chicago: University of Chicago Press, 1998), 223, 238 n. 18. I have no difficulty with the proposition that the map-like qualities of the painting might owe nothing to European influence. It is interesting, however, that Dr. Galloway provides no examples of southeastern "event transcriptions" that preserve cardinal direction in a rough way so as to have a colorable claim to being a map.

72. For these, see Samuel Wilson Jr., "The Drawings of François Benjamin Dumont de Montigny," and Samuel Wilson Jr., "Louisiana Drawings by Alexandre De Batz," in Jean M. Farnsworth and Ann M. Masson, eds., *The Architecture of Colonial Louisiana: Collected Essays of Samuel Wilson, Jr., F.A.I.A.* (Lafayette: Center for Louisiana Studies, 1987), 105–7, 261–74. The Le Bouteux drawing of New Biloxi is reproduced in Arnold, *Colonial Arkansas,* 10–11.

Chapter IV
French and Spanish Hearts as One?

1. Dickinson, ed., *New Travels,* 45.

2. See Aubry to the minister, 25 February 1765, ANC, C¹³ᴬ 45:41; Alvord and Carter, eds., *The Critical Period, 1763–1765,* 175, 352, 362, 368, 378, 379, 383, 456; John Richard Alden, *John Stuart and the Southern Colonial Frontier* (Ann Arbor: University of Michigan Press, 1944), 201, 203.

3. La Grandcour to Ulloa, 21 April 1766, AGI, PC, *leg.* 107:606.

4. Spanish judicial records, 15 October 1769, Louisiana History Center, New Orleans; DeClouet to O'Reilly, 14 November 1769, AGI, PC, *leg.* 107:23. See also DeClouet to Aubry (?), AGI, PC, *leg.* 107:36. Cf. Desmazellières to Unzaga, 15 May 1770, AGI, PC, *leg.* 107:89 (commandant assures Quapaws that the Spanish had the same affection for them that the French had and that the Spanish thought the same way that the French did).

5. DeClouet to Aubry (?), 14 February 1769, AGI, PC, *leg.* 107:7.

6. DeClouet to O'Reilly (?), 20 September 1769, AGI, PC, *leg.* 107:18.

7. DeClouet to O'Reilly, 13 December 1769, AGI, PC, *leg.* 107:26.

8. Desmazellières to O'Reilly, 15 January 1770, AGI, PC, *leg.* 107:76.

9. Desmazellières to O'Reilly, 15 May 1770, AGI, PC, *leg.* 107:89.

10. Desmazellières to Unzaga, 18 August 1770, AGI, PC, *leg.* 107:124.

11. Leyba to Unzaga, 22 November 1771, AGI, PC, *leg.* 107:267.

12. Unzaga to Leyba, 14 March 1772, AGI, PC, *leg.* 107:282.

13. Leyba to Unzaga, 25 March 1773, AGI, PC, *leg.* 107:359; Leyba to Unzaga, 18 June 1773, AGI, PC, *leg.* 107:360.

14. Leyba to Unzaga, 6 June 1771, AGI, PC, *leg.* 107:247.

15. Leyba to Unzaga, 18 June 1773, AGI, PC, *leg.* 107:360.

16. Orieta to Unzaga, 6 June 1774, AGI, PC, *leg.* 107:190.

17. Orieta to Unzaga, 14 July 1774, AGI, PC, *leg.* 107:191.

18. There is a great deal of correspondence in the record on the subject of these insignia. See, e.g., Desmazellières to O'Reilly, [1770], AGI, PC, *leg.* 107:93; Orieta to Unzaga, 14 July 1774, AGI, PC, *leg.* 107:191; Leyba to Unzaga, 10 May 1771, AGI, PC, *leg.* 107:241; Leyba to Miró, 22 November 1771, AGI, PC, *leg.* 107:267 (medals); Leyba to Unzaga, 19 December 1771, AGI, PC, *leg.* 107:273; Leyba to Unzaga, 18 April 1772, AGI, PC, *leg.* 107:287 (medals); Leyba to Unzaga, 9 October 1772, AGI, PC, *leg.* 107:326 (medals); Leyba to Unzaga, 25 March 1773, AGI, PC, *leg.* 107:344 (medals); Leyba to Unzaga, 26 November 1773, AGI, PC, *leg.* 107:374 (medals); Villiers to Gálvez, 12 October 1777, AGI, PC, *leg.* 190:117 (medals); Villiers to Miró, 31 December 1787, AGI, PC, *leg.* 13:876 (patents and medals); Miró to Villiers, 11 February 1788, AGI, PC, *leg.* 5:312 (patents and medals); Miró to Navarro, 24 April 1788, AGI, PC, *leg.* 87 (draft) (medals and gorgets); Miró to Vallière, 12 May 1788, AGI, PC, *leg.* 119:553 (draft) (medals and gorgets); Miró to Vallière, 24 May 1788, AGI, PC, *leg.* 5:621 (medals); Vallière to Miró, 22 December 1788, AGI, PC, *leg.*

14:676 (medals and gorgets); Delinó to Carondelet, 10 May 1792, AGI, PC, *leg.* 25:439; Delinó to Carondelet, 15 May 1793, AGI, PC, *leg.* 26:921 (patents and medals); Salcedo to Caso y Luengo, 7 May 1803, AGI, PC, *leg.* 76:998 (medal and patent).

19. Delanglez, ed., "Journal of Father Vitry," 51.

20. DuBreuil to Miró, 31 January 1785, AGI, PC, *leg.* 107:558.

21. Vallière to Miró, 4 April 1789, AGI, PC, *leg.* 15:342; Miró to Vallière, 27 May 1789, AGI, PC, *leg.* 6:690.

22. Quapaw census of 17 April 1784, AGI, PC, *leg.* 107:510.

23. Census of the Quapaws, 3 August 1777, AGI, PC, *leg.* 190:112.

24. Vilemont to Governor, 5 August 1798, AGI, PC, *leg.* 215A:273.

25. Governor to Vilemont, 22 August 1798, AGI, PC, *leg.* 215A:274 (draft).

26. For the *cabanne de valeur,* see Arnold, *Unequal Laws,* 25.

27. Orieta to Unzaga, 18 March 1776, AGI, PC, *leg.* 189B:48.

28. Villiers to Gàlvez, 22 March 1778, AGI, PC, *leg.* 191:229.

29. Desmazellières to Unzaga, [1770?], AGI, PC, *leg.* 107:93.

30. Leyba to Unzaga, 25 May 1773, AGI, PC, *leg.* 107:359.

31. Leyba to Unzaga, 18 June 1773, AGI, PC, *leg.* 107:360.

32. See, e.g., Arnold, *Unequal Laws,* 69.

33. Villiers to Piernas, 1 December 1781, AGI, PC, *leg.* 194:76.

34. Villiers to Governor, 31 March 1782, AGI, PC, *leg.* 195:200.

35. DuBreuil to Miró, 17 January 1783, AGI, PC, *leg.* 107:387; DuBreuil to Miró, 18 February 1783, AGI, PC, *leg.* 107:393; DuBreuil to Miró, 1 March 1783, AGI, PC, *leg.* 107:396.

36. Gunsmiths could augment their meager salaries by doing contract black-smith work for the garrison. See, e.g., AGI, PC, *leg.* 107:489 (bill for handcuffs and nails manufactured by Antoine Lepine, dated 30 January 1784). Gunsmiths/black-smiths no doubt also did work for the hunters, merchants, and *habitants,* like making horseshoes and chandeliers.

37. Leyba to Unzaga, 10 May 1771, AGI, PC, *leg.* 107:241.

38. Leyba to Unzaga, 6 June 1771, AGI, PC, *leg.* 107:247.

39. Villiers to Gálvez, 19 July 1779, AGI, PC, *leg.* 192:168. See also Villiers to Gálvez, 15 September 1779, AGI, PC, *leg.* 192:185. It is a reasonable guess that he was the son of Pierre Joseph Lambert, who was a soldier in the French garrison on 31 December 1758.

40. Gálvez to Villiers, 9 August 1779, AGI, PC, *leg.* 112:155 (draft in AGI, PC, *leg.* 192:177).

41. Villiers to Gálvez, 15 September 1779, AGI, PC, *leg.* 192:182.

42. DuBreuil to Morales, 8 August 1783, AGI, PC, *leg.* 608:28; DuBreuil to Miró, 11 August 1783, AGI, PC, *leg.* 107:460; Dubreuil to Navarro, 11 August 1783, AGI, PC, *leg.* 608:22.

43. DuBreuil to Miró, 14 April 1785, AGI, PC, *leg.* 107:565.

44. DuBreuil to Miró, 15 October 1785, AGI, PC, *leg.* 107:577.

45. Miró to DuBreuil, 20 December 1785, AGI, PC, *leg.* 107:585.

46. DuBreuil to Miró, 9 August 1786, AGI, PC, *leg.* 13:38.

47. Miró to DuBreuil, 29 August 1786, AGI, PC, *leg.* 117A:55 (draft in AGI, PC, *leg.* 4:541).

48. Vilemont to Gayoso, 20 April 1799, and Vilemont to Gayoso, 20 August 1799, in "Memorial of the Heirs of Carlos de Vilemont," *Documents of the 24th Congress, 2d Session,* No. 89 (Washington: 1837).

49. Shea, ed., *Discovery and Exploration,* 48.

50. Ibid., 169–70.

51. *JR,* 67:255.

52. Orieta to Unzaga, 19 May 1774, AGI, PC, *leg.* 107:179 (Quapaws agree not to allow Englishmen in Arkansas); Villiers to Unzaga, 28 September 1776, AGI, PC, *leg.* 189B:61 (same).

53. Leyba to Unzaga, AGI, PC, *leg.* 107:325 (chief complained about his present).

54. DeClouet to Aubry, 27 February 1768, AGI, PC, *leg.* 107:36; Desmazellières to O'Reilly, 15 January 1770, AGI, PC, *leg.* 107:76.

55. For references to these trips, see, e.g., DeClouet to Aubry (?), 14 February 1769, AGI, PC, *leg.* 107:7; Villiers to Gálvez, 30 August 1778, AGI, PC, *leg.* 191:268; DuBreuil to Miró, 16 December 1786, AGI, PC, *leg.* 13:51; Delinó to Carondelet, 9 June 1792, AGI, PC, *leg.* 25:610.

56. La Grandcour to Ulloa, 21 April 1766, AGI, PC, *leg.* 107:606; DeClouet to Aubry, 14 February 1769, AGI, PC, *leg.* 107:7; DeClouet to O'Reilly, AGI, PC, *leg.* 107:18; Desmazellières to Unzaga, AGI, PC, 15 May 1770, *leg.* 107:89; Orieta to Unzaga, 6 June 1774, AGI, PC, *leg.* 107:190; Orieta to Unzaga, 14 July 1774, AGI, PC, *leg.* 107:191.

57. See, e.g., Orieta to Unzaga, 15 May 1770, AGI, PC, *leg.* 107:142, for a report of an occasion on which the Quapaws and *habitants* joined together (*se juntáron*) to come see the commandant, and they had a meeting (*consulta*) about a threat of attack from the Choctaws.

58. See, e.g., Leyba to Unzaga, 30 April 1773, AGI, PC, *leg.* 107:353; Orieta to Unzaga, 17 October, 1774, AGI, PC, *leg.* 107:200; Orieta to Unzaga, 12 November 1774, AGI, PC, *leg.* 107:207.

59. Desmazellières to Unzaga, 7 August 1770, AGI, PC, *leg.* 107:121; Desmazellières to Unzaga, 18 August 1770, AGI, PC, *leg.* 107:124.

60. Desmazellières to Unzaga, 7 October 1770, AGI, PC, *leg.* 107:134; Leyba to Unzaga, 10 May 1771, AGI, PC, *leg.* 107:241; Leyba to Unzaga, 6 June 1771, AGI, PC, *leg.* 107:247.

61. Desmazellières to Unzaga (?), 4 March 1770, AGI, PC, *leg.* 107:60; Desmazellières to Unzaga, 26 May 1770, AGI, PC, *leg.* 107:60; Desmazellières to Unzaga, AGI, PC, *leg.* 107:96.

62. Ulloa (?) to DeClouet, [1768], AGI, PC, *leg.* 107:3v.

63. Unzaga to Orieta, 20 July 1770, AGI, PC, *leg.* 107:150.

64. Unzaga to Desmazellières, 27 July 1770, AGI, PC, *leg.* 119.

65. DeClouet to Mon Commandant, 26 December 1768, AGI, PC, *leg.* 107:54.

66. Desmazellières to Unzaga [1770], AGI, PC, *leg.* 107:93.

67. Leyba to Unzaga, 18 April 1772, AGI, PC, *leg.* 107:287.

68. Leyba to Unzaga, 9 October 1772, AGI, PC, *leg.* 107:326.

69. Leyba to Unzaga, 30 April 1773, AGI, PC, *leg.* 107:357.

70. Leyba to Unzaga, 22 November 1771, AGI, PC, *leg.* 107:267.

71. Orieta to Unzaga, 25 December 1775, AGI, PC, *leg.* 189B:29.

72. Leyba to Unzaga, 30 April 1773, AGI, PC, *leg.* 107:355.

73. Villiers to Gálvez, 20 June 1780, AGI, PC, *leg.* ?:129.

74. ANC, C^{13A} 40:357 (Sarrazin was interpreter); ANC, C^{13A} 40:381 (François Sossier was interpreter). See also, Dickinson, ed., *New Travels,* 46, where Bossu mentions "[t]he interpreter whom I had asked for (because during my stay in France I had somewhat forgotten the *Akanças* language)." For a treatment of the duties of Indian interpreters during the French colonial period in Louisiana, see Patricia Galloway, "Talking with Indians: Interpreters and Diplomacy in French Louisiana," in Winthrop D. Jordan and Sheila L. Skemp, eds., *Race and Family in the Colonial South* (Jackson: University Press of Mississippi, 1987), 109–29.

75. Already in 1722 La Harpe employed as interpreter a soldier of the Arkansas garrison, "who spoke several dialects of the country." Cain, Koenig, and Conrad, eds., *Historical Journal,* 147. In 1733, Coulange wrote that he had told the Quapaws that if they joined in the war against the Chickasaws he would march with them along with an interpreter. It is unclear whether this person was a regular employee of the garrison. See ANC, C^{13A} 17:256.

76. Orieta to Unzaga, 1 June 1770, AGI, PC, *leg.* 107:144.

77. Orieta to Unzaga, 5 December 1770, AGI, PC, *leg.* 107:159. See also *SMV,* 2:406, where Delinó revealed that he had sent two hunters who "know how to speak several Indian languages" to an Indian congress near the St. Francis River that included representatives from the Chickasaw, Mascouten, Cherokee, Shawnee, Abenaki, and Sauk tribes, to learn what they were up to.

78. ANC, C^{13A} 40:354; Leyba to Unzaga, 10 May 1771, AGI, PC, *leg.* 107:241.

79. Leyba to Unzaga, 27 July 1771, AGI, PC, *leg.* 107:256.

80. Leyba to Miró, 22 November 1771, AGI, PC, *leg.* 107:267. Landroni served as interpreter from 1 May until the end of September 1771. Leyba to Unzaga, 2 August 1773, AGI, PC, *leg.* 107:363.

81. Leyba to Miró, 22 November 1771, AGI, PC, *leg.* 107:267.

82. Leyba to Unzaga, 18 April 1772, AGI, PC, *leg.* 107:287.

83. See Robert R. Rea, "Redcoats and Redskins on the Lower Mississippi, 1763–1776: The Career of Lt. John Thomas," *Louisiana History* 11 (Winter 1970): 5–35.

84. Leyba to Unzaga, 12 June 1772, AGI, PC, *leg.* 107:308.

85. Rea, "Redcoats and Redskins," 25.

86. Leyba to Unzaga, 15 June 1772, AGI, PC, *leg.* 107:310.

87. Dickinson, ed., *New Travels,* 40.

88. Leyba to Unzaga, 15 June 1772, AGI, PC, *leg.* 107:310. Further details on the interpreters and their activities can be found in Appendix II.

89. See Layssard to ?, 13 December 1758, ANC, C^{13A} 40:339.

90. Delanglez, ed., "Journal of Father Vitry," 35. See also ANC, C^{13A} 17:356, where Coulange wrote to Bienville that the Quapaws had told him that Bienville had promised them a present during their recent visit to New Orleans.

91. For lists of presents, see, e.g., AGI, PC, *leg.* 107:225 (1775 present); AGI, PC, *leg.* 189B:52 (1776 present); AGI, PC, *leg.* 193A:165 (1780 present); AGI, PC, *leg.* 608:39 (1783 present); AGI, PC, *leg.* 107:511–19 (1784 present); AGI, PC, *leg.* 95:9 (1802 present); AGI, PC, *leg.* 2359:211 (undated).

92. AGI, PC, *leg.* 107:225.

93. DeClouet to Mon General [Aubry], 21 May 1768, AGI, PC, *leg.* 107:44.

94. Desmazellières to O'Reilly [1770], AGI, PC, *leg.* 107:63v.

95. Villiers to Gálvez, 28 May 1777, AGI, PC, *leg.* 190:100.

96. For complaints, see DeClouet to Mon General [Aubry], 31 March 1768, AGI, PC, *leg.* 107:41; for promises to send, see Aubry (?) to DeClouet, 23 July 1768, AGI, PC, *leg.* 107:4v; same to DeClouet, 16 October 1768, AGI, PC, *leg.* 107:5.

97. *SMV,* 1:154.

98. Desmazellières to O'Reilly, 4 March 1770, AGI, PC, *leg.* 107:80 (extract in AGI, PC, *leg.* 107:60v).

99. Leyba to Unzaga, 6 June 1771, AGI, PC, *leg.* 107:247.

100. Leyba to Unzaga, 24 June 1772, AGI, PC, *leg.* 107:312.

101. Leyba to Unzaga, 9 October 1772, AGI, PC, *leg.* 107:326.

102. Leyba to Unzaga, 17 December 1772, AGI, PC, *leg.* 107:337.

103. Leyba to Unzaga, 6 April 1773, AGI, PC, *leg.* 107:348.

104. Villiers to Unzaga, 28 May 1777, AGI, PC, *leg.* 189B:57. The 1776 present may have been sent in February of that year. See Unzaga to Villiers, 29 February 1776, AGI, PC, *leg.* 189B:41. If so, it should have arrived in the middle of April.

105. ? to Villiers, 6 February 1781, AGI, PC, *leg.* 194:50. A general scarcity of goods during the Revolutionary War made it difficult for the Spanish to honor their commitments to their Indian allies. Din and Nasatir, *The Imperial Osages,* 120–21.

106. For other correspondence concerning the annual present, see Villiers to Gálvez, 1 June 1778, AGI, PC, *leg.* 191:252 (going to distribute present even though guns are missing); Gálvez to Villiers, 26 August 1778, AGI, PC, *leg.* 1:633 (items missing from present delivered to Mme. Villiers); Villiers to Piernas, 23 December 1780, AGI, PC, *leg.* 193A:175 (Quapaws' present late; promised Angaska that he can come to see governor if it has not arrived by the end of the year); Morales to DuBreuil, 13 February 1783, AGI, PC, *leg.* 608:38 (bill of lading for present sent) (another copy, AGI, PC, *leg.* 84:812); Morales to DuBreuil, 26 February 1783, AGI, PC, *leg.* 608:39 (list of goods in Quapaw present); Morales to DuBreuil, 20 July 1784, AGI, PC, *leg.* 84:820 (bill of lading of Quapaw present sent); DuBreuil to Morales, 31 January 1785, AGI, PC, *leg.* 608:30 (received Quapaw present, much of it missing and of bad quality); Navarro to DuBreuil, 23 December 1785, AGI, PC, *leg.* 7:37 (Quapaw present coming on Illinois convoy); ? to DuBreuil, 4 March 1786, AGI, PC, *leg.* 608:40 (Quapaw present loaded on boat); Navarro to DuBreuil, 31 January 1787, AGI, PC, *leg.* 87:700 (bill of lading for Quapaw present); Navarro to Vallière, 28 February 1788, AGI, PC, *leg.* 87:706 (bill of lading for Quapaw present); Vallière

to Miró, 4 April 1789, AGI, PC, *leg.* 15:340 (received Quapaw present for 1789); Vallière to Miró, 1 October 1789, AGI, PC, *leg.* 15:485 (received Quapaw present for next year); Miró to Delinó, 3 March 1791, AGI, PC, *leg.* 8:287 (bill of lading for Quapaw present); Delinó to Carondelet, 15 May 1793, AGI, PC, *leg.* 26:924 (received Quapaw present); Vilemont to Carondelet, 28 July 1794, AGI, PC, *leg.* 29:682 (received Quapaw present); Gayoso to Vilemont, 13 March 1795, AGI, PC, *leg.* 43:1013 (Quapaw present loaded on galley); Vilemont to Gayoso, 28 April 1795, AGI, PC, *leg.* 48:1618 (received Quapaw present from Mississippi squadron); Vilemont to Governor, 24 March 1798, AGI, PC, *leg.* 215A:254 (Quapaws' present late); Vilemont to Lopez, 10 April 1801, AGI, PC, *leg.* 608:46 (received Quapaw presents); Morales to Caso, 29 May 1802, AGI, PC, *leg.* 608:60 (bill of lading for Quapaw present sent) (bill of lading attached); Caso to Morales, 6 August 1803, AGI, PC, *leg.* 608:52 (received Quapaw present).

Chapter V
Competing Fathers and Quapaw European Policy

1. Desmazellières to Unzaga, 4 March 1770, AGI, PC, *leg.* 107:60v (extract).

2. Desmazellières to Unzaga [undated], AGI, PC, *leg.* 107; Desmazellières to Unzaga [1770 ?], AGI, PC, *leg.* 107:93.

3. Desmazellières to Unzaga, 4 March 1770, AGI, PC, *leg.* 107:60v (extract); Desmazellières to Unzaga, 26 May 1770, AGI, PC, *leg.* 107:91.

4. Desmazellières to Unzaga, 7 June 1770, AGI, PC, *leg.* 107:98.

5. Leyba to Unzaga, 22 November 1771, AGI, PC, *leg.* 107:267.

6. Leyba to Unzaga, 26 November 1773, AGI, PC, *leg.* 107:374.

7. Unzaga to Orieta, 27 June 1775, AGI, PC, *leg.* 107:230.

8. Orieta to Unzaga, 25 December 1775, AGI, PC, *leg.* 189B:29.

9. ? to DeClouet, 3 May 1768, AGI, PC, *leg.* 107:3; ? to DeClouet, [1768], AGI, PC, *leg.* 107:3v; DeClouet to Mon General, 28 April 1768, AGI, PC, *leg.* 107:43; DeClouet to Mon General, 8 July 1768, AGI, PC, *leg.* 107:48.

10. ? to DeClouet, 3 May 1768, AGI, PC, *leg.* 107:3; Leyba to Unzaga, 18 April 1772, AGI, PC, *leg.* 107:287; Leyba to Unzaga, 27 April 1772, AGI, PC, *leg.* 107:291. The Tunicas at this time were located on the English side of the Mississippi about two miles upriver from Pointe Coupée. See Jeffrey P. Brain, *Tunica Archaeology* (Cambridge: Peabody Museum of Archaeology and Ethnology, 1988), 42. The reference to the Tunicas here, however, is probably a reference to the English post at Manchac.

11. DeClouet to Mon General, 8 July 1768, AGI, PC, *leg.* 107:48.

12. DeClouet to Mon General, 26 July 1768, AGI, PC, *leg.* 107:50. DeClouet identifies the Englishman only as Stuart, but he was no doubt Charles Stuart, whom John Stuart (no relation) had appointed to the post of Deputy Superintendent of Indian Affairs for West Florida in 1765. See Helen Louise Shaw, *British Administration of Southern Indians, 1756–1783* (Lancaster, Pa.: Lancaster Press, 1931), 43–44.

13. Orieta to Unzaga, 31 May 1775, *leg.* 107:226. It was also called "the English Arkansaws." *SMV,* 1:264.

14. John Bradley had established himself in the fort at Natchez when it was abandoned in 1768. See *SMV,* 1:71.

15. Desmazellières to O'Reilly [1770], AGI, PC, *leg.* 107:86.

16. Leyba to Unzaga, 27 April 1772, AGI, PC, *leg.* 107:291.

17. For this official's activities, see Rea, "Redcoats and Redskins."

18. Leyba to Unzaga, 26 May 1772, AGI, PC, *leg.* 107:301.

19. DeClouet to Aubry, 14 February 1769, AGI, PC, *leg.* 107:7.

20. DeClouet to Aubry, 25 February 1769, AGI, PC, *leg.* 107:9. Orieta reported the next year that the "Englishwoman who established herself on the other side of the Mississippi" had "left for Manchac." Orieta to Unzaga, 1 June 1770, AGI, PC, *leg.* 107:144.

21. Orieta to Unzaga, 1 June 1770, AGI, PC, *leg.* 107:144. Four years later, there were three Englishmen living in the Quapaw village who were married to Quapaw women. See Orieta to Unzaga, 14 July 1774, AGI, PC, *leg.* 107:191.

22. Leyba to Unzaga, 26 November 1773, AGI, PC, *leg.* 107:374.

23. Orieta to Unzaga, 14 July 1774, AGI, PC, *leg.* 107:191.

24. Ibid.; Orieta to Unzaga, 30 October 1774, AGI, PC, *leg.* 107:205.

25. Villiers to Unzaga, 28 September 1776, AGI, PC, *leg.* 189B:61.

26. Villiers to Unzaga, 26 October 1776, AGI, PC, *leg.* 190:70.

27. Villiers to Unzaga, 4 November 1776, AGI, PC, *leg.* 190.

28. Villiers to Unzaga, 29 November 1776, AGI, PC, *leg.* 190.

29. Denombrement du Poste des Akanzas . . . , 3 August 1777, AGI, PC, *leg.* 190:111.

30. Villiers to Gálvez, 22 March 1778, AGI, PC, *leg.* 229.

31. Villiers to Gálvez, 16 April 1777, AGI, PC, *leg.* 190:96.

32. DeClouet to Aubry, 13 January 1769, AGI, PC, *leg.* 107:6.

33. DeClouet to Aubry, 14 February 1769, AGI, PC, *leg.* 107:7.

34. Desmazellières to Aubry, 2 June 1770, AGI, PC, *leg.* 107:96.

35. Desmazellières to O'Reilly, 4 June 1770, AGI, PC, *leg.* 107:66.

36. Desmazellières to O'Reilly, 16 June 1770, AGI, PC, *leg.* 107:101.

37. Cazenonpoint to O'Reilly, 12 September 1770, AGI, PC, *leg.* 107:131.

38. Orieta to Unzaga, 1 May 1775, AGI, PC, *leg.* 107:222. The war party returned a few weeks later without engaging the enemy. Orieta to Unzaga, 31 May 1775, AGI, PC, *leg.* 107:226.

39. Cazenonpoint to Unzaga, 12 September 1770, AGI, PC, *leg.* 107:131.

40. DeClouet to Aubry (?), 25 February 1769, AGI, PC, *leg.* 107:9.

41. Orieta to Unzaga, 25 December 1775, AGI, PC, *leg.* 189B:29.

42. Delanglez, ed., "Journal of Father Vitry," 42.

43. DeClouet to O'Reilly (?), 20 September 1769, AGI, PC, *leg.* 107:18.

44. La Grandcour to Ulloa, 24 April 1766, AGI, PC, *leg.* 107:606.

45. Leyba to Unzaga, 6 June 1771, AGI, PC, *leg.* 107:247.

46. DeClouet to Aubry, 1 September 1769, AGI, PC, *leg.* 107:16.

47. Aubry (?) to DeClouet [1768], AGI, PC, *leg.* 107:3v.

48. For a comment on this well known fact of life in colonial Louisiana, see Din, ed., *Louisiana in 1776*, 63.

49. Desmazellières to Unzaga, 6 October 1770, AGI, PC, *leg.* 107:133.

50. Orieta to Unzaga, 12 November 1770, AGI, PC, *leg.* 107:156.

51. Orieta to Unzaga, 18 April 1776, AGI, PC, *leg.* 189B:48. The machinations of the British at Manchac were well known to the Spanish government. "The English sub-delegate in Manchac," Francisco Bouligny wrote, "does nothing else daily but attempt to attract the Indians who are on our lands, particularly the Arkansas." Din, *Louisiana in 1776*, 67.

52. Villiers to Gálvez, 28 May 1777, AGI, PC, *leg.* 190:100.

53. Census of the Quapaw nation, 3 August 1777, AGI, PC, *leg.* 190:112.

54. Villiers to Gálvez, 28 May 1777, AGI, PC, *leg.* 190:100.

55. Census of the Quapaw nation, 3 August 1777, AGI, PC, *leg.* 190:112.

56. Villiers to Gálvez, 14 August 1777, AGI, PC, *leg.* 190:115.

57. DuBreuil to Miró, 17 January 1783, AGI, PC, *leg.* 107:387; DuBreuil to Miró, 18 February 1783, AGI, PC, *leg.* 107:393; DuBreuil to Miró, 1 March 1783, AGI, PC, *leg.* 107:396.

58. Villiers to Gálvez, 29 July 1780, AGI, PC, *leg.* 193A:163.

59. For this incident, see Samuel Dorris Dickinson, trans., *Spain and the Cherokee and Choctaw Indians in the Second Half of the Eighteenth Century, by Manuel Searrano y Sanz* (Idabel, Okla.: Potsherd Press, 1995), 9.

60. *SMV,* 1:430–31.

61. Villars to Gálvez, 6 August 1782, AGI, PC, *leg.* 195:528.

62. DuBreuil to Miró, 5 May 1783, AGI, PC, *leg.* 107:403.

63. DuBreuil to Miró, 22 May 1783, AGI, PC, *leg.* 107:433.

64. Miró to DuBreuil, 12 May 1784, AGI, PC, *leg.* 107:533.

65. DuBreuil to Miró, 14 April 1785, AGI, PC, *leg.* 107:565. See also DuBreuil to Navarro, 14 April 1785, AGI, PC, *leg.* 602:32.

66. Din and Nasatir, *The Imperial Osages,* 59, 73–74, 77, 108, 109, 122, 125, 135, 138, 170, 203, 213, 223, 237, 239, 282, 283, 307, 341.

67. Ibid., 340.

68. See the 1791 census of Arkansas Post in Arnold and Core, eds., *Arkansas Colonials,* 42–46.

69. See, e.g., Din and Nasatir, *Imperial Osages,* 47 n. 41.

70. See, e.g., ibid., 66–67, 73, 76, 83, 163.

71. Leyba to Unzaga, 30 April 1773, AGI, PC, *leg.* 107:353.

72. Din and Nasatir, *Imperial Osages,* 95.

73. Ibid., 114, 124.

74. Ibid., 169.

75. Rollings, *The Osages,* 140. Professor Rollings emphasizes the amount of cooperation that existed between the Osages and the Quapaws in the eighteenth century and the evidence that their enmity was not as strong as that between the Osages

and other tribes connected with the prairie-plains region. See ibid., 138–42. Because there were numerous groups and bands of the Osages by the end of the eighteenth century, it is somewhat risky to generalize about Quapaw and "Osage" relations.

Chapter VI
Whose Law, Whose Religion?

1. A distinguished example of this genre is Robert A. Williams Jr., *The American Indian in Western Legal Thought: The Discourses of Conquest* (New York: Oxford University Press, 1990). Despite its comprehensive title, Professor Williams's book does not deal with French legal attitudes toward the Indians or with the experience in Louisiana. Other recent contributions recognize the uniqueness of Louisiana and the extent to which the Indian nations there retained their sovereignty. For an excellent example, see Michael James Forêt, "Red over White: Indians, Deserters, and French Colonial Louisiana," in Patricia Galloway, ed., *Proceedings of the Seventeenth Meeting of the French Colonial Historical Society* (Lanham, Md.: University Press of America, 1993), 79–89. The invasion metaphor had some currency in earlier twentieth-century historiography, but it was probably popularized by Francis Jennings, *The Invasion of America: Indians, Colonialism, and the Cant of Conquest* (Chapel Hill: University of North Carolina Press, 1976).

2. Yasuhide Kawashima, *Puritan Justice and the Indian: White Man's Law in Massachusetts, 1630–1763* (Middletown, Conn.: Wesleyan University Press, 1986), 21–41.

3. Ibid., 34. For examples of treaties purporting to extend English law over Indians, see Colin G. Calloway, ed., *Dawnland Encounters: Indians and Europeans in Northern New England* (Hanover, N.H.: University Press of New England, 1991), 100–14.

4. James P. Ronda, "Red and White at the Bench: Indians and the Law in Plymouth Colony, 1620–1691," *Essex Institute Historical Collections* 110 (1924): 200–15.

5. W. Stitt Robinson Jr., "The Legal Status of the Indian in Colonial Virginia," *Virginia Magazine of History and Biography* 61 (July 1953): 247–59. For a treatment of efforts to extend European law over Indians and into Indian territory in seventeenth- and eighteenth-century South Carolina, see John Phillip Reid, *A Better Kind of Hatchet: Law, Trade, and Diplomacy in the Cherokee Nation during the Early Years of European Contact* (University Park: Pennsylvania State University Press, 1976).

6. See generally Woodrow Borah, *Justice by Insurance: The General Indian Court of Colonial Mexico and the Legal Aides of the Half-Real* (Berkeley and Los Angeles: University of California Press, 1983); Gretchen Koch Markov, "The Legal Status of Indians under Spanish Rule," Ph.D. dissertation, University of Rochester, 1983.

7. S. L. Cline, "A Legal Process at the Local Level: Estate Division in Late Sixteenth-Century Culhuacan," in Ronald Spores and Ross Hassig, eds., *Five Centuries of Law and Politics in Central Mexico* (Nashville, Tenn.: Vanderbilt University, 1984), 39–53.

8. See generally Susan Kellogg, *Law and the Transformation of Aztec Culture,*

1500–1700 (Norman: University of Oklahoma Press, 1995). See also P. E. B. Coy, "Justice for the Indian in Eighteenth Century Mexico," *American Journal of Legal History* 12 (January 1968): 41–49. For Indian successes in pressing their claims in courts in the Spanish borderlands, see Charles R. Cutter, "Indigenous Communities and Spanish Colonial Law," *Indiana Academy of the Social Sciences: Proceedings, 1992* 27 (1992): 1–9.

9. Charles R. Cutter, *The Legal Culture of Northern New Spain, 1700–1810* (Albuquerque: University of New Mexico Press, 1995), 98; *Recopilacion de leyes de los reinos de las Indias* (Libro 5, Titulo 10, Ley 13) (Madrid: 5th ed., 1841), 2:196.

10. For general accounts of the original assimilationist policy of the colonial government in New France, see Mason Wade, "The French and the Indians," in Howard Peckham and Charles Gibson, eds., *Attitudes of Colonial Powers toward the American Indian* (Salt Lake City: University of Utah Press, 1969), 61–80; George F. G. Stanley, "The Policy of 'Francisation' as Applied to the Indians during the Ancien Regime," *Revue d'histoire de l'Amérique française* 3 (December 1949): 333–48.

11. John A. Dickinson, "Native Sovereignty and French Justice in Early Canada," in Jim Phillips, Tina Loo, and Susan Lewthwaite, eds., *Essays in the History of Canadian Law* (Toronto: University of Toronto Press, 1994), 17, 27–29.

12. Ibid., 29–30.

13. Ibid., 39 n. 80.

14. Ibid., 29.

15. Ibid., 30.

16. Ibid., 29.

17. This event is recounted and discussed in Arnold, *Unequal Laws*, 1–3.

18. Records of the Superior Council of Louisiana, 15 October 1769, Louisiana History Center, New Orleans.

19. For interesting treatments of what other Indian tribes meant when they addressed white officials as "father," see Richard White, *The Middle Ground: Indians, Empires, and Republics in the Great Lakes Region, 1650–1815* (Cambridge: Cambridge University Press, 1991), 85 et passim; Patricia Galloway, "'The Chief Who Is Your Father': Choctaw and French Views of the Diplomatic Relation," in Wood, Waselkov, and Hatley, eds., *Powhatan's Mantle*, 254–78.

20. Actually, in 1744 the Quapaws had interceded with the French on behalf of a French deserter named Boisson. See *VP,* 193.

21. ANC, C[13A] 39:177–80. For further discussion of this important event, see George Sabo III, "Inconsistent Kin," 105, 125–28.

22. Berryer to Kerlérec and Bobé Descloseaux, 14 July 1769, ANC, B[109]: 487–88. I erroneously stated in Arnold, *Unequal Laws,* 28, 204, and Arnold, *Colonial Arkansas,* 134, that these French deserters did not receive a trial and that the facts surrounding the homicide that Bernard committed had not been developed. In fact, inquiries were made into these matters by a council of war held at the Illinois on 11 October 1755 and, in the case of the homicide that Bernard committed, it appears that the Superior Council convicted him of the killing and of fighting in a fortress. But since

Captain de Reggio, commandant of Arkansas Post, had written on 29 February 1756 that Bernard had killed Nicolet in self-defense, Kerlérec thought that a pardon was warranted. See ANC, C¹³ᴬ 39:175–76.

23. For liability for international homicide under Cherokee law, see John Phillip Reid, *A Law of Blood: The Primitive Law of the Cherokee Nation* (New York: New York University Press, 1970), 157.

24. I shall frequently characterize actions by Indians as illegal, even though they were not illegal under relevant Indian legal principles, because they were illegal from the point of view of the Europeans who were in charge of the Louisiana government. This strategy is appropriate because this chapter deals with the question of the extent to which Europeans imposed their own legal norms on Indians. The reader will want to remember that many of these acts were lawful under the relevant native legal regime, a fact that created a tension that would obviously make it extremely difficult to apply European legal norms to them.

25. Vallière to Miró, July 1788, AGI, PC, *leg.* 14:379; Miró to Vallière, 11 August 1788, AGI, PC, *leg.* 5:998; Miró to Vallière, 12 August 1788, AGI, PC, *leg.* 5:1000; legal proceedings, 31 July 1788, AGI, PC, *leg.* 14:451.

26. The relevant provisions of the Treaty of Mobile executed on 14 July 1784 are set out in Abelardo Levaggi, "Aplicación de la politica española de tratados a los indios de la Nueva España y sus confines: el caso de la Luisiana y las Floridas (1781–1790)," *Revista de Investigaciones Jurídicas* 20 (1996): 371, 395–96.

27. This event is discussed briefly in Din, "Between a Rock and a Hard Place," 112, 125; in Faye, "Indian Guests," 106; and in Faye, "The Arkansas Post of Louisiana: Spanish Domination," 697.

28. Vallière to Miró, 4 April 1789, AGI, PC, *leg.* 15:346.

29. Vallière to Miró, 22 December 1788, AGI, PC, *leg.* 14:674; Vallière to Miró, 9 May 1789, AGI, PC, *leg.* 15. Din, "Between a Rock and a Hard Place," 125, and Faye, "Indian Guests," 106, assert that an Abenaki Indian was executed as well, but I have been unable to verify this from their citations. In any case, the execution of an Abenaki would not affect the analysis here.

30. Miró to Vallière, 27 May 1789, AGI, PC, *leg.* 6:694.

31. The Quapaws' kinsmen the Osages bent every effort to compose intratribal homicides by attempting to persuade a victim's clan to accept compensation to "cover" the death. See Rollings, *The Osage,* 48. For the possibility of buying off the blood feud under Cherokee law even in the case of international homicide, see Reid, *Law of Blood,* 93–112. In 1734, the Osages came to Arkansas Post to make compensation for a slave whom they had killed on the Arkansas River. The Osages were said to "have covered the death of a slave" ("ont couvert cette mort d'un ecclave"). See synopsis of Bienville's letters of 15 March and 26 April 1734, ANC, C¹³ᴬ 18:226v. For the view that the Indians of New France preferred compensation to blood revenge, see White, *Middle Ground,* 76–77.

32. DeClouet to O'Reilly, 10 March 1763, AGI, PC, *leg.* 107:42. DeClouet's words are that the Quapaw chief wanted "aller frapper sur les Chactas pour vanger

selon lui un homme de sa famille qui a eté tué par eux il y á nombre d'années." This letter also reveals that the slain Quapaw was the "father" of the chief seeking vengeance. Europeans sometimes mistook maternal uncles for fathers when dealing with tribes that had a matrilineal kinship system, because in such systems the mother's brother assumed duties and exercised authority associated with fathers in the European patriarchal family. But since the kinship system of the Quapaws is said to have been patrilineal (see Baird, *The Quapaw Indians,* 12–13), it seems likely that the slain Quapaw was the literal father of the chief who was seeking vengeance. We can deduce from this event, then, that under Quapaw law the duty to retaliate would sometimes fall on the son of the victim.

Although this is a case of international homicide, it probably exposes to view the Quapaws' customs with regard to intratribal homicide as well.

33. See text, *supra* at note 23, this chapter.

34. On the Cherokees' version of the law applicable to intertribal homicide, see John Phillip Reid, "A Perilous Rule: The Law of International Homicide," in Duane H. King, ed., *The Cherokee Indian Nation: A Troubled History* (Knoxville: University of Tennessee Press, 1979), 33–45. Lieutenant Governor DeMézières said that it was a rule as old as Natchitoches itself that friendly Indian tribes would bring the commandant the heads of Indians who had murdered whites, and that the Europeans did the same for friendly Indian tribes if Europeans killed Indians. See *ADM,* I, 164, 186–87; II, 119.

35. Rollings, *The Osage,* 48.

36. See Patricia Galloway, "The Barthelemy Murders: Bienville's Establishment of the *Lex Talionis* as a Principle of Indian Diplomacy," in E. P. Fitzgerald, ed., *Proceedings of the Eighth Annual Meeting of the French Colonial Historical Society, 1982* (Lanham, Md.: University Press of America, 1985), 91–103.

37. Clarence E. Carter, ed., *The Territorial Papers of the United States* (Washington: Government Printing Office, 1949), 14:221.

38. I have borrowed this phrase from White, *Middle Ground.* See ibid., 75–93, for resolutions reached in similar cases in the Great Lakes region in the eighteenth century. In the North American West, it seems that white fur traders adopted the Indian law of vengeance themselves when dealing with Indians. See John Phillip Reid, "Principles of Vengeance: Fur Trappers, Indians, and Retaliation for Homicide in the Transboundary North American West," *Western Historical Quarterly* 24 (February 1993): 21–43.

39. I have borrowed the metaphors that are employed in White, *Middle Ground,* ix.

40. Leyba to Unzaga, 22 November 1771, AGI, PC, *leg.* 107:270–71.

41. Leyba to Unzaga, 6 June 1771, AGI, PC, *leg.* 107:247.

42. DuBreuil to Miró, 19 March 1785, AGI, PC, *leg.* 107:563.

43. DuBreuil to Miró, 28 December 1785, AGI, PC, *leg.* 107:590.

44. Delinó to Carondelet, 24 December 1792, AGI, PC, *leg.* 25:733; Delinó to Carondelet, 20 February 1793, AGI, PC, *leg.* 26:245; Delinó to Carondelet, 15 May, 1793, AGI, PC, *leg.* 25:922; Delinó to Carondelet, 15 November 1793, AGI, PC, *leg.*

32:393; Delinó to Carondelet, 5 May 1794, AGI, PC, *leg.* 31:1073; Vilemont to Gayoso, 29 August 1794, AGI, PC, *leg.* 47:73; Vilemont to Carondelet, 7 September 1794, AGI, PC, *leg.* 30:386.

45. Delinó to Carondelet, 17 December 1793, AGI, PC, *leg.* 27:431.

46. Delinó to Carondelet, 15 November 1793, AGI, PC, *leg.* 32:393.

47. See, e.g., Delinó to Carondelet, 20 February 1793, AGI, PC, *leg.* 26:245; Delinó to Carondelet, 15 November 1793, AGI, PC, *leg.* 32:393.

48. For the relevant provisions of the Treaty of Mobile of 22 and 23 June 1784, see Levaggi, "Aplicación de la politica española de tratados a los indios," 388–89. Arkansas Post is specifically mentioned in this section of the treaty.

49. Delinó to Carondelet, 17 December 1793, AGI, PC, *leg.* 27:431 (Carondelet's marginal note that "compensation will be sought from the Chickasaw nation").

50. Carondelet to Delinó, 24 December 1793, AGI, PC, *leg.* 19:393.

51. Carondelet to Vilemont, 12 February 1796, AGI, PC, *leg.* 22:652.

52. Carondelet to Vilemont, 10 December 1795, AGI, PC, *leg.* 22:1468; Vilemont to Carondelet, 19 March 1796, AGI, PC, *leg.* 33:643.

53. In 1801, Vilemont was still complaining that the Chickasaws were stealing his *habitants'* horses and killing their livestock. Vidal to Vilemont, 9 December 1801, AGI, PC, *leg.* 137:178.

54. The Spanish government encouraged the Choctaws to seek game in the trans-Mississippi West in order to minimize intertribal competition for the depleted hunting lands on the east side of the river. See Richard White, *The Roots of Dependency: Subsistence, Environment, and Social Change among the Choctaws, Pawnees, and Navajos* (Lincoln: University of Nebraska Press, 1983), 92–93, 98.

55. Vilemont to Gayoso, 2 November 1794, AGI, PC, *leg.* 47:74.

56. Vilemont to Gayoso, 1 July 1795, AGI, PC, *leg.* 48:1619. A year later, the famous Natchez trader Anthony Glass appeared at the Post in the company of some Choctaw hunters. See Carondelet to Vilemont, 30 November 1796, AGI, PC, *leg.* 34:673. On Glass's later activities, see Dan L. Flores, ed., *Journal of an Indian Trader: Anthony Glass and the Texas Trading Frontier, 1790–1810* (College Station: Texas A & M University Press, 1985).

57. Vilemont to ?, 8 July 1797, AGI, PC, *leg.* 213:210.

58. See the provisions of the Treaty of Mobile of 14 July 1784 in Levaggi, "Aplicación de la politica española de tratados a los indios," 395.

59. Vilemont to ?, 30 January 1798, AGI, PC, *leg.* 215A:236; Vilemont to ?, 24 March 1798, AGI, PC, *leg.* 215A:254.

60. Desmazellières to Unzaga, 7 August 1770, AGI, PC, *leg.* 107:121.

61. Desmazellières to Unzaga, 18 August 1770, AGI, PC, *leg.* 107:124; *ADM,* I, 180.

62. Desmazellières to Governor (?), 7 October 1770, AGI, PC, *leg.* 107:134.

63. Governor (?) to Desmazellières, 19 December 1770, AGI, PC, *leg.* 107:136.

64. Vilemont to Carondelet, 2 April 1796, AGI, PC, *leg.* 33:644.

65. Victor Collot, *A Journey in North America* (Paris: 1826), 2:40.

66. Villiers to Piernas, 7 September 1781, AGI, PC, *leg.* 194:71.

67. Piernas to Villiers, 24 September 1781, AGI, PC, *leg.* 114:727 (draft in AGI, PC, *leg.* 194:75).

68. Governor to Delinó, 27 August 1791, AGI, PC, *leg.* 122A.

69. Vilemont to Carondolet (?), 31 May 1796, AGI, PC, *leg.* 33:359.

70. Degoutin to Carondolet, 10 November 1796, AGI, PC, *leg.* 34:839.

71. Vallière to Miró, 25 June 1787, AGI, PC, *leg.* 13:482.

72. Collot, *A Journey in North America,* 2:39–40.

73. The allusion here, of course, is to Francis Parkman's famous dictum that "Spanish civilization crushed the Indian; English civilization scorned and neglected him; French civilization embraced and cherished him." Francis Parkman, *The Jesuits in North America in the Seventeenth Century* (Boston: Little, Brown, and Company, 1867), 131.

74. See, e.g., Piernas (?) to Villiers, 24 September 1781, AGI, PC, *leg.* 194:75; Miró to DuBreuil, 20 July 1782, AGI, PC, *leg.* 117A:189–90v.

75. Treat to Dearborn, 1 April 1807, *APLB,* 171.

76. This inventory is in AGI, PC, *leg.* 140, and is published in Arnold and Core, eds., *Arkansas Colonials,* 92–95.

77. These records are in the Louisiana History Center in New Orleans.

78. These records are calendared in May Wilson McBee, ed., *The Natchez Court Records, 1767–1805: Abstracts of Early Records* (Baltimore: Genealogical Publishing Company, 1979).

79. These records are at the Missouri Historical Society in St. Louis.

80. Derek N. Kerr, *Petty Felony, Slave Defiance, and Frontier Villainy: Crime and Criminal Justice in Spanish Louisiana, 1770–1803* (New York: Garland Publishing, 1993).

81. On this, see *ADM,* 1:66–79, reprinted in John Francis Bannon, ed., *Bolton and the Spanish Borderlands* (Norman: University of Oklahoma Press, 1964), 172–84.

82. For a discussion of some of the Louisiana governors' correspondence concerning Indian crime, see Kerr, *Petty Felony,* 53–54.

83. Vallière's petition to Miró, AGI, PC, *leg.* 15:479.

84. For a seminal article on the resistance of Indians to attempts to incorporate them into the religious and legal order in New France, see Cornelius J. Jaenen, "The Meeting of the French and Amerindians in the Seventeenth Century," *Revue de l'Université d'Ottawa* 43 (January–March 1973): 128. Missionaries occasionally referred to the need to impose French law on the native peoples as part of a general process of cultural assimilation. For an example, see Cornelius J. Jaenen, *Friend and Foe: Aspects of French-Amerindian Cultural Contact in the Sixteenth and Seventeenth Centuries* (New York: Columbia University Press, 1976), 166.

85. Baird, *The Quapaw Indians,* 17.

86. Bienville's *mémoire* [undated], ANC, C13A 1:362.

87. See, e.g., Smith, "Exploration," 350.

88. Henri de Tonty, *An Account of Monsieur de la Salle's Last Expedition and Discoveries in North America* (London: 1698), 83. These remarks, however, do not appear in Tonty's original memoir. See Falconer, ed., *On the Discovery of the Mississippi,* 64.

89. Smith, "Exploration," 350; See also Cain, Koenig, and Conrad, eds., *Historical Journal,* 148.

90. Feiler, ed., *Bossu's Travels,* 63–64.

91. Ibid., 63 n. 7.

92. Lottinville, ed., *Travels into Arkansas Territory,* 98.

93. But see Alice C. Fletcher and Francis La Flesche, *The Omaha Tribe* (Lincoln: University of Nebraska Press, 1992), 2:592, where it is said that the Omahas, Dhegihan Sioux cousins of the Quapaws, placed food on graves as an act of remembrance and not "because of a belief that the dead needed or partook of food."

94. Kellogg, *A Journal,* 2:231. See also Dickinson, ed., *New Travels,* 39, where Bossu claims that his long absence had caused the Quapaws to fear that he had gone to "the land of *spirits,*" that is, that he had died. See also Lottinville, ed., *Travels into Arkansas Territory,* 98, where Nuttall remarks of the Quapaws that their "heaven for hunters is at least as rational as that of some of our own fanatics."

95. Bienville, *mémoire* [undated, but 1726], ANC, C¹³ᶜ 1:362.

96. Mereness, ed., *Travels,* 58.

97. See, e.g., Shea, ed., *Early Voyages,* 134, for the complaint that the Tunicas were "so close-mouthed as to all the mysteries of their religion that the missionary could not discover anything about it."

98. Delanglez, *The French Jesuits in Lower Louisiana,* 33–34.

99. *JR,* 68:219.

100. *JR,* 70:241.

101. For the church in Arkansas in the eighteenth century, see Arnold, *Colonial Arkansas,* 88–97.

102. See, e.g., Wilfred Bovey, "Some Notes on Arkansas Post and St. Philippe in the Mississippi Valley," *Transactions of the Royal Society of Canada* (Section II, 1939), 40; Dorothy Jones Core and Nicole Wable Hatfield, eds., *Abstract of the Catholic Register of Arkansas (1764–1858)* (DeWitt, Ark.: Grand Prairie Historical Society, 1976), 12.

103. See, e.g., Core and Hatfield, eds., *Abstract of the Catholic Register,* 23–24.

104. See, e.g., ibid., 13–14.

105. Ibid., 18, 23, 25. All three of these women were Paducahs.

106. Ibid., 14, 32, 36.

107. Baird, *The Quapaw Indians,* 38. Jones, "Conversion of the Tamaroas and the Quapaws," identifies a number of matters that contributed to the failure of early French efforts to convert the Quapaws, among them the dispersal of the Indian villages, language barriers, polygyny among the Quapaws, a lack of funds, the difficulty of communicating with superiors, and the un-Christian activities of the local French *coureurs de bois.*

Chapter VII
Fin de Siècle/Fin del Siglo/End of an Era

1. Perrin du Lac, *Voyage dans les deux Louisianes,* 367.

2. Records of the Superior Council, 10156903, Louisiana State History Center, New Orleans.

3. Records of the Superior Council, 10156902, Louisiana State History Center, New Orleans.

4. García to Unzaga, 18 June 1776, AGI, PC, *leg.* 189B:53.

5. Vallière to Miró, 22 December 1788, AGI, PC, *leg.* 14:673.

6. See, e.g., G. W. Featherstonhaugh, *Excursions through the Slave States* (London: John Murray, 1844), 2:230, where, speaking of the wife of Antoine Barraqué, who lived in Jefferson County, Featherstonhaugh observed that "from appearances, Madame has no small portion of the Quapaw blood in her, which is not an uncommon thing, as most of the Creole French who lived out of New Orleans connected themselves with Indian women: her mother no doubt was of that stock, but she is a very good-looking woman notwithstanding her Indian blood, has *French* manners, and has produced a fine young family."

7. But see Tanis C. Thorne, *The Many Hands of My Relations: French and Indians on the Lower Missouri* (Columbia: University of Missouri Press, 1996), 152, for the view that some upper-class Louisiana Frenchmen were "raised in a household that included Indian people and accepted mixed-blood kin and acquaintances as intimate family friends and business partners."

8. See Jacqueline Peterson, "The People in Between: Indian-White Marriage and the Genesis of a *Métis* Society and Culture in the Great Lakes Region, 1680–1830," Ph.D. dissertation, University of Illinois at Chicago Circle, 1981.

9. Bovey, "Some Notes on Arkansas Post and St. Philippe," 40; *VP,* 142, 152; ANC, C^{13A} 50:128; *Diocese of Baton Rouge Catholic Church Records* (Baton Rouge, La.: Catholic Diocese of Baton Rouge, 1978), 1:219. Sarazin may have been the son of a former *garde magasin* who was living on Chartres Street in New Orleans in 1725. See Faye, "The Arkansas Post of Louisiana: French Domination," 710 n. 20.

10. For the unsuccessful efforts to locate this window, see Burney McClurkan, "The Saracen Window," *Jefferson County Historical Quarterly* 2 (1970): 3–6.

11. DuBreuil to Miró, 5 May 1783, AGI, PC, *leg.* 107:403, 404. There are two very bad attempts in print at translating this important letter, one in Anna Lewis, *Along the Arkansas* (Dallas: Southwest Press, 1932), 177–83, and the other in Anna Lewis, "An Attack upon the Arkansas Post, 1783," *AHQ* 2 (September 1943): 261–67. In the first, Dr. Lewis unaccountably omits the tomahawk incident altogether; and in the second, she quite wrongly attributes the planting of the tomahawk to Colbert's band, not to a Quapaw. Faye, "The Arkansas Post of Louisiana: Spanish Domination," 685, makes much more accurate use of this letter; and both Faye and Corbitt, the latter in Duvon Clough Corbitt, "Arkansas in the American Revolution," *AHQ* 1

(December 1942): 290, 302, correctly attribute the tomahawk-throwing to a Quapaw. The letter is put to excellent use in the narratives in Gilbert C. Din, "Arkansas Post in the American Revolution," *AHQ* 40 (Spring 1981): 3, 23–26, and in Edwin C. Bearss, *Special History Report: The Colbert Raid* (Denver: National Park Service, 1974), 51–56; but no reference is made to a Quapaw throwing a tomahawk in either of these accounts.

12. Timothy Flint, *Recollections of the Last Ten Years* (Boston: Cummings, Hilliard, and Company, 1826), 270–71.

13. William F. Pope, *Early Days in Arkansas* (Little Rock, Ark.: Frederick W. Allsopp, 1895), 138–39.

14. Ibid., 139.

15. Baird, *The Quapaw Indians,* 71.

16. Carter, ed., *Territorial Papers,* 20:497.

17. Baird, *The Quapaw Indians,* 79. For more on Saracen, see Bob Lancaster, *The Jungles of Arkansas: A Personal History of the Wonder State* (Fayetteville: University of Arkansas Press, 1989), 31–32; James W. Leslie, *Saracen's Country: Some Southeast Arkansas History* (Little Rock, Ark.: Rose Publishing Co., 1974), 124–28; and Fred W. Allsopp, *Folklore of Romantic Arkansas* (New York: Grolier Society, 1931), 1:262–63, 272–74.

18. Arnold, "Testament II: François Menard," 26.

19. J. W. Bocage, "Old and New Pine Bluff," *Jefferson County Historical Quarterly* 4 (1973): 25, 28–29.

20. Villiers to Gálvez, 19 July 1779, AGI, PC, *leg.* 192:168; Villiers to Gálvez, 21 July 1779, AGI, PC, *leg.* 192:172.

21. Arnold, *Unequal Laws,* 71. For more on the subject of native Americans and liquor at Arkansas Post, see Din, "Between a Rock and a Hard Place," 121–22; Samuel Dorris Dickinson, "Health and Death in Early Arkansas, 1541–1803" in Edwina Walls, ed., *Contributions to Arkansas Medical History* (Charlotte, N.C.: Delmar Printing Company, 1990), 5, 54. For a general treatment of the ill effects of alcohol on the early North American indigenous population, see Peter C. Mancall, *Deadly Medicine: Indians and Alcohol in Early America* (Ithaca, N.Y.: Cornell University Press, 1995).

22. See, e.g., White, *The Roots of Dependency,* 146.

23. Early contributions to this literature are H. Scott Gordon, "The Economic Theory of a Common Property Resource: The Fishery," *J. Pol. Econ.* 62 (1954): 124–42; Harold Demsetz, "Toward a Theory of Property Rights," *Am. Econ. Rev.* 573 (1967): 347–59; Garrett Hardin, "The Tragedy of the Commons," *Science* 162 (December 1968): 1243–48.

24. For information on prehistoric Indian trade routes in the West, see William Brandon, *Quivira: Europeans in the Region of the Santa Fe Trail, 1540–1820* (Athens: Ohio University Press, 1990).

25. See Appendix I.

26. See Elizabeth A. H. John, *Storms Brewed in Other Men's Worlds: The Confrontation of Indians, Spanish, and French in the Southwest, 1540–1795* (College Station: Texas A & M University Press, 1975).

27. On this, see generally, Matt Ridley, *The Origins of Virtue: Human Instincts and the Evolution of Cooperation* (Viking Penguin, 1997).

28. See, e.g., White, *Middle Ground,* 94–95.

29. On Labuxière's unhappy fate, see Kerr, *Petty Felony,* 79–80.

Appendix I
Quapaw Population, 1682–1805

1. Jean Delanglez, ed., "Tonti Letters," *Mid-America* 21 (1939): 209, 229.

2. Ibid., 229 n. 35.

3. Shea, ed., *Early Voyages,* 72.

4. Kellogg, ed., *Journal of a Voyage,* 2:229.

5. Vaudreuil to the minister, 20 March 1748, ANC, C¹³A 32:28.

6. Theodore Calvin Pease and Ernestine Jenison, eds., *Illinois on the Eve of the Seven Years' War, 1747–1755* (Springfield: Illinois State Historical Library, 1940), 739.

7. Villiers to Gálvez, 10 December 1777, AGI, PC, *leg.* 191:187.

8. Villiers to Piernas, 1 December 1781, AGI, PC, *leg.* 194:76.

9. For an interesting and detailed discussion of the difficulties that inhere in estimating Louisiana Indian populations, see Zitomersky, *French Americans-Native Americans.*

Appendix II
Arkansas Post Interpreters

1. Leyba to Unzaga, 17 December 1772, AGI, PC, *leg.* 107:337.

2. Leyba to Unzaga, 30 April 1773, AGI, PC, *leg.* 107:354.

3. Unzaga to Leyba, 18 June 1773, AGI, PC, *leg.* 78:68.

4. Lajeunesse to Unzaga, 19 December 1773, AGI, PC, *leg.* 107:373. There is a similar petition dated 8 October 1773, in which Lajeunesse claims that he has seven children. See AGI, PC, *leg.* 107:372.

5. Leyba to Unzaga, 20 December 1773, AGI, PC, *leg.* 107:378.

6. Leyba to Unzaga, 11 January 1774, AGI, PC, *leg.* 107:381.

7. Villiers to Unzaga, 23 September 1776, AGI, PC, *leg.* 189B:58. Gálvez had given Lajeunesse his permission to quit sometime in 1776. See Gálvez to Villiers, 29 February 1776, AGI, PC, *leg.* 189B:41. A month later, Lajeunesse was still acting as interpreter and was sent with a party of twenty Quapaws and four soldiers to pillage English intruders. Villiers to Unzaga, 26 October 1776, AGI, PC, *leg.* 190:70.

8. Gálvez to Villiers, 25 March 1777, AGI, PC, *leg.* 1:129.

9. Villiers to Gálvez, 9 April 1782, AGI, PC, *leg.* 195:204.

10. Miró to Villiers, 22 May 1782, AGI, PC, *leg.* 3:249 (draft in AGI, PC, *leg.* 195:213).

11. Villars to Miró, 5 July 1782, AGI, PC, *leg.* 195:223.

12. Memorial from Lajeunesse to Miró, 5 July 1782, AGI, PC, *leg.* 195:243.

13. Miró to Villars, 13 July 1782, AGI, PC, *leg.* 3:279 (draft in AGI, PC, *leg.* 195:240).

14. Villars to Miró, 12 August 1782, AGI, PC, *leg.* 195:273; Miró to Villars, 23 August 1782, AGI, PC, *leg.* 3:310.

15. DuBreuil to Navarro, 12 October 1785, AGI, PC, *leg.* 602:38.

16. DuBreuil to Miró, 7 August 1786, AGI, PC, *leg.* 13:38.

17. Piernas to DuBreuil, 29 August 1786, AGI, PC, *leg.* 117A:55 (draft in AGI, PC, *leg.* 4:541).

18. Vallière to Miró, 4 April 1789, AGI, PC, *leg.* 15:337; Memorial from Sossier to Vallière, 6 April 1789, AGI, PC, *leg.* 15:359; Miró to Vallière, 27 May 1789, AGI, PC, *leg.* 6:691.

19. Treat to Saussier, 31 December 1808, *APLB,* 230.

Bibliography

Alden, John Richard. *John Stuart and the Southern Colonial Frontier.* Ann Arbor: University of Michigan Press, 1944.

Allain, Mathé. *"Not Worth a Straw": French Colonial Policy and the Early Years of Louisiana.* Lafayette: Center for Louisiana Studies, 1988.

Allsopp, Fred W. *Folklore of Romantic Arkansas.* New York: Grolier Society, 1931.

Alvord, Clarence Walworth. *The Illinois Country, 1673–1818.* Urbana and Chicago: University of Illinois Press, 1987.

Alvord, Clarence Walworth, and Clarence Edwin Carter, eds. *The Critical Period, 1763–1765.* Springfield: Illinois State Historical Library, 1915.

Anderson, Melville B., ed. *Relation of the Discovery of the Mississipi River, Written from the Narratives of Nicolas de La Salle.* Chicago: The Caxton Club, 1898.

———. *Relation of Henri de Tonty Concerning the Explorations of LaSalle from 1678 to 1683.* Chicago: The Caxton Club, 1898.

Arnold, Morris S. *Colonial Arkansas, 1686–1804: A Social and Cultural History.* Fayetteville: University of Arkansas Press, 1991.

———. "Eighteenth-Century Arkansas Illustrated." *AHQ* 53 (Summer 1994): 119–36.

———. "The Myth of John Law's German Colony on the Arkansas." *Louisiana History* 31 (Winter 1990): 83–88.

———. "The Significance of Arkansas's Colonial Experience." In *Cultural Encounters in the Early South: Indians and Europeans in Arkansas,* edited by Jeannie M. Whayne, 131–41. Fayetteville: University of Arkansas Press, 1995.

———. "Testament II: François Menard." *GPHSB* 37 (April 1994): 23–26.

———. *Unequal Laws unto a Savage Race: European Legal Traditions in Arkansas, 1686–1804.* Fayetteville: University of Arkansas Press, 1985.

Arnold, Morris S., and Dorothy Jones Core, eds. *Arkansas Colonials.* DeWitt, Ark.: Grand Prairie Historical Society, 1986.

Arrest du conseil déstat du Roy . . . du 9 May 1720.

Bailey, Garrick A., ed. *The Osage and the Invisible World from the Works of Francis La Flesche.* Norman: University of Oklahoma Press, 1995.

Baird, W. David. *The Quapaw Indians: A History of the Downstream People.* Norman: University of Oklahoma Press, 1980.

Baker, Vaughan B. "*Cherchez les Femmes:* Some Glimpses of Women in Early Eighteenth-Century Louisiana." *Louisiana History* 31 (Winter 1990): 21–35.

Ballesteros Gaibrois, Manuel. "Pieles de bisonte pintadas: tres ejemplares de Museo Arqueologico Nacional," *Tierra Firme* (1935), 65.

Ballesteros Gaibrois, Manuel, and Paul Kirchoff. *Arte antiguo norteamericano: pieles de bisonte pintadas*. Madrid: Tipografía de Archivos, 1934.

Bannon, John Francis, ed. *Bolton and the Spanish Borderlands*. Norman: University of Oklahoma Press, 1964.

Barbeau, Marius. *Indian Days on the Western Prairies*. Ottawa: National Museum of Canada, 1960.

Baudry des Lozieres, Louis N. *Voyage a la Louisiane, et sur le continent de l'Amérique septentrionale*. Paris: 1802.

Bearss, Edwin C. *Special History Report: The Colbert Raid*. Denver: National Park Service, 1974.

Bell, Ann Linda, and Patricia Galloway, eds. "Voyage Made from Canada Inland Going Southward during the Year 1682." In *La Salle, the Mississippi, and the Gulf: Three Primary Documents,* edited by Robert S. Weddle, 29–68. College Station: Texas A & M University Press, 1987.

Blaine, Martha Royce. "The French Efforts to Reach Santa Fe: André Fabry de la Bruyère's Voyage up the Canadian River in 1741–42." *Louisiana History* 20 (Spring 1979): 133–57.

Bocage, J. W. "Old and New Pine Bluff." *Jefferson County Historical Quarterly* 4 (1973): 25–29.

Borah, Woodrow. *Justice by Insurance: The General Indian Court of Colonial Mexico and the Legal Aides of the Half-Real*. Berkeley and Los Angeles: University of California Press, 1983.

Bossu, Jean Bernard. *Nouveaux voyages dans l'Amerique septentrionale*. Amsterdam: 1777.

Bougés, ———. "Colonie de la Louisiane, journal historique." Tulane University Library, Special Collections, M 955.

Bovey, Wilfrid. "Some Notes on Arkansas Post and St. Philippe in the Mississippi Valley." *Transactions of the Royal Society of Canada* (Section II, 1939), 29–47.

Brain, Jeffrey P. *Tunica Archaeology*. Cambridge: Peabody Museum of Archaeology and Ethnology, 1988.

Brandon, William. *Quivira: Europeans in the Region of the Santa Fe Trail, 1540–1820*. Athens: Ohio University Press, 1990.

Brasseaux, Carl A. "The Moral Climate of French Colonial Louisiana, 1699–1763." *Louisiana History* 27 (Winter 1986): 27–41.

Brotherston, Gordon. *Book of the Fourth World: Reading the Native Americas through Their Literature*. Cambridge: Cambridge University Press, 1992.

Brown, Margaret Kimball. *"Allons, Cowboys."* *Illinois Historical Journal* (1983): 273–82.

Brownstone, Arni. *War Paint: Blackfoot and Sarcee Painted Buffalo Robes in the Royal Ontario Museum.* Toronto: Royal Ontario Museum, 1993.

Bushnell, David I., Jr. "Native Villages and Village Sites East of the Mississippi." *Bulletin of the Bureau of American Ethnology* (Washington: Government Printing Office, 1919), 69:68–69.

Cabello Carro, Paz. *Coleccionismo americano indígena en la España del siglo xviii.* Madrid: Ediciones de Cultura Hispánica, 1989.

Cabinet de Curiosités et d'Objets d'Art de la Bibliothèque Publique de la Ville de Versailles, Catalogue. Versailles, 1869.

Cain, Joan, Virginia Koenig, and Glenn R. Conrad, eds. *The Historical Journal of the Establishment of the French in Louisiana.* Lafayette: Center for Louisiana Studies, 1971.

Calloway, Colin G., ed. *Dawnland Encounters: Indians and Europeans in Northern New England.* Hanover, N.H.: University Press of New England, 1991.

Carter, Clarence E., ed. *The Territorial Papers of the United States* (Washington: Government Printing Office, 1949), vols. 14 and 20.

Cline, S. L. "A Legal Process at the Local Level: Estate Division in Late Sixteenth-Century Culhuacan." In *Five Centuries of Law and Politics in Central Mexico,* edited by Ronald Spores and Ross Hassig, 39–53. Nashville, Tenn.: Vanderbilt University, 1984.

Collot, Victor. *A Journey in North America.* Paris: 1826.

Conrad, Glenn R. *The First Families of Louisiana.* Baton Rouge, La.: Claitor's Publishing Division, 1970.

Corbitt, Duvon Clough. "Arkansas in the American Revolution." *AHQ* 1 (December 1942): 290–306.

Core, Dorothy Jones. "Canadian Baugis to Arkansas Bogy." *GPHSB* 18 (October 1975): 3–6.

———. "Canadian Baugis to Arkansas Bogy (Part II)." *GPHSB* (April 1976): 19–23.

———. "Canadian Baugis to Arkansas Bogy (Part III)." *GPHSB* 19 (October 1976): 36–38.

———. "First Bankruptcy in Arkansas County Records." *GPHSB* 16 (October 1973): 8–13.

———. "Imbeau–A First Family of Arkansas." *GPHSB* 27 (October 1984): 5–12.

———. "Imbeau–A First Family of Arkansas (Part II)." *GPHSB* 28 (October 1985): 2–8.

———. "Pierre Lefevre of Arkansas." *GPHSB* 17 (April 1974): 14–17.

———. "Pierre Lefevre of Arkansas (Part Two)." *GPHSB* 17 (October 1974): 9–14.

———. "Pierre Lefevre of Arkansas (Part Three)." *GPHSB* 18 (April 1975): 17–20.

————. "Testament François Menard." *GPHSB* 20 (April 1977): 23–24.

————. "Valliere Documents." *GPHSB* 32 (April 1989): 2–9.

————. "The Vaugine Arkansas Connection." *GPHSB* 21 (April 1978): 6–24.

Core, Dorothy Jones, and Nicole Wable Hatfield, eds. *Abstract of Catholic Register of Arkansas (1764–1858)*. DeWitt, Ark.: Grand Prairie Historical Society, 1976.

Coy, P. E. B. "Justice for the Indian in Eighteenth Century Mexico." *American Journal of Legal History* 12 (January 1968): 41–49.

Crane, Verner W. *The Southern Frontier, 1670–1732*. Ann Arbor: University of Michigan Press, 1929.

Cutter, Charles R. "Indigenous Communities and Spanish Colonial Law." *Proceedings of the Indiana Academy of the Social Sciences: Proceedings, 1992* 27 (1992): 1–9.

————. *The Legal Culture of Northern New Spain, 1700–1810*. Albuquerque: University of New Mexico Press, 1995.

Davis, Hester A., ed. *Arkansas before the Americans*. Fayetteville: Arkansas Archeological Survey, 1991.

Delanglez, Jean. *The French Jesuits in Lower Louisiana (1700–1763)*. Washington: Catholic University of America, 1935.

————. *Journal of Jean Cavalier*. Chicago: Institute of Jesuit History, 1938.

————, ed. "Journal of Father Vitry of the Society of Jesus, Army Chaplain during the War against the Chickasaws." *Mid-America* 28 (1941): 30–59.

————. "M. Le Maire on Louisiana." *Mid-America* 19 (1937): 124–54.

————. "Tonti Letters." *Mid-America* 21 (1939): 209–38.

Demsetz, Harold. "Toward a Theory of Property Rights." *American Economic Review* 573 (1967): 347–59.

De Ville, Winston. *Louisiana Colonials: Soldiers and Vagabonds*. Baltimore: Genealogical Publishing Co., 1963.

Dickinson, John A. "Native Sovereignty and French Justice in Early Canada." In *Essays in the History of Canadian Law,* edited by Jim Phillips, Tina Loo, and Susan Lewthwaite, 17–40. Toronto: University of Toronto Press, 1994.

Dickinson, Samuel Dorris. "An Early View of the Ouachita Region." *The Old Time Chronicle* 3 (July 1990): 12–18.

————. "Health and Death in Early Arkansas, 1541–1803." In *Contributions to Arkansas Medical History,* edited by Edwina Walls, 5–62. Charlotte, N.C.: Delmar Printing Company, 1990.

————. "Lake Mitchegamas and the St. Francis." *AHQ* 43 (Autumn 1984): 197–207.

————, ed. *New Travels in North America by Jean-Bernard Bossu, 1770–1771*. Natchitoches: Northwestern Louisiana State University Press, 1982.

————. "Quapaw Indian Dances." *Pulaski County Historical Review* 32 (Fall 1984): 42–50.

————. "Shamans, Priests, Preachers, and Pilgrims at Arkansas Post." In *Arkansas before the Americans,* edited by Hester A. Davis, 95–104. Fayetteville: Arkansas Archeological Society, 1991.

————, trans. *Spain and the Cherokee and Choctaw Indians in the Second Half of the Eighteenth Century, by Manuel Searrano y Sanz.* Idabel, Okla.: Potsherd Press, 1995.

Din, Gilbert C. "Arkansas Post in the American Revolution." *AHQ* 40 (Spring 1981): 3–30.

————. "Between a Rock and a Hard Place: The Indian Trade in Spanish Arkansas." In *Cultural Encounters in the Early South: Indians and Europeans in Arkansas,* edited by Jeannie M. Whayne, 112–30. Fayetteville: University of Arkansas Press, 1995.

————, ed. *Louisiana in 1776: A Memoria of Francisco Bouligny.* New Orleans: 1977.

————. and A. P. Nasatir. *The Imperial Osages: Spanish-Indian Diplomacy in the Mississippi Valley.* Norman: University of Oklahoma Press, 1983.

Diocese of Baton Rouge Catholic Church Records, vol. 1. Baton Rouge, La.: Catholic Diocese of Baton Rouge, 1978.

Dorsey, James Owen. "Kwapa Folk-Lore." *Journal of American Folklore* 8 (January–March 1895): 130–31.

Dubroca, Louis. *L'Itinéraire des Français dans la Louisiane.* Paris: 1802.

Dumont de Montigny, François Benjamin. *Mémoires historiques sur la Louisiane.* Paris: 1753.

"An Early Letter from Arkansas Post." *Jefferson County Historical Quarterly* 4 (1973): 29.

Ekberg, Carl J. *French Roots in the Illinois Country: The Mississippi Frontier in Colonial Times.* Urbana: University of Illinois Press, 1998.

Ewers, John Canfield. *Plains Indian Painting: A Description of an Aboriginal Art.* Stanford University, Calif.: Stanford University Press, 1939.

Falconer, Thomas, ed. *On the Discovery of the Mississippi.* London: Samuel Clarke, 1844.

Falconer, W. H., ed. "Arkansas and the Jesuits in 1727–A Translation." *Publications of the Arkansas Historical Association* 4 (1917): 352–78.

Farnsworth, Jean M., and Ann M. Masson, eds. *The Architecture of Colonial Louisiana: Collected Essays of Samuel Wilson, Jr., F.A.I.A.* Lafayette: Center for Louisiana Studies, 1987.

Faye, Stanley. "The Arkansas Post of Louisiana: French Domination." *LHQ* 26 (July 1943): 633–721.

————. "The Arkansas Post of Louisiana: Spanish Domination." *LHQ* 27 (July 1944): 629–716.

————. "Indian Guests at the Spanish Arkansas Post." *AHQ* 4 (Summer 1945): 93–108.

Featherstonhaugh, G. W. *Excursions through the Slave States*. London: John Murray, 1844.

Feiler, Seymour, ed. *Jean-Bernard Bossu's Travels in the Interior of North America, 1751–1762*. Norman: University of Oklahoma Press, 1962.

Fishman, Laura Schrager. "How Noble the Savage?: The Image of the American in French and English Travel Accounts." Ph.D. dissertation, City University of New York, 1979.

Fitzgerald, E. P., ed. *Proceedings of the Eighth Annual Meeting of the French Colonial Historical Society, 1982*. Lanham, Md.: University Press of America, 1985.

Fletcher, Alice C., and Francis La Flesche. 2 vols. *The Omaha Tribe*. Lincoln: University of Nebraska Press, 1992.

Fletcher, Mary P. "A Sketch of Peter Le Fevre." *AHQ* 13 (Spring 1954): 86–89.

Flint, Timothy. *Recollections of the Last Ten Years*. Boston: Cummings, Hilliard, and Company, 1826.

Flores, Dan L., ed. *Journal of an Indian Trader: Anthony Glass and the Texas Trading Frontier, 1790–1810*. College Station: Texas A & M University Press, 1985.

Forêt, Michael James. "Red over White: Indians, Deserters, and French Colonial Louisiana." In *Proceedings of the Seventeenth Meeting of the French Colonial Historical Society, Chicago, May 1991*, edited by Patricia Galloway, 79–89. Lanham, Md.: University Press of America, 1993.

A Full and Impartial Account of the Company of the Mississippi. London: 1720.

Galloway, Patricia. "The Barthelemy Murders: Bienville's Establishment of the *Lex Talionis* as a Principle of Indian Diplomacy." In *Proceedings of the Eighth Annual Meeting of the French Colonial Historical Society*, edited by E. P. Fitzgerald, 91–103. Lanham, Md.: University Press of America, 1985.

————. "The Chief Who Is Your Father: Choctaw and French Views of the Diplomatic Relation." In *Powhattan's Mantle: Indians in the Colonial Southeast*, edited by Peter H. Wood, Gregory A. Waselkov, and M. Thomas Hatley. Lincoln: University of Nebraska Press, 1989.

————. "Couture, Tonti, and the English-Quapaw Connection: A Revision." In *Arkansas before the Americans*, edited by Hester A. Davis, 74–94. Fayetteville: Arkansas Archeological Survey, 1991.

————. "Debriefing Explorers: Amerindian Information in the Delisles' Mapping of the Southeast." In *Cartographic Encounters: Perspectives on Native American Mapmaking and Map Use*, edited by G. Malcolm Lewis, 223–40. Chicago: University of Chicago Press, 1998.

————, ed. *Mississippi Provincial Archives: French Dominion, 1749–1763*. Baton Rouge: Louisiana State University Press, 1984.

————, ed. *Proceedings of the Seventeenth Meeting of the French Colonial Historical Society, Chicago, May 1991*. Lanham, Md.: University Press of America, 1993.

————. "Talking with Indians: Interpreters and Diplomacy in French Louisiana." In *Race and Family in the Colonial South,* edited by Winthrop D. Jordan and Sheila L. Skemp, 109–29. Jackson: University Press of Mississippi, 1987.

Gerstaeker, Frederick. *Wild Sports in the Far West.* London and New York: Geo. Routledge & Co., 1854.

González López-Briones, M. Carmen. "Spain in the Mississippi Valley: Spanish Arkansas, 1752–1804." Ph.D. thesis, Purdue University, 1983.

Gordon, H. Scott. "The Economic Theory of a Common Property Resource: The Fishery." *Journal of Political Economy* 62 (1954): 124–42.

Habig, Marion A. *The Franciscan Père Marquette, A Critical Biography of Father Zénobe Membré, O. F. M.* New York: Joseph F. Wagner, 1934.

Hagan, William T. *American Indians.* Chicago: University of Chicago Press, 3d ed., 1993.

Hall, Gwendolyn Midlo. *Africans in Colonial Louisiana: The Development of Afro-Creole Culture in the Eighteenth Century.* Baton Rouge: Louisiana State University Press, 1992.

Hardin, Garrett. "The Tragedy of the Commons." *Science* 162 (December 1968): 1243–48.

Hodges, Dr. and Mrs. T. L. "Possibilities for the Archaeologist and Historian in Eastern Arkansas." *AHQ* 2 (June 1943): 141–63.

Hoffman, Michael P. "Quapaw Structures, 1673–1834, and Their Comparative Significance." In *Arkansas before the Americans,* edited by Hester A. Davis, 55–68. Fayetteville: Arkansas Archeological Survey, 1991.

Holder, Preston. "The Fur Trade as Seen from the Indian Point of View." In *The Frontier Re-examined,* edited by John Francis McDermott, 129–39. Urbana: University of Illinois Press, 1967.

Horse Capture, George P. "From Museums to Indians: Native American Art in Context." In *Robes of Splendor: Native American Painted Buffalo Hides,* 61–91. New York: New Press, 1993.

————. "Gallery of Hides." In *Robes of Splendor: Native American Painted Buffalo Hides,* 93–139. New York: New Press, 1993.

House, John H. "Buffalo Bones Identified at Lincoln County Archaeological Site," *Field Notes,* Arkansas Archeological Survey, No. 248, September/October 1992, 3.

Hudson, Charles. *The Southeastern Indians.* Knoxville: University of Tennessee Press, 1976.

Ingersoll, Thomas N. *Mammon and Manon in Early New Orleans.* Knoxville: University of Tennessee Press, 1999.

Jackson, Robert H., ed. *New Views of Borderlands History.* Albuquerque: University of New Mexico Press, 1998.

Jaenen, Cornelius J. *Friend and Foe: Aspects of French-Amerindian Cultural Contact in the Sixteenth and Seventeenth Centuries*. New York: Columbia University Press, 1976.

———. "The Meeting of the French and Amerindians in the Seventeenth Century." *Revue de l'Université d'Ottawa* 43 (January–March 1973): 128–44.

Jennings, Francis. *The Invasion of America: Indians, Colonialism, and the Cant of Conquest*. Chapel Hill: University of North Carolina Press, 1976.

John, Elizabeth A. H. *Storms Brewed in Other Men's Worlds: The Confrontation of Indians, Spanish, and French in the Southwest, 1540–1795*. College Station: Texas A & M University Press, 1975.

Jones, Linda Carol. "Conversion of the Tamaroas and the Quapaws: An Unlikely Outcome in the Missions of the Seminary of Québec." M.A. thesis, University of Arkansas, 1997.

Jordan, Winthrop D., and Sheila L. Skemp, eds. *Race and Family in the Colonial South*. Jackson: University Press of Mississippi, 1987.

Joutel, Henri. "Remarques de Joustel sur l'ouvrage de Tonty relatif à la Louisiane." Service Hydrographique Archives, Paris, 115–19, no. 12.

Kawashima, Yasuhide. *Puritan Justice and the Indian: White Man's Law in Massachusetts, 1630–1763*. Middletown, Conn.: Wesleyan University Press, 1986.

Kellogg, Louise Phelps, ed. *Early Narratives of the Northwest, 1634–1699*. New York: Charles Scribner's Sons, 1917.

———. *Journal of a Voyage to North America*. Chicago: The Caxton Club, 1923.

Kellogg, Susan. *Law and the Transformation of Aztec Culture*. Norman: University of Oklahoma Press, 1995.

Kerr, Derek N. *Petty Felony, Slave Defiance, and Frontier Villainy: Crime and Criminal Justice in Spanish Louisiana, 1770–1803*. New York: Garland Publishing, 1993.

King, Duane H., ed. *The Cherokee Indian Nation: A Troubled History*. Knoxville: University of Tennessee Press, 1979.

Lahontan, Louis-Armand de Lom d'Arce, Baron de. *New Voyages to North-America*. London: 1735.

———. *Nouveaux voyages de Mr le baron de Lahontan, dans l'Amerique septentrionale*. The Hague: 1709.

Lancaster, Bob. *The Jungles of Arkansas: A Personal History of the Wonder State*. Fayetteville: University of Arkansas Press, 1989.

Le Page du Pratz, Antoine Simon. *Histoire de la Louisiane*. Paris: 1758.

Leslie, James W. *Saracen's Country: Some Southeast Arkansas History*. Little Rock, Ark.: Rose Publishing Co., 1974.

Levaggi, Abelardo. "Aplicación de la politica española de tratados a los indios de la Nueva España y sus confines: el caso de la Luisiana y las Floridas (1781–1790)." *Revista de Investigaciones Jurídicas* 20 (1996): 371–403.

Lévine, Daniel, ed. *Amérique continent imprévu: la rencontre de deux mondes.* Paris: Bordas, 1992.

Lewis, Anna. *Along the Arkansas.* Dallas: Southwest Press, 1932.

―――. "An Attack upon the Arkansas Post, 1783." *AHQ* 2 (September 1943): 261–67.

Lewis, G. Malcolm, ed. *Cartographic Encounters: Perspectives on Native American Mapmaking and Map Use.* Chicago, University of Chicago Press, 1998.

―――. "Hiatus Leading to a Renewed Encounter." In *Cartographic Encounters: Perspectives on Native American Mapmaking and Map Use,* edited by G. Malcolm Lewis, 55–67. Chicago: University of Chicago Press, 1998.

―――. "Indicators of Unacknowledged Assimilations from Amerindian *Maps* on Euro-American Maps of North America: Some General Principles Arising from a Study of La Vérendrye's Composite Map, 1728–29." *Imago Mundi* 38 (1986): 9–34.

―――. "The Indigenous Maps and Mapping of North American Indians." *Map Collector* 9 (1979): 25–32.

Lottinville, Savoie, ed. *A Journal of Travels into the Arkansas Territory during the Year 1819.* Norman: University of Oklahoma Press, 1980.

McBee, May Wilson, ed. *The Natchez Court Records, 1767–1805: Abstracts of Early Records.* Baltimore: Genealogical Publishing Co., 1979.

McClurkan, Burney. "The Saracen Window." *Jefferson County Historical Quarterly* 2 (1970): 3–6.

McDermott, John Francis, ed. *Captain Philip Pittman's The Present State of the European Settlements on the Missisippi.* Memphis, Tenn.: Memphis State University Press, 1977.

―――. *The Frontier Re-examined.* Urbana: University of Illinois Press, 1967.

Mancall, Peter C. *Deadly Medicine: Indians and Alcohol in Early America.* Ithaca: Cornell University Press, 1995.

Markov, Gretchen Koch. "The Legal Status of Indians under Spanish Rule." Ph.D. dissertation, University of Rochester, 1983.

Martin, Fontaine. *A History of the Bouligny Family and Allied Families.* Lafayette: Center for Louisiana Studies, 1990.

Mereness, Newton D., ed. *Travels in the American Colonies.* New York: Macmillan Co., 1916.

Moniteur de la Louisiane, 13 November 1802.

Murphy, Edmund Robert. *Henry de Tonty, Fur Trader of the Mississippi.* Baltimore: Johns Hopkins Press, 1941.

Nasatir, Abraham P. *Spanish War Vessels on the Mississippi, 1792–1796.* New Haven, Conn.: Yale University Press, 1968.

Odell, George H. *Final Report on Archaeological Excavations Conducted between May and July, 1988, at the Lasley Vore Site (34TU-65), Jenks, Oklahoma, 1989.*

Parkman, Francis. *The Jesuits in North America in the Seventeenth Century*. Boston: Little, Brown, and Company, 1867.

Pease, Theodore Calvin, and Ernestine Jenison, eds. *Illinois on the Eve of the Seven Years' War, 1747–1755*. Springfield: Illinois State Historical Library, 1940.

Peckham, Howard, and Charles Gibson, eds. *Attitudes of Colonial Powers toward the American Indian*. Salt Lake City: University of Utah Press, 1969.

Perrin du Lac, François Marie. *Voyage dans les deux Louisianes*. Lyon: 1805.

Peterson, Charles E. "French Landmarks Along the Mississippi." *Magazine Antiques* 53 (April 1948): 286–88.

Peterson, Jacqueline. "The People in Between: Indian-White Marriage and the Genesis of a *Métis* Society and Culture in the Great Lakes Region, 1680–1830." Ph.D. dissertation, University of Illinois at Chicago Circle, 1981.

Peyser, Joseph L. "The Chickasaw Wars of 1736 and 1740: French Military Drawings and Plans Document the Struggle for the Lower Mississippi." *Journal of Mississippi History* 44 (February 1982): 1–25.

Phillips, Jim, Tina Loo, and Susan Lewthwaite, eds. *Essays in the History of Canadian Law*. Toronto: University of Toronto Press, 1994.

Pittman, Philip. *The Present State of the European Settlements on the Missisippi*. London: 1770.

Platt, Steven G., and Christopher G. Brantley. "Canebrakes: An Ecological and Historical Perspective." *Castanea* 62 (March 1997): 8–21.

Pope, John. *A Tour through the Southern and Western Territories of the United States of North America; the Spanish Dominions on the River Mississippi, and the Floridas; the Countries of the Creek Nations; and Many Uninhabited Parts*. Richmond, Va.: John Dixon, 1792.

Pope, William F. *Early Days in Arkansas*. Little Rock, Ark.: Frederick W. Allsopp, 1895.

Rea, Robert R. "Redcoats and Redskins on the Lower Mississippi, 1763–1776: The Career of Lt. John Thomas." *Louisiana History* 11 (Winter 1970): 5–35.

Read, William A. *Louisiana-French*. Baton Rouge: Louisiana State University Press, 1931.

Recopilacion de leyes de los reinos de las Indias. Madrid: 5th ed., 1841.

Records of the Superior Council. Louisiana State History Center, New Orleans.

Reid, John Phillip. *A Better Kind of Hatchet: Law, Trade, and Diplomacy in the Cherokee Nation during the Early Years of European Contact*. University Park: Pennsylvania State University Press, 1976.

———. *A Law of Blood: The Primitive Law of the Cherokee Nation*. New York: New York University Press, 1970.

———. "A Perilous Rule: The Law of International Homicide." In *The Cherokee Indian Nation: A Troubled History,* edited by Duane H. King, 33–45. Knoxville: University of Tennessee Press, 1979.

———. "Principles of Vengeance: Fur Trappers, Indians, and Retaliation for Homicide in the Transboundary North American West." *Western Historical Quarterly* 24 (February 1993): 21–43.

Resancement General des habitants, voyageurs, femmes, enfans, esclaves, chevaux, beufs, vaches, cochons, etc., de Post des Akansa, 1749. Vaudreuil Papers, LO 200, Huntington Library, San Marino, California.

Ridley, Matt. *The Origins of Virtue: Human Instincts and the Evolution of Cooperation.* Viking Penguin, 1997.

Robertson, James Alexander, ed. *Louisiana under the Rule of Spain, France, and the United States, 1785–1807.* Cleveland, Ohio: Arthur H. Clark Company, 1911.

Robes of Splendor: Native American Painted Buffalo Hides. New York: New Press, 1993.

Robin, C. C. *Voyages dans l'intérieur de la Louisiane.* Paris, 1807.

Robinson, W. Stitt, Jr. "The Legal Status of the Indian in Colonial Virginia." *Virginia Magazine of History and Biography* 61 (July 1953): 247–59.

Rollings, Willard H. "Living in a Graveyard: Native Americans in Colonial Arkansas." In *Cultural Encounters in the Early South: Indians and Europeans in Arkansas,* edited by Jeannie M. Whayne, 38–60. Fayetteville: University of Arkansas Press, 1995.

———. *The Osage: An Ethnohistorical Study of Hegemony on the Prairie-Plains.* Columbia: University of Missouri Press, 1992.

Ronda, James P. "Red and White at the Bench: Indians and the Law in Plymouth Colony, 1620–1691." *Essex Institute Historical Collections* 110 (1924): 200–15.

Ross, Margaret Smith. "Squatters Rights: Some Pulaski County Settlers Prior to 1814." *Pulaski County Historical Review* 4 (June 1956): 17–27.

Rosselli, Bruno. *Vigo: A Forgotten Builder of the American Republic.* Boston: Stratford Company, 1933.

Rostlund, Erhard. "The Geographic Range of the Historic Bison in the Southeast." *Annals of the Association of American Geographers* 50 (June 1960): 395–407.

Sabo, George III. "Encounters and Images: European Contact and the Caddo Indians." *Historical Reflections/Réflexions Historiques* 21 (Spring 1995): 217–42.

———. "Inconsistent Kin: French-Quapaw Relations at Arkansas Post." In *Arkansas before the Americans,* edited by Hester A. Davis, 105–30. Fayetteville: Arkansas Archeological Survey, 1991.

———. *Paths of Our Children: Historic Indians of Arkansas.* Fayetteville: Arkansas Archeological Survey, 1992.

———. "Rituals of Encounter: Interpreting Native American Views of European Explorers." In *Cultural Encounters in the Early South: Indians and Europeans in Arkansas,* edited by Jeannie M. Whayne, 76–87. Fayetteville: University of Arkansas Press, 1995.

Sánchez Garrido, Araceli. "Plains Indian Collections of the Museo de América." *European Review of Native American Studies* 6 (1992): 21, 25.

Schoolcraft, Henry R. *Journal of a Tour into the Interior of Missouri and Arkansaw.* London: 1821.

Shaw, Helen Louise. *British Administration of Southern Indians, 1756–1783.* Lancaster, Pa.: Lancaster Press, 1931.

Shea, John Gilmary, ed. *Discovery and Exploration of the Mississippi Valley.* New York: Redfield, 1852.

———, ed. *Early Voyages up and down the Mississippi.* Albany, N.Y.: Joel Munsell, 1861.

———, ed. *Journal de la guerre du Micissippi contre les chicashas.* New York: Presse Cramoisy, 1859.

———, ed. *Relation de la Mission du Missisipi du Seminaire de Québec en 1700.* New York: Presse Cramoisy, 1861.

Smith, Ralph A. "Exploration of the Arkansas River by Benard de la Harpe." *AHQ* 10 (Winter 1951): 339–63.

Spores, Ronald, and Ross Hassig, eds. *Five Centuries of Law and Politics in Central Mexico.* Nashville, Tenn.: Vanderbilt University, 1984.

Stanley, George F. G. "The Policy of 'Francisation' as Applied to the Indians during the Ancien Regime." *Revue d'histoire de l'Amérique française* 3 (December 1949): 333–48.

Stern, Peter. "Marginals and Acculturation in Frontier Society." In *New Views of Borderlands History,* edited by Robert H. Jackson, 157–88. Albuquerque: University of New Mexico Press, 1998.

Stiles, Henry Reed, ed. *Joutel's Journal of La Salle's Last Voyage, 1684–7.* Albany, N.Y.: Joseph McDonough, 1906.

Stoddard, Amos. *Sketches, Historical and Descriptive, of Louisiana.* Philadelphia: Mathew Carey, 1812.

Surrey, N. M. Miller. *The Commerce of Louisiana during the French Régime, 1699–1763.* New York: Columbia University Press, 1916.

Sutton, Keith, ed. *Arkansas Wildlife: A History.* Fayetteville: University of Arkansas Press, 1998.

Thorne, Tanis C. *The Many Hands of My Relations: French and Indians on the Lower Missouri.* Columbia: University of Missouri Press, 1996.

Thwaites, Reuben Gold, ed. *New Voyages to North-America by the Baron de Lahontan.* Chicago: A. C. McClurg & Co., 1905.

Tonty, Henri de. *An Account of Monsieur de la Salle's Last Expedition and Discoveries in North America.* London: 1698.

———. *Dernieres decouvertes dans l'Amerique septentrionale de M. de la Sale.* Paris: 1697.

Usner, Daniel H., Jr. "The Frontier Exchange Economy of the Lower Mississippi Valley in the Eighteenth Century." *William and Mary Quarterly,* 3d ser., 44 (April 1987): 165–92.

———. *Indians, Settlers, and Slaves in a Frontier Exchange Economy: The Lower Mississippi Valley before 1783.* Chapel Hill: University of North Carolina Press, 1990.

Vaughan, Myra. "Genealogical Notes of the Valliere-Vaugine Family." *AHQ* 15 (Winter 1956): 304–18.

Vitart, Anne. "Chronique d'une rencontre en terre de Canada." In *Amérique continent imprévu: la rencontre de deux mondes,* edited by Daniel Lévine, 89, 106. Paris: Bordas, 1992.

———. "From Royal Cabinets to Museums: A Composite History." In *Robes of Splendor: Native American Painted Buffalo Hides,* 27–57. New York: New Press, 1993.

Wade, Mason. "The French and the Indians." In *Attitudes of Colonial Powers toward the American Indian,* edited by Howard Peckham and Charles Gibson, 61–80. Salt Lake City: University of Utah Press, 1969.

Wallis, Dave, and Frank Williamson, eds. *A Baptismal Record of the Parishes Along the Arkansas River, August 5, 1796 to July 16, 1802.* Pine Bluff, Ark.: Jefferson County Historical Society, 1982.

Walls, Edwina, ed. *Contributions to Arkansas Medical History.* Charlotte, N.C.: Delmar Printing Company, 1990.

Walthall, John A., and Thomas E. Emerson, eds. *Calumet & Fleur-de-Lys: Archaeology of Indian and French Contact in the Midcontinent.* Washington: Smithsonian Institution Press, 1992.

Waselkov, Gregory A. "French Colonial Trade in the Upper Creek Country." In *Calumet & Fleur-de-Lys: Archaeology of Indian and French Contact in the Midcontinent,* edited by John A. Walthall and Thomas E. Emerson, 35–53. Washington: Smithsonian Institution Press, 1992.

———. "Indian Maps of the Colonial Southeast." In *Powhatan's Mantle: Indians in the Colonial Southeast,* edited by Peter H. Wood, Gregory A. Waselkov, and M. Thomas Hatley, 292–343. Lincoln: University of Nebraska Press, 1989.

Weddle, Robert S., ed. *La Salle, the Mississippi, and the Gulf: Three Primary Documents.* College Station: Texas A & M University Press, 1987.

Wedel, Mildred Mott. "Claude-Charles Dutisné: A Review of His 1719 Journeys." *Great Plains Journal* 12 (Fall 1972): 5–25 (Part I).

———. "Claude-Charles Dutisné: A Review of His 1719 Journeys." *Great Plains Journal* 12 (Spring 1973): 147–73 (Part II).

———. *The Deer Creek Site, Oklahoma: A Wichita Village Sometimes Called Ferdinandina, An Ethnohistorian's View.* Oklahoma City: Oklahoma Historical Society, 1981.

———. "J. B. Bénard, Sieur de La Harpe: Visitor to the Wichitas in 1719." *Great Plains Journal* 10 (Spring 1971): 37–70.

Whayne, Jeannie M., ed. *Cultural Encounters in the Early South: Indians and Europeans in Arkansas*. Fayetteville: University of Arkansas Press, 1995.

White, Richard. *The Middle Ground: Indians, Empires, and Republics in the Great Lakes Region, 1650–1815*. Cambridge: Cambridge Unversity Press, 1991.

———. *The Roots of Dependency: Subsistence, Environment, and Social Change among the Choctaws, Pawnees, and Navajos*. Lincoln: University of Nebraska Press, 1983.

Williams, C. Fred. "The Bear State Image: Arkansas in the Nineteenth Century." *AHQ* 39 (Summer 1980): 99–111.

Williams, Robert A., Jr. *The American Indian in Western Legal Thought: The Discourses of Conquest*. New York: Oxford University Press, 1990.

Wilson, Samuel, Jr. "The Drawings of François Benjamin Dumont de Montigny." In *The Architecture of Colonial Louisiana: Collected Essays of Samuel Wilson, Jr., F.A.I.A.,* edited by Jean M. Farnsworth and Ann M. Masson, 105–7. Lafayette: Center for Louisiana Studies, 1987.

———. "Louisiana Drawings by Alexandre De Batz." In *The Architecture of Colonial Louisiana,* edited by Jean M. Farnsworth and Ann M. Masson, 261–74. Lafayette: Center for Louisiana Studies, 1987.

Wood, Peter H., Gregory A. Waselkov, and M. Thomas Hatley, eds. *Powhatan's Mantle: Indians in the Colonial Southeast*. Lincoln: University of Nebraska Press, 1989.

Wright, J. Leitch, Jr. *The Only Land They Knew: The Tragic Story of the American Indians in the Old South*. New York: Free Press, 1981.

Zitomersky, Joseph. *French Americans–Native Americans in Eighteenth-Century French Colonial Louisiana: The Population Geography of the Illinois Indians, 1670s–1760s*. Lund, Sweden: Lund University Press, 1994.

Index

Abeka Indians, 25; attack Arkansas Post in 1749, 26

Abenaki Indians, 126, 190n. 77, 197n. 29; trade with, 56, 58, 136–37

Alabaman Indians, 133; ally with Choctaws to destroy Caddos and Quapaws, 130

alcohol. *See* liquor

altruism, 152

American Revolution: Quapaws' role in, 113–14, 153; Spain sides with Americans, 86

Americans at Arkansas Post, 13

Angaska (a Quapaw chief), 84, 86–87; accepts English medal and flag, 112–13; complains about interpreter, 162; death of, 114; role in American Revolution of, 113–14, 153

annual presents to Quapaws. *See* presents to Quapaws

Apache Indians, 60

Arkansas: name for Quapaws, xix, 64

Arkansas County, 73

Arkansas Indians, *See* Quapaw Indians

Arkansas Post: archives of, 135; attacked in 1749, 26, 67; attacked in 1783, 113–14, 153; buildings at, 66–67, 73; church at, 12; in Desha County, 72; described, in 1727, 15–16; —, in 1738, 16; —, in 1739, 61; —, in 1765, 73; —, in 1802, 143; —, in 1809, 14; founded, xix, 10; merchants at, 46, 47, 53, 58, 62, 177n. 90; moved, xix, 24, 67; origin of name, 15, 168n. 63; population of, 44–45, 61–62; seat of territorial government, xix; weakness of garrison at, 62, 125, 131; *et passim*

Arkansas River: bankrupts on, 44–45; buffaloes on, 32; hunters on, 44; *et passim*

d'Artaguiette, Diron Benard: on buffaloes, 32; on demand for Quapaw paintings, 69; on Quapaw population, 158–59; on

Quapaw religious beliefs and practices, 6, 73, 140; on Quapaw women's work, 8; on sexual practices of Indian women, 10

assemblies, 54; of Quapaws and Spanish, 85–86, 89–90

Aubry, Charles Phillippe (governor of Louisiana), 111

Baird, W. David: on Quapaws' religion, 142

bankrupts: on Arkansas River, 44, 58

Barthelemy, ———, 49

Bartholome, ———: Quapaw attacks, 128

Bastrop, Baron de: granted exclusive trade rights on Ouachita River, 57

bear meat, 39, 41, 174n. 57

Bearnoud, François (New Orleans trader), 49

bears, 35, 39–41, 61, 105

bearskins, 43

bear's oil, 34, 39–41, 43, 47, 68, 105, 174n. 58, 175n. 62; production of, 40–41; uses of, 40, 175n. 61

bear tongues, 34

beaver pelts, 41, 42–43, 107, 136–37, 143, 175n. 70

Bénard de La Harpe, Jean-Baptiste. *See* La Harpe

Bernard, Jean-Baptiste: accused of murder, 120, 122

Berryer, Nicholas René (minister of the marine), 122

Bienville, Jean-Baptiste Lemoyne de (governor of Louisiana), 15, 45, 191n. 90; complains about Quapaw deerskin production, 20; describes Arkansas Post in 1739, 61; on Quapaw attitude towards their dead, 140; on Quapaw population, 159; on Quapaw religious beliefs, 138; on Quapaw women, 41; recruits Quapaw warriors, 25; seeks trade connection with Wichitas, 60

New Mexico, 18, 19, 38, 106, 119, 151

New Orleans, 12, 14, 20, 32, 35, 43, 44, 49, 50, 51, 57, 78, 87, 93, 107, 108, 110, 115, 130, 131, 148, 200n. 77; courts at, 135; hunters from, 33, 34; Quapaws visit governor in, 80, 84, 89, 120, 162, 191n. 90; revolution against Spanish in, 79, 89–90

New Spain, 119; application of Spanish law to Indians in, 118–19

Nicolet, Jean: murdered at Post, 120

Nitar(d), Pedro (merchant at Arkansas Post), 53, 136–37

North Africa: Labuxière imprisoned in, 153

notaries: in La Salle's company, 120; Indian notaries in Mexico, 118

Nuttall, Thomas: on Quapaw's religious practices, 201n. 94; on Quapaw women's hairstyles, 68

Ohio River, 27, 111

Omaha Indians: kinsmen of Quapaws, xix, 201n. 93; religious practices of, 201n. 93

O'Reilly, Alexander (governor of Louisiana), 79, 108, 144

d'Orgon, Henri: reports epidemics among Quapaws, 157–58

Orhan (son-in-law of Quapaw chief), 84

Orieta, Josef (commandant at Arkansas Post), 84, 90, 92, 100; conversations with Quapaws, 91–92; Quapaws perform mourning rite on death of, 146; reports on Angaska's acceptance of English flag and medal, 112; reports on English attempts to undermine Quapaw alliance, 104–5; reports Quapaw inclination to move to English territory, 101; reports on trespassing Englishmen, 105

Osage Indians: 27, 48; attack Quapaws and French hunters, 60, 178n. 103; buffalo hunting techniques of, 174n. 52; cosmology of, 186n. 64; enemies of Quapaws, 4, 20, 73, 75, 92, 100, 108, 115; kill French hunters, 114–15; kill slave on Arkansas River, 197n. 31; law of, 197n. 31; kinsmen of Quapaws, xix, 138, 186n. 64, 197n. 31; produce deerskins, 42; refuse to produce buffalo hides, 51; right of chief to execute manslayer, 127; rob hunters of Arkansas region, 125; trade with, 45, 50, 52, 57, 62; traders among, 174n. 50; war with, 153

Osotouy: Quapaw village, 64, 72, 133

Ouachita Post, 57

Ouachita River: trade on, 57

Ouhappatisay (a Quapaw chief), 86

Paducah Indians, 60

Panis Indians, 47, 59. See also Wichitas

Parkman, Francis, 134

Pasemony (a Quapaw chief), 83

patents: distributed to Quapaws, 81, 86

Pénicaut, André-Joseph: describes Quapaw women, 4

Pensacola: Quapaws treat with English at, 101, 103

Peoria Indians, 70

Périer, Étienne de (governor of Louisiana): avenges Natchez massacre, 23; reestablishes Post garrison, 24

Perrin du Lac, François Marie: describes Post in 1802, 143

philosophes, 149

Pichart, ———: Osages attack, 60

Piernas, Pierre, 163–64

Pine Bluff, 146, 148, 149

Pittman, Philip: describes Post in 1765, 73; describes Quapaws, 59; reports on Quapaw population, 159

Plains Indians, 184n. 31

plantation Indians: in Massachusetts, 118

Plymouth Colony: application of English law to Indians in, 118

Pointe Coupée, 32, 34, 49, 50, 92, 192n. 10

Ponca Indians: kinsmen of Quapaws, xix

Pontiac's rebellion: Quapaws participate in, 70, 78

poste: meaning of, 15, 168n. 63

presents to Quapaws, 80, 86, 87, 89, 90, 97–99, 100, 105, 109, 110, 113, 114, 162–63, 191n. 90; during French period, 97; goods included in, 97; importance of to alliance with Spain, 97–98

private property: Quapaws sense of, 152

prostitution, 103

Quapaw Indians: accept Louis XIV as "master of their lands," 120; adopt English trader, 103–4; adoption rituals, 16, 68, 95–96, 151; agricultural activities of, 7; and American Revolution, 86–87, 99, 113–14, 115–16, 147; application of European law to, 120, 125–29, 131, 133; assemblies with Spanish, 85; attachment to homeland, 91–92, 101, 140; attend English war council in 1708, 15; avenge massacre on Chickasaws, 78;

Vivier, Father Louis: on Quapaw population, 159
voyageurs, 11, 12, 44, 62

Wabash River. *See* Ohio River
Wah-ḳon-tah: Quapaw life force, 138
Welch, Thomas (English trader), 15
West Florida, 78
White River, 41, 42, 102, 133; buffaloes on, 33, 34; Cherokees on, 56; Englishmen on, 105; hunters on, 44; *voyageurs* on, 62
Wichita Indians, 23; ally with Quapaws, 108; cannibals, 60; French refugees among, 48; raid Arkansas hunters, 48; trade with, 19, 59–62; women, work of, 61

"wildcats," 43
wild horses, 172n. 20
Wilson, Carrie V. (Quapaw NAGPRA representative), xiv
Wilson, Edna, xiv
Wilson, Robert: killed by Quapaws, 125
women: French women at Arkansas Post, 11–12; produce paintings among Plains Indians, 184n. 31; sexual practices of, 10. *See also* Quapaw Indians; Wichita Indians

Yazoo Indians, 23
Yazoo River, 15, 26, 31, 32, 174n. 57